Crime and Punishment in England

Crime and Punishment in England

An Introductory History

John Briggs
Christopher Harrison
Angus McInnes
David Vincent
University of Keele

St. Martin's Press
New York

CRIME AND PUNISHMENT IN ENGLAND

St. Martin's Press, Scholarly and Reference Division, 175 Fifth Avenue, New York, N.Y. 10010

First published in 1996 by UCL Press
The name of University College London (UCL) is a registered trade mark used by UCL Press with the consent of the owner.

First published in the United States of America in 1996

Printed in Great Britain

ISBNs
0-312-16330-4 (cloth)
0-312-16331-2 (pbk)

Library of Congress Cataloging-in-Publication Data

Crime and punishment in England, 1100–1990 : an introductory history / John Briggs . . . [et al.].
    p. cm.
    Includes bibliographical references and index.
    ISBN 0-312-16330-4 (cloth). – ISBN 0-312-16331-2 (paper)
    1. Criminal justice, Administration of –England–History.
2. Crime–England–History. 3. Punishment–England–History.
I. Briggs, John, 1938–
HV9960.G7C73   1996
364.941–dc20   96-20019
                                                                        CIP

Contents

Preface   vii

1 The medieval origins of the English criminal justice system   1

Part I: The early modern period   15
2 Crime and the courts in early modern England   17
3 Church courts and manor courts   33
4 The machinery of law enforcement   47
5 Imposing the law   61
6 Punishment   73
7 Socio-political crime   87

Part II: Crime, police and punishment in England
after the Industrial Revolution, 1800–75   101
8 The ordering of society   103
9 The changing nature of crime in the nineteenth century   121
10 The policing of society   141
11 Patterns of punishment   157

Part III: The making of the modern criminal,
1875–1960   175
12 Patterns of crime   177
13 Bad behaviour   193
14 Professional law   209
15 Ordering punishment   227
16 Epilogue   245

Glossary   253
Bibliography   257
Index   261

Preface

Ours is a society obsessed with crime. According to popular myth, it confronts us in our homes and on the streets, at work and on holiday, at home and abroad. The problem of crime is one of the political issues of our day. We spend an enormous amount of public money through the police and prison services and in the criminal courts attempting to control or at least to contain the "problem". To that massive figure one must add the private and corporate money spent on insurance and preventive measures.

We fear crime but we also gain a vicarious pleasure from it through television series, films, crime and detective novels and through "true-crime" accounts. Nor does interest stop at mere entertainment. Popular and professional studies on the police, the prisons, criminals, the criminal law, the sociology of crime and the history of crime abound.

But is crime the potential threat to the very survival of our society that many now fear? Is the situation now worse than it was in the past? In what ways does the modern criminal problem differ from that of past ages? Can we learn nothing from the past about how to tackle today's problems? In brief, what sort of contribution can historians make to the present debate?

This was the challenge posed us by the criminologists at Keele University. Could we help their students, most of whom are not historians, to place the present in its historical context? We tried through lectures and tutorials. It rapidly became clear that while there are many excellent books on various aspects and periods of the history of crime, there was no general textbook available. We have written this book to meet that need.

The chapters that follow have emerged out of the lectures we wrote for these non-historians. Our aim was and is to tell the complex story of the history of crime and punishment in England over a millennium as simply as we could. We are, of course, dependent in part upon the scholarship of others, and our debt to those scholars is reflected in the bibliography.

We hope and believe that this history will be of interest to people other than students of criminology. Police officers and prison officers, probation officers and social workers, lawyers and magistrates may welcome a brief historical introduction to the practical problems they confront. Even television and newspaper journalists, whose writings so influence public response to crime, might benefit by being better informed. Dare we hope that even a few of the politicians and civil servants whose decisions on our behalf determine the state's response to crime will read this book? It is to be hoped so, for any attempt to tackle today's problems without reference to the past is likely to be inept. We also hope that historians and students of history will find this work of interest, for the history of crime is as much a part of our national history and heritage as the history of dynasties. Last but not least we hope that general readers will welcome this exploration into the dark side of our nation's historical psyche.

Chapter 1

The medieval origins of the English criminal justice system

What was the role of law in English medieval society? What did contemporaries understand by the concept of law? Did the practice of law change over the Middle Ages, and if so how? What was the medieval legacy for the English criminal justice system?

Anglo-Saxon society

Land lay at the heart of Anglo-Saxon and later medieval society. Wealth and power were reflected and expressed in the amount of land one held. Furthermore, how one held land determined one's rights and duties at law. A landed thegn or aristocrat had many legal rights, a ceorl or freeman fewer. But most Anglo-Saxons were unfree, that is slaves, landless labourers, and peasants who held land by a bond tenure. What rights in law did they have? Not many, but even they had some because from the earliest times it was recognized that even the unfree needed some protection at law.

So from the outset there were really two strains in English medieval law: the protection of the individual regardless of landed status, and the protection of property, particularly landed property.

All land was held directly or indirectly from a lord. In theory and in practice no-one owned land. There was then in Anglo-Saxon England a hierarchy of lords, headed by the king. And the basis of that hierarchy was land. Thus, great lords held land from the king, lesser lords from the greater lords, and so on. Think of it as a pyramid of power with the king at the head, great lords or thegns below him, and lesser lords below them. Even that great institution the Church held land from the Crown. How was this hierarchy managed? Mainly through landholding. Each lord from the king down had his vassals, who held land from him in return for rents and services. These vassals were often themselves lords with vassals under them, owing rents and services.

The relationship of lord and vassal was the key to much law. When a lord granted land to a freeman (the notion of freedom here is important), a tripartite ceremony occurred in which a freeman did homage and swore fealty (loyalty) to his lord. In return for this surrender and promise of service, the vassal was rewarded by the lord with his fief, that is his land, in what became known as the investiture. Once this ceremony had taken place both lord and vassal acquired rights and duties, and these formed the basis of much medieval law.

One of the principal duties of a lord was to uphold the rights of his vassals, that is to provide them protection. First the vassal's rights on his land had to be protected. Secondly, where a lord's vassals were in conflict one with another, he had to make judgements between them. In short, the lord needed a court. Thus, one of the principal elements in lordship was the right (even the duty) to hold a court. In that court vassals got justice and the lord got honour, power and profit. In theory every freeman was either a lord or the vassal of a lord. In theory this relationship was voluntary, but in practice there was increasing pressure on men to take a lord. For example, the Anglo-Saxon king, Aethelstan insisted that all his subjects take a lord:

> With regard to lordless men from whom no [legal] satisfaction can be obtained, we have declared that their relatives shall be commanded to settle them in a fixed residence where they shall become amenable to public law, and find them a lord at a public meeting. If, however, on the appointed day they [the relatives] will not or cannot, he shall be henceforth an outlaw [a man outside of the protection of the law], and he who encounters him may assume him to be a thief and kill him.

There was then a strong incentive for the individual to take a lord, for to be without a lord was to be outside of the protection of the law. There was, too, a strong pressure on him from the community for, as Aethelstan's law says, he who was lordless could give no legal satisfaction, that is the community could not get legal redress from a lordless man.

Clearly, the more vassals one had the richer and more powerful one was. Thus, the greatest lords were the kings because, in general, they had the most vassals. Kings had a special place in the hierarchy of power. They were not only pre-eminent, they were essentially different from other lords. They had no lords over them; by their coronation and anointing, they enjoyed a quasi-sacerdotal status. They were, in a sense, protected by God and the Church.

Gradually kings came to extend their jurisdiction directly or indirectly over all their subjects, not just their immediate vassals. How did this come about? First, the king had a need to adjudicate in disputes between his officers and his subjects, particularly on questions of taxation. Where could a subject go who had a complaint against a royal official except to the king's court, the witan? Then there were groups in society who, for a variety of reasons, did not have secular lords, for example the clergy, women, foreigners and the Jews. The king extended his protection or peace to these groups. Then he extended his protection over special places such as the king's highway (200 yards either side of the main road) to protect merchants and other travellers, and the lands of the Church. In this way, the king's court became in time the nation's court, the final and supreme court of justice.

Alongside this development of direct royal justice emerged the acceptance that only the monarch could grant legal franchises, rights or, as they were known, "liberties". If a town wanted to become a borough, that is to have the right, *inter alia*, to hold its own courts, then it needed a royal charter.

It was this combination of the extension of royal justice and the control of private justice that led to the development of the medieval concept of the state as that area over which a monarch ruled and in which he had the duty to protect all according to their estates or, as we would now say, their socio-economic group or class. Thus by the mid-twelfth century, English kings began to call themselves king of England (the place) rather than king of the English (the people). By the thirteenth century the law was firmly established as an integral and central part of society; indeed, in a sense it defined it.

The law and courts of Anglo-Saxon England

The first and most important thing to note about Anglo-Saxon England is that it was a slave society. In most cases the protection of the law applied only to freemen and above.

Secondly, for much of the Anglo-Saxon period, England was not a unified kingdom, and even when nominally under a single king its areas had different laws. The most significant regional difference was between the Danelaw of eastern England and the rest. In Danelaw, that part of England settled by the Viking invaders, there were more freemen lower down the social scale than in the old Anglo-Saxon kingdoms, and it had fewer slaves. Because of raiding and irregular invasions there were different laws applying on the Welsh and Scottish borders. London seems to have developed its own system of justice from an early date.

Thirdly, law was made by the king in consultation with his senior clerics and secular lords. When an Anglo-Saxon king issued or "made" his laws, they were presented as simply the writing down of already customarily agreed precepts. What made them special, what gave them enhanced authority was that they were written down. In a society largely based on oral transmission of information, anything written down had a high status.

Fourthly, the laws as written down covered only a very narrow area: manslaying, theft, particularly the theft of stock such as cattle and horses, the abduction of heiresses and the maltreatment of maidservants.

By the end of the tenth century, England was divided up for administrative and legal purposes into shires (counties), each headed by a sheriff (who was the king's agent) and an earl, who was the largest landholder in the county. Each shire was divided into hundreds, each in turn headed by a bailiff appointed by the sheriff. The hundred was in origin a fiscal or tax unit, dependent on a royal manor, at which the king's taxes and other revenues were collected. In theory, a hundred consisted of 100 hides, each hide being the land necessary to maintain one household.

The principal courts of public justice in Anglo-Saxon England were the county courts and the hundred courts. At the hundred court all freemen were required to attend. There the sheriff and other magnates took the view of frankpledge. This was the system whereby young freemen were sworn in to maintain the king's peace. They joined a tithing, a group of neighbours responsible for each other's actions.

Minor cases were heard at a hundred court. More serious cases and those involving more important people were heard in a shire court, to which representatives from all the manors and all the local magnates came. In both hundred and shire courts, the judges were local noblemen and ecclesiastics.

Thus, all freemen were subject to royal justice through this hierarchy of courts. There was one exception to this general rule, the borough courts. Burghs or boroughs were special places. In origin they were fortified settlements established to protect England from the ravages of the Danes. In return for this, the townsmen were given special legal privileges or "franchises" as they became known. Here the suitors, jurymen and judges were the townsmen themselves. No superior lord was involved, and justice was not dependent upon landholding and vassalage.

Cases involving very important persons, such as thegns or bishops, and those involving people from different shires could be tried in the king's court, the witan, before the king. As Alan Harding writes: "There was then a single hierarchy of meetings or synods from the king's court down through the shire to the hundred in which ecclesiastical and lay judges sat side by side." This hierarchy was reflected in the frequency of meetings of the various courts: the witan met as and when necessary; shire courts every six months; borough courts every four months; hundred courts every four weeks.

In general this system of justice described applied only to freemen. Where did the unfree go for justice? In addition to the courts of public justice, there were many private courts applying what came to be called customary law. Each lord held his own court in each of his villages and manors. In these he administered justice to his own peasants and slaves. In many cases the lord had rights up to and including the passing of capital sentences on these unfree men. The unfree looked to their local lord for justice and were largely denied the protection of royal justice.

Methods of trial

There were two basic methods of trial in Anglo-Saxon England: compurgation and ordeal.

In trial by compurgation, the jury or *juratores* (those sworn), usually numbering twelve, were summoned to swear to the truth of the submission of the defendant or complainant. They did so on the basis not of evidence presented in the court but of their knowledge of the disputants and the alleged offences. It was, says Warren, a form of arbitration with a tendency towards compromise.

If compurgation was not possible then one was thrown back on trial by ordeal. Such a trial was conducted by a priest in a church before witnesses. God not man was determining the guilt or innocence of the accused. It was an arational system of trial. There were three basic forms of trial by ordeal: by hot water or hot iron; by consecrated bread (the *corsnaed*); by cold water.

In the hot water ordeal, a stone was placed in a cauldron of water, which was then heated. The fire was removed and witnesses and the accused admitted to the church. Prayers were then said, and the water and stone allowed to cool a little. The accused then had to take the still hot stone out of the cauldron. In the ordeal of iron the accused had to carry a heated weight of iron a certain distance. In both cases the accused was considered innocent if after three days his injured hand had healed without festering.

In the ordeal by consecrated bread, the accused was forced to swallow a piece of consecrated bread after it had been abjured to choke the guilty. This form of ordeal was used on clerics.

In the ordeal by cold water, the accused was tied up in a crouching position with his wrists under and between his legs. A rope came up between his legs and a knot was tied in it at the length of his hair. He was let down gently into water so as not to make a splash. If he sank down to the knot he was adjudged innocent; if he floated he was guilty. Trial by this form of ordeal was considered particularly undignified and was reserved for serfs.

Criminal law

Alan Harding has said that "The origin of the criminal law [was] the assumption by the state of the responsibility for avenging personal injuries." What, in the case of England, did this mean in practice? The Anglo-Saxon system of criminal justice was mainly concerned to resolve feuds by financial compensation, either for the victim or his family. Consider these early seventh-century laws of Aethelberht: a pierced ear was to be compensated with 3 shillings, a lacerated ear with 6 shillings, and a severed ear with 12 shillings.

Financial compensation was preferred to corporal punishment. Even some forms of murder could be paid for through a money-payment. (In general, prison was a place where one was held before trial rather than a place one was sent to for punishment on conviction. The only exception to this general rule was for clerics, who could be and were imprisoned for felonies.) The following law of King Ine illustrates the way a felony (an offence punishable by death) could be mitigated by a money payment: "If a thief is caught [in the act] he shall die the death or his life shall be redeemed by the payment of his wergeld." Wergeld was what you had to pay if you killed a man – the sum varied according to the status of the person killed; an earl's wergeld was larger than a ceorl's. This sum was paid to the dead person's relatives or kindred. In this case we can see that the wergeld applied also to offences other than murder. Only if the criminal was a notorious evil-doer and a danger to the whole community was corporal punishment insisted upon, as illustrated here by another of Ine's laws: "If a commoner has often been accused of theft and is at last proved guilty his hand or foot shall be struck off." Perhaps the most striking feature of the Anglo-Saxon system of criminal justice was the preference for financial compensation for victims or their surviving relatives. However, persistent offenders got short shrift, and the punishments were cruel.

The Norman conquest of England and the law

The Norman conquest of England in 1066 led to some radical changes in English criminal law. With the Conquest, and for the first time, all land was held directly or indirectly from the Crown. In Anglo-Saxon England some land had fallen outside of the crown's control. Now, all tenants-in-chief (i.e. the principal landholders) owed suit to the king's court (the *curia regis*) for their land. The tenants-in-chief had their own tenants who owed suit to their courts, the so-called honorial courts. The tenurial revolution of the Conquest, by which Anglo-Saxon lords were replaced by Norman and French lords, created a revolution in land law.

Up to one-third of England was designated "forest". In these areas "forest law" applied. Thus, much of England, albeit the more sparsely populated areas, came under a new law and new courts. Forest law was not true law, its rules were arbitrary and its introduction was deeply resented by the Anglo-Saxons.

Independent church courts were established. This led in time to the separation of ecclesiastical and secular law. Church law went in one direction, closer to the old Roman law, state law went another. There was a sharp decline in slavery, that is most men became subjects. The language of pleading became Norman-French, the language of record Latin, which created problems of translation. In Anglo-Saxon England the language of pleading and record had been English. The dominance of Latin as the language of record was not to be challenged until the Commonwealth under Oliver Cromwell in the mid-seventeenth century.

The Normans introduced a new method of trial called trial by battle. In such a trial defendant and complainant fought either in person or by proxy through the use of a champion. Such champions could be used only in disputes over land. Where felonies such as murder were concerned, the defendant had to appear in person. The two combatants fought to a stand-still. The loser, if not already killed in battle, was subsequently hanged. As in ordeals, the theory was that God gave the judgment. God would not permit an innocent man to be defeated, therefore the defeated man was guilty. Because of the uncertain outcome of such a system of trial, most litigants tried to avoid it. However, it was still common in the thirteenth and four-teenth centuries, and as late as 1536 the Yorkshire rebels challenged Thomas Cromwell to decide the issue between them by trial by battle.

Despite these changes, the Norman kings were anxious to stress con-tinuity in law as in other aspects of government. William the Conqueror confirmed the laws of Edward the Confessor; Henry I confirmed his father's laws. In theory, at least, the law of England did not change at the Conquest. In reality, the above changes were themselves revolutionary.

Later innovations

Henry I (1100–35), the son of William the Conqueror, tried to use the law to control his magnates. The most important instrument he employed was the Exchequer, the principal revenue-raising office of the Crown. It was through the Exchequer that the king collected his rents, taxes and other dues. These were collected on the king's behalf by the sheriffs, the Anglo-Saxon shire reeves. When there was a dispute the case was taken before the barons of the Exchequer, who in effect sat as judges. They developed prec-edents, that is they started to make law. This so-called "judge-made law" remains an important part of the English legal system. The court met twice a year at set times and in a set place, Westminster. It had a set procedure and started to keep records, the so-called pipe-rolls. The decisions of the Exchequer gained the full force of law, and the Exchequer became under Henry I, in effect, a national court of law, the first permanent national court.

Henry's other major innovation was to take royal justice into the shires, to make it more accessible. He sent royal justices into the shires to hear royal pleas, that is pleas hearable before the king. So instead of needing to find the king or his justiciar, one could turn to the king's nominated travelling jus-tices, the so-called justices in eyre. In so doing Henry inevitably extended royal justice and its influence.

These innovations came to nought during the civil war and anarchy of Stephen's reign (1135–54), when law and order broke down completely. Men were dispossessed of their lands; churches sacked; hostages taken; men murdered; women raped; heiresses abducted. Justice was virtually impossible to find; lawlessness ruled. The experience of this anarchy led to a desire for law and order. It was recognized, perhaps for the first time in English history, that a lawless society in the end benefited nobody. This was the problem that confronted both the people of England and their new monarch Henry II (1154–89), who was neither English nor Norman but a Frenchman from Anjou. He had many continental territories to govern in addition to the kingdom of England. How could one man govern them all?

The first thing he did was re-establish the office of justiciar, one first created under Henry I but which had lapsed during the Anarchy. The justiciar was the king's first and personal representative, necessary now England was part of a continental "empire". Thus, when the king was abroad one went to the justiciar; one no longer had to follow the king to get justice.

Secondly, Henry brought increasing pressure to bear on his royal officials in the shires, the sheriffs, through the Exchequer. The court was strengthened, and the reforms first introduced by Henry I were re-implemented. For the first time a continuous set of financial records, the pipe-rolls, were kept. Now the court had a written memory. Debts due from the sheriff and not paid within one year were carried over to the next year. Sheriffs who failed to pay their dues were subject to imprisonment.

Thirdly, in 1166 Henry established or re-established the eyre system, whereby royal justices perambulated the country, not only hearing royal pleas but checking up on the activities of the sheriffs to make sure they were administering royal justice without fear or favour. This was formally introduced at the Assize of Clarendon of 1166. (An assize was a modification of the customary law.) It established that sheriffs and county justices had to hold inquiries into all murders, robberies and thefts in their counties, and to name the alleged criminals and those harbouring them. But how were these suspects to be identified? Representatives of the hundreds and villages were sworn on to local juries of presentment. They testified under oath to all crimes committed in their areas and named those responsible. By this means the community rather than the family became responsible for bringing prosecutions.

It was the sheriff's responsibility to produce the accused before the justices in eyre. They were to hunt down and imprison suspects without regard to franchises; for example, offenders living in boroughs were not exempt from the sheriff's jurisdiction in this case.

Those indicted were to be tried by ordeal by water, which was considered a particularly offensive device since it was normally restricted to the lower orders. The chattels of the convicted were to go to the king, and their lands were to revert to their lord.

Within two years a twice yearly visit to the shires by itinerant royal justices was instituted. Thus, for the first time, royal justice was brought there on a regular basis. Widespread local corruption was revealed in these early eyres, and in 1170 an inquiry into the sheriffs was undertaken, and 22 of the 29 were dismissed. They were replaced by officials from the king's *curia*, the so-called *ministrales*. Thus, the office of sheriff ceased to be a purely seigneurial preserve; the sheriff now owed his office not to the accident of birth but to royal promotion.

In 1176 the Assize of Northampton revised the Assize of Clarendon and increased the powers of the itinerant justices and the penalties they could impose. Thus, for example, a convicted murderer was to lose not only one foot, as under Clarendon, but also the right hand; even one who had successfully passed trial by ordeal was to be banished.

An illustration of the effectiveness of the new system is the recorded increase in Crown income from cases heard in the shires. In 1129–30 around 60 recorded debts generated *c.* £2,250. In 1176–7 around 200 recorded debts generated *c.* £7,900.

The fourth innovation arose directly from the above. The justices in eyre heard not only criminal but also civil cases. Men flocked to bring pleas before the royal justices, particularly pleas of land. The result was that the itinerant justices became overwhelmed by the number of cases being brought before them. In 1178 a permanent court (later to be known as the Court of Common Pleas) was established in Westminster to hear some of these cases. Not long after, a permanent Westminster court called King's Bench was also established in Westminster to hear criminal cases. Thus it was during Henry's reign that the three great permanent courts of Exchequer (finance), Common Pleas (land) and King's Bench (criminal) were established.

Coroners

Despite these reforms, the administration of criminal justice in England remained less than ideal. In 1194, under Henry's son Richard I (1189–99), a further innovation was made with the appointment of new county officers called coroners. They, with a sworn jury, were required to inquire into all sudden and unnatural deaths and report these to the Crown, in effect to the visiting justices in eyre. If an offence such as murder was alleged, the coroner had to inform the sheriff, who was then required to arrest and imprison the felon until the next eyre. The system was designed to ensure that all serious offences were brought to the attention of the court.

The Crown was entitled to the value of the instrument that had caused the death (this was called the *deodand*) whether or not it had been a murder instrument, such as a knife, or a non-murder instrument, something that just happened accidentally to cause the death. For example, if a wain fell on a man and killed him, the Crown was entitled to the value of the wain and the beasts (horses or oxen) that were pulling it at the time. (It is a law we might consider re-introducing; imagine that whenever someone is killed by a car the car is seized by the state, regardless of fault, to pay for the states's costs caused by the accident.)

The coroner had another duty, to oversee the banishment of those felons who had taken sanctuary. If a felon could reach the sanctuary of a church, he came under the protection of the church for forty days (the same length of time that Christ spent in the wilderness). At the end of these forty days, the felon had two choices: either to surrender and submit himself for trial or to accept banishment. If, as most did, he opted for the latter, he was dressed in sackcloth and given a wooden cross to carry (these were to identify him as a man who had been banished and was proceeding overseas); he was then sent by the shortest or most direct route along the king's highway to the nearest port, where he had to embark on the first ship going to a foreign port. It was the coroner's job to oversee this exercise.

Trial juries

In the Lateran Council of 1215, the Church withdrew its participation in trial by ordeal because, it was argued, churchmen should not be involved in the taking of the life of a fellow Christian. Since such trials could not be conducted without the assistance of priests, trial by ordeal ceased. The only trial systems left were pre-Conquest compurgation and trial by battle; alternatives were needed.

The writs of *novel disseisin* and *mort d'ancestor* used *de facto* trial juries to decide land cases. Juries of presentment for criminal cases had also worked quite well since their institution in 1166. It was not a difficult or large jump, therefore, to adapt the civil juries used in land cases to criminal cases. Thus emerged one of the linchpins of the English criminal justice system: trial juries. These consisted of local men under oath who would decide the truth or falsity of a criminal charge brought against a person by the juries of presentment or other means. It is important to note that these trial juries gave verdicts not on the basis of evidence presented to them in court but on the basis of their knowledge of what had taken place.

Approvers

Approvers were convicted felons who turned king's evidence to escape the death penalty. They had to "prove" ten cases, that is to say they had to give evidence leading to the conviction of ten felons before they could escape hanging. If they failed to do so, they were hanged; if they succeeded, then they were not freed but banished.

Justices of the peace

Keepers of the peace, later justices of the peace, emerged in the fourteenth century. They were county gentlemen entrusted with the enforcement of the king's peace in their counties. For the first time the gentry, as opposed to the military aristocracy, were formally incorporated into the administration of justice as judges. The magistracy, as they became, was to remain a central element in the administration of criminal justice in the counties. Gradually other tasks were added to their commission. For example, in 1351 they were ordered to enforce the repressive labour legislation passed in the parliament of that year. The office of justice of the peace became and remains a crucial element in the administration of English criminal justice to this day. Most criminal cases are heard before magistrates, the modern successors to the medieval JPs.

The civil law

In many respects, the criminal law was unsophisticated and limited compared with the civil law. For example, there was a massive growth in the number of different writs for initiating a civil action: c. 1087 there were 2 writs; c. 1216 there were 50 to 60 writs; c. 1272 there were 120 writs; and c. 1320 there were 890 writs. Which writ should be used to initiate an action? The answer was to employ an expert pleader or lawyer to act on one's behalf. Slowly it became the case that only accredited lawyers from the Inns of Court could plead in the central royal courts. The expertise these men developed to deal with civil pleas was extended to cover the (less lucrative) Crown pleas, that is criminal cases.

The law became the technical preserve of experts, and textbooks were written for them. The first English lawbook, titled *Glanvil on the laws and customs of England*, was written between 1187 and 1189. Slightly earlier than that was the *Dialogus de Scaccario*, which both describes the procedures of the Exchequer and raises issues of Exchequer law. By the thirteenth century year-books were being issued. These detailed cases of legal interest heard during the year and recorded the reasons given by judges for arriving at their judgments. These became the precedents cited in subsequent similar cases. New law textbooks were issued. In the fourteenth century student textbooks appeared.

Church law

From the mid-twelfth century, the Church began to hold its own courts and to administer its own justice. Church jurisdiction extended not only to clerics and church buildings, but also to a number of other activities. What we would now call family law, sexual offences and testamentary affairs were the concern of the Church courts. Thus, for example, if one had committed adultery, borne a bastard child, committed fornication, or had a dispute over a will one appeared not before a secular court but before a church court. These courts were arranged diocese by diocese, each diocese being divided into archdeaconries, each of which had its own court. Major cases went to the provincial courts at York or Canterbury. These courts had their own officials and their own lawyers.

Manor courts

For most people most of the time, the courts that most impinged on their lives were the local manor courts. These were held by the local lord or more usually his steward. In it the peasants could and did sue each other, transfer bond land and make by-laws for the running of the common fields. Peasants could be and were charged, tried by local juries and convicted of such criminal offences as affray and theft. In other words, the court had a criminal as well as a civil jurisdiction. By the thirteenth century, punishments were restricted to fines or amercements, although in the pre- and post-Conquest period they also had the right in some cases to hang offenders. Court records were maintained from the late thirteenth century. In many cases, although they were the most junior of the courts, these were the most important for most people. It is significant that these courts administered a mixture of private and public justice, that is they made their own laws but also enforced the king's.

Conclusion

The law, as a body of authoritative knowledge, had arrived. What did these developments mean? For the first time since the collapse of Roman civilization there was a body of authoritative knowledge exclusive of the Church. The Church's monopoly on learning was ended. Secondly, the development of rules of law provided an objective check on arbitrary action by rulers and other great lords. The law became a control over royal and seigneurial power. Secular authority was no longer absolute. Thirdly, the law by its self-definition helped, in a sense, to define the state; for good or ill, it created the state.

On a practical level, the medieval period bequeathed to the English criminal justice system the following elements:

(a) the King's Bench – the settled Westminster court to hear important criminal cases;

(b) royal justice taken into the counties through the eyre system;

(c) the county and the hundred as the basic units of administration of criminal justice;

(d) the sheriff, albeit increasingly circumscribed and controlled, as county peace-keeping officer;

(e) juries of presentment, later to become the grand juries;

(f) trial juries;

(g) coroners and coroner's juries for investigating violent death;

(h) justices of the peace, by which landed gentry were given a central role in the county criminal justice system.

Part I

The early modern period

Chapter 2

Crime and the courts
in early modern England

Introduction

Some time between the seizure of power by Henry Tudor in 1485 and the restoration of the monarchy in 1660 there was a significant change in both attitudes to and the perception of crime in England. What were these changes and why did they occur?

Later medieval kings were first and foremost concerned to control the rich and the powerful. It was the aristocrats and their armed retainers who threatened the integrity of the kingdom. On the whole the common people did not present a serious threat. The main exception was the massive outburst of popular protest that culminated in the Great Revolt of 1381. By 1660 the perception of crime had changed. More and more, disorder among and crimes by the common people were seen as threats to society, what they called the common weal or commonwealth; it was not just the monarch who felt threatened, but also the aristocrats, gentry and merchants. Legislation was passed to meet that perceived challenge to privilege and order. The two concepts, an ordered society and a society of privilege, were seen as near synonyms and certainly as symbiotic the one on the other. Thus, the criminal law became increasingly an instrument of social control or, as Marxists would say, of class dominance.

How and why did our rulers come to fear the common people? The first thing to notice is that there were just more of them! The population of England and Wales rose from 2.25 million in the early 1520s to 4.11 million by the end of the century. Sharp changes in population, whether up or down, tend to cause tensions within a society. All other things being equal, more people means more crime. It is certainly the case that in nearly every court, both national and local, the volume of business increased during the sixteenth and early seventeenth centuries.

Secondly, the common people became poorer. Prices, especially of basic foodstuffs, rose. The real value of wages fell. The transfer of monastic and other ecclesiastical estates from the Church to secular landlords led to a more aggressive exploitation of those estates. Real rents, particularly of the smaller holdings, rose. Peasants found it harder to keep their holdings. Some were dispossessed, others forced on to the part-time labour market to

17

supplement their income from their land. In brief there was a monetary crisis and economic and tenurial changes that led to the economic decline of poor people. The landless labourer became a cause of real concern to the authorities; as we shall see, the vagabond became the paradigm of the early modern criminal.

Thirdly, this period saw for the first time the widespread prosecution of ideological offenders. At the Reformation, England abandoned Catholicism for its own peculiar brand of Protestantism. But not everyone gave up Catholicism, particularly in the northwest, and not everyone was happy with the new Anglican version of Protestantism, particularly in London and the southeast. Nor was the process of change from Catholic to Protestant state a smooth one. Under Mary (1553–8) there was a bloody restoration of Catholicism. Then in the 1580s and 1590s Catholics were actively persecuted. The state used the criminal law in a vain attempt to enforce religious conformity. In 1559 a new jurisdiction, the High Commission, was introduced to enforce conformity, and from 1580 responsibility for enforcing attendance at church was transferred from the church courts to JPs.

A curious side-effect of the Reformation was the increase in criminal legislation. Parliament met more frequently. This meant that changes to the criminal law could be and were introduced more easily than hitherto. By the end of the sixteenth century there were more statute offences to commit.

Fourthly, the period saw an unprecedented outbreak of popular uprisings, with four in the period 1536 to 1554. There were further disturbances in the Midland Revolt of 1607. And of course the period ended with a civil war, which is the ultimate form of popular uprising. The unsurprising response of the authorities to these disturbances was to introduce more and more controls: over wages, over residence, over religious practice, over the poor and over criminals.

This brief summary is given to illustrate the crucial point that criminal justice, like most other aspects of a country's history, is affected by general trends and changes in a society. The history of crime and punishment cannot be divorced from demographic, economic, religious or political events of the time.

The popular myth

The archetypal medieval criminal was an outlaw, literally a man outside the law. Outlaws operated in gangs, which through extortion, kidnapping and murder came to dominate some areas to the near exclusion of local justice. An outlaw was a vicious and surely undesired figure on the medieval landscape; the poor as well as the rich suffered from him. Yet he was also the subject of popular romantic myth, as in the Robin Hood ballads.

How Ratsey escaped out of Lincolnshire into Noiffolke when watch was laide for him in euery place.

The many Robberies that Ratsey had done in Lincolneshire caused the Country to make search, and watch to be layd in euery place for him: which he not knowing how to auoyde, thought it the best course for him and his companye to disguise themselues, and to attyre his Page very richly in greene Veluet: which beeing done, for all their brauery they became seruants to the Moone, for the Sunne was to hot for them in those parts and yeilded them small comfort. Therefore reuoluing with himselfe how to escape, hauing trauelled a great part of a wonderfull stormy night of rayne hayle and winde, at last they came to a great house, a Iustice of Peace, within three or foure miles of Wybyche, whose Warrant was gone forth for Ratsey and the rest. But he thought he would place his hopes vpon a desperate hazzard, and sent his Page to the Gentlemans house, where knocking at the doore, desired speach with the Gentleman from his mayster, but the olde gentleman was in bed, yet the Gentlewoman comming vnto the doore, Ratsey began to tell her, that being a stranger in those parts, by his small knowledge of the Countrey, and the foulenesse of the weather that night, both hee and his men were driuen out of his way, therfore desired to do a gentle. that fauor as to pleasure him with

8

Figure 2.1 From *Ratsey's ghost* (1605) (a coney-catching chap-book).

In the Tudor period, the outlaw was supplanted by the vagabond as the archetypal criminal. The change in myth reflected a changing reality. Gangs of outlaws no longer terrorized the countryside; but at the same time there was a growing army of vagabonds, "idle and suspect persons living suspiciously" as an act of 1495 described them. Of course, not all the homeless poor were criminals, but it was believed many were. In both the popular and the official mind, vagabond and rogue were synonyms. ("Criminal" was not used as a noun until 1626, and "crime" as an abstract concept was not widely used until the early nineteenth century.)

Within this growing group of vagrants there existed in and around London a core of professional criminals, professionals in that all their income came from the proceeds of crime and in that individuals tended to specialize in particular crimes. The horse thief, a "prigger of prancers", was unlikely also to be an "abram-man", one who pretended madness in order to get charity, who again was unlikely also to be an "angler", someone who used a pole with a hook to lift items from rooms with unglazed windows. It was alleged that different nationalities had their own specialities; English xenophobia, which charges strangers in our midst with special criminal attributes, has a long history. The Irish were notorious as beggars; the Welsh were alleged to feign dumbness in order to get charity. As one Elizabethan writer put it, "these dummerers are a lewd and most subtle people. They will never speak, unless to hold down their tongues doubled groaning for your charity and holding up their hands full piteously so that with their deep dissimulation they get very much."

There was a strict hierarchy within this group mirroring the social system it had rejected. At their head was the "uprightman", the gentleman of crime. It was he who arranged the robberies, exacted protection money from the lesser rogues and beggars and had the pick of the many "bawdy baskets", "morts" and "doxies" who accompanied the menfolk. Beneath the uprightmen were those with special skills, such as the horse thieves and card-sharps. These were the yeomen of crime. Below them were the beggars and prostitutes, the peasantry of crime.

Crime was a trade with, in some cases, an apprenticeship scheme. In 1585 a London alehouse keeper was arrested and charged with running a school for pickpockets and cutpurses. Boys who could lift counters from a pocket hung with bells were adjudged "public foisters", those who could cut a purse similarly decorated without ringing the bells were called "judicious nippers". Fagin had his real-life predecessor three hundred years before Dickens invented him.

This secret society had its own language called "canting". (The use by criminals of a specialized language was reported by Dickens and Mayhew in the nineteenth century and remains a feature of some groups to this day, especially in the drug subculture.) This enabled initiates to pass information from one to the other without revealing their purposes to the casual hearer. Many of these terms survive: some such as "nipper" (boy) and "cove" (man) have entered into our common language; others such as "prat" (bottom) and "doxy" or "moll" (thief's woman) retain the dubiety of their origin.

This criminal subculture was first described in 1566 by Thomas Harman in his *Caveat for common cursitors*. Greene and Dekker drew heavily on it. Plays and chap-books (short, cheap pamphlets widely distributed) about these "cony-catchers" were as popular with the Elizabethans and Jacobeans as detective novels and television soap operas about the police are today.

There is little doubt that these London-based professional criminals and their esoteric subculture existed, but they were not the only criminals even in London and they were not typical of criminality in the country as a whole. For a true account of criminality, we must look beyond the myth, starting first with London.

London

London, not only the city but also Westminster, Southwark and the suburbs, was the thief's Mecca, because it was unique and had unique opportunities for the criminal. It was larger and grew faster than any other English city. The population in 1520 was 60,000, in 1582 120,000, and by 1605 about 200,000. In the early 1520s, Norwich had 12,000 people, Bristol 10,000, York, Exeter and Salisbury 8,000 each; by the end of the century their populations had risen, Norwich to 15,000, Bristol to 12,000, York to 11,000, Exeter to 9,000, Salisbury to 7,000. In both absolute numbers and percentage increases these provincial capitals did not rival London, which continued to grow reaching over half a million by 1700.

How London grew is relevant to the history of its crime. The resident population could not maintain let alone increase its numbers. Smallpox, typhoid and other endemic diseases, and the occasional but devastating outbreaks of sweating sickness, plague and influenza prevented natural demographic growth. The rise in London's population was due to large-scale immigration. In truth we know little about the immigrants. No doubt some came willingly, believing that in London their fortunes would be made, but one suspects that many, such as the dispossessed cottagers and copyholders, the unemployed rural labourers, orphans and unmarried mothers, came unwillingly, forced there by economic and social pressures. Many of these immigrants were young and single; youth crime was a constant worry to the authorities. Most Londoners were recent arrivals; most were young and poor; most had little to lose if they turned to crime. The city was also the natural home of unattached people, such as disbanded soldiers and sailors, the Jews, foreigners and religious refugees from both home and abroad.

Temporary residents swelled the total numbers. The nobility and gentry and their entourages visited London regularly, for business, for pleasure and for reasons of social prestige. Their sons attended the Inns of Court. Their estate officials came to the capital to conduct legal and financial business on behalf of their masters. The royal courts at Westminster attracted a constant stream of litigants, witnesses and jurymen, many of them members of the lower social orders. Many yeomen's sons came to London for their apprenticeships, returning on qualification to their home counties. Figures from 1551 to 1553 show that out of 1,088 young men admitted as freemen in London only 244 came from the city, 80 from the Home Counties and 764 from elsewhere (168 from Yorkshire alone). And, as always, London attracted a whole army of itinerant traders, suppliers and carriers: badgers and brokers, carters and drovers, packhorse men and sailors.

The size and mobility of this population gave the criminals two important advantages. First, London had a higher concentration of portable and hence stealable wealth than the rest of the country. The London palaces of the monarch and the London homes of the aristocrats and bishops were rich in pickings, as were the residences of city merchants. The many temporary residents needed money to pay for lodgings, services and goods. Those who traded had money to carry back with them to the provinces. Secondly, the size and mobility of the population made it impossible to isolate or control London's criminals. The absence of a co-ordinated peace-keeping agency, a multiplicity of criminal jurisdictions (the city, Westminster, Southwark and Middlesex) and sheer numbers meant that crime was not detected or prevented, it was discovered. The greatest incentive to the criminal is a low arrest rate.

To these practical advantages one must add the capital's traditional reputation for thievery and vice, for tradition was as powerful a force for the criminal as for the rest of early modern society. Tradition told the rogue where to go as it had done since at least the twelfth century, when a Winchester monk wrote:

> When you reach England, if you come to London pass through it quickly. Each race brings its own vices and its own customs to the city. No-one lives in it without falling into some sort of crime. Every quarter of it abounds with grave obscenities. Whatever evil or malicious thing that can be found in any part of the world, you will find it in that one city. Actors, jesters, smooth-skinned lads, Moors, flatterers, pretty boys, effeminates, pederasts, singing and dancing girls, quacks, belly-dancers, sorceresses, extortioners, night-wanderers, magicians, mimes, beggars, buffoons: all this tribe fill all the houses. Therefore, if you do not want to dwell with evildoers do not live in London.

For all these reasons, London crime was probably different from and more extensive than crime elsewhere.

Hard data on crime in early modern London is hard to come by. Between 1550 and 1625 in the Middlesex Quarter Sessions, which had jurisdiction over some London suburbs, 93 per cent of all indictments for felonies were for property offences. The only other major category was homicide and infanticide. But this, alas, tells us little about the level of crime in the capital overall. Many serious offences were heard in the central courts, of which we have little hard data. We have no good statistical evidence on London crime.

One is therefore forced to infer criminal activity from cony-catching chapbooks, diaries, chronicles and letters.

There is no doubt that the professional thieves described by Harman existed, but they do not seem to have posed a great threat to law and order; that at least seems a reasonable inference from the absence of contemporary action on them. The same was not the case for vagabondage generally. This was perceived as a problem even at the beginning of the sixteenth century, when the Lord Mayor ordered small prison houses, complete with stocks, to be built in each ward for the punishment of "sterke beggars and vagabundys". Such primitive lock-ups still existed in the suburbs in the 1560s. At Newington, for example, it consisted of a simple cage built in the middle of the street. It was recognized that not all vagrants were criminals. In the mid-sixteenth century the London Bridewell was established to provide relief and work for destitute and homeless vagrants. But these laudable aims were soon abandoned. In a survey of the Bridewell made in 1609, 1,700 inmates were being held in temporary detention of whom only 130 were being set to work. Institutional charity for the vagrant poor was largely ineffective. One probable reason for this was that, despite prohibition, begging could more than fill the gap. The counterfeit-crank Nicholas Jennings got 13s 3d for a single day's begging in 1566; an unskilled wage labourer would be lucky to earn 6d a day at that time.

The judicial response to vagabondage was crude and cruel. As we have seen, the Bridewell soon lost its humanitarian function and became just a temporary prison. Those waiting there for return to their home parishes would already have been punished. On a first conviction, the vagrant was burned through the gristle of the right ear with a hot iron, then secured to the back of a cart and whipped until the back was bloody; women were treated the same as men. On a second conviction, the vagrant was burned through the other ear, whipped again and then put to service. On a third conviction the vagrant was hanged. At the Middlesex Sessions between 1572 and 1575, 44 vagabonds were branded (and presumably whipped), 8 set to service, and 5 hanged. On a single day in January 1552, seven female vagrants were whipped through the city. Such numbers were typical and reflect the extent of the problem and authority's response to it.

Another serious if irregular problem for London was the sudden appearance of large numbers of discharged soldiers. In 1589 over 500 unpaid soldiers threatened to loot Bartholomew's Fair; a similar situation arose in 1598. In both cases martial law was declared. The provost marshal was instructed "to apprehend all such [soldiers] as shall not be readily reformed and corrected by the ordinary officers of justice and them without delay to execute upon the gallows". Martial law implied summary capital punishment.

Rebellion provided its crop of London victims; 59 rebels were hanged in London and Southwark after Wyatt's Revolt in 1554. Most acts could count as treason. In May 1555, a youth was carted and whipped through London for claiming to be Edward VI. (The boy-king had died two years earlier.) Ten months later, the same boy was convicted of the same offence. This time he was executed.

The fate of the Marian martyrs is too well known to need retelling, but Mary was not the only Tudor to burn heretics. An old man suffered that punishment for heresy in 1500. Nor was burning necessarily the cruellest punishment for the religiously deviant. In 1535 a number of Carthusian monks were convicted of treason for refusing to swear the Oath of Supremacy. They were hanged, cut down while still alive and tied to a board, when their bowels were cut out and burnt before them. Only then were they killed by beheading.

Vagabondage, treason, heresy, these are the crimes most commonly associated with Tudor London, but there were many others, many of them serious. From the numerous references it would seem that murder was not uncommon. Punishment could follow swiftly on the act. The murderers of two Italians were tried, convicted and hanged a mere five days after the offence. A prisoner on trial at the Old Bailey pulled a knife and killed another in the court. For this murder he was summarily convicted and taken outside, the hand that struck the blow was amputated, and he was hanged on improvised gallows.

Poisoning was not unknown. Women poisoners were burnt, male poisoners boiled alive. Thus, the cook convicted of attempting to poison the Bishop of Rochester was "boiled in a caldron he was locked in a chain and pulled up and down with a gibbet at divers times til he was dead".

Piracy, which in this context almost certainly meant theft from shipping in the port of London, was common. The punishment was designed to fit the crime. The convicted pirate was hung in chains at low water and then left to drown from the incoming tide.

A multitude of other offences, such as coin-clipping, rape, horse theft, cutpursing and the theft of any item valued at 40 shillings or more, were subject to the death penalty. These frequent executions were held in public.

Judicial brutality was just as much a feature of the lesser punishments. Consider the pillory. This consisted of a thick wooden post against which the convicted criminal was made to stand for up to four hours by the simple expedient of nailing his ear to the post. At the end of that time the ear was cut off. This was a crude form of criminal record keeping. For a second offence the criminal lost the other ear, for a third one was hanged. The instruction for a whipping was that it should continue until the offender's back was bloody. In the mid-sixteenth century, London vagrants were branded.

Only in the area of trade offences and vandalism do the punishments seem reasonable to the modern mind. A merchant who used a false yard-measure when selling cloth was stocked for a couple of hours. A baker who sold an underweight loaf was set in the pillory with the offending loaves hung round his neck. Two youths who broke street lights in Southwark were led from the Counter (a prison) to Southwark with the broken lanterns tied front and rear. The punishment was clearly intended to shame as much as to harm.

London was an early home to puritan sentiment. This led to an attempt by the city authorities to enforce a stricter sexual morality. The Southwark brothels were closed down – until then they had been officially licensed and regulated. Thereafter prostitutes were regularly whipped and/or pilloried. One peculiar London punishment much feared by prostitutes was to be dragged through the Thames, at the end of a rope drawn by a boat, from Lambeth to Westminster. In its attacks on prostitution, London seems to have set an example followed later by the rest of the country.

There are three important features of crime in early modern London. First, most offenders were not the professional criminals described by Harman and others. The criminal problem even in the capital was not primarily organized crime. Secondly, while it is not possible to state in detail the incidence of crime, there certainly seems to have been a lot of it, especially when we remember that cases recorded in journals and diaries refer to incidents leading to conviction and do not in general record unsuccessful prosecutions or unsolved or unreported crime. Thirdly, despite what may have been a high incidence of crime, particularly theft, there are few contemporary expressions of fear. Londoners seemed to be able to live with their criminals.

What of the rest of England? Was there as much crime there, *pro rata*, as in London. Was it of the same type? Did it lead to serious anxiety among the population at large or the authorities in particular? Who were the criminals? What was the criminal justice system in early modern England, and how effective was it?

The criminal justice system outside London

The county
Since the early eleventh century England had been divided for administrative purposes into counties, and each county into hundreds, in some places called wapentakes. The county remained the basis for the administration of criminal justice in the early modern period.

The sheriff and the coroner
The chief peace-keeping officer of the county remained, in theory at least, the sheriff, an annually appointed local landholder. He had his own court, the county court, but by 1500 this dealt only with civil cases. However, it retained one important criminal function, outlawing those accused who failed to appear before a higher court.

Another medieval officer who continued to function in this period was the coroner. There were three or four per county. In addition, some boroughs had their own coroners. Very little work has been done on the early modern coroner, but as far as we can tell he continued much as before, investigating sudden and violent deaths and reporting to the sheriff those suspected of homicide. He was also the officer who, at the county court, declared outlaws those suspects who had failed to appear at trial.

Three cases must suffice to illustrate the roles of the coroner. On 6 July 1614 a cart-load of hay broke free of its horses, ran down a steep hill and over one of the carters, Thomas Wood, killing him. The following day the Stafford coroner sitting with a jury of fifteen accepted this account and recorded a verdict of accidental death. In September the same year a coroner and jury of fourteen investigated a suspected case of child abuse in Stafford leading to the death of a nine-year-old at the hands of the child's stepmother. Again they returned a verdict of accidental death, but it is clear from the surviving papers that there was sufficient suspicion to justify an inquiry.

The third case is even more startling in its revelation of the investigatory role of the coroner's jury. In the summer of 1546 Thomas Lockett was murdered. A coroner's jury of nineteen was sworn in, and, *before* they were called to hear the case, they visited the home of one of the suspects to check on his alibi. The suspect's son gave his father an alibi but, at the full hearing before the jury and coroner, changed the hour. It is clear that in this case at least the coroner's jury made its own enquiries between the time it was sworn in and the time it was called to hear the case. These three cases illustrate the way the coroner and his jury acted as an investigative agent in the criminal justice system.

Justices of the peace and quarter sessions

The most high-profile peace-keeping officers of the early modern period were the justices of the peace. By and large they consisted of the landed gentry of a county for, although bishops, aristocrats and resident judges appear on the commissions of the peace, they seldom intervened in person. Crucial as the role of JPs was in the administration of criminal justice, one must be careful not to exaggerate it. A county would not have more than about twenty active JPs at any one time. (In Elizabethan Staffordshire the number was lower, about twelve.) These unpaid, part-time justices had other interests and duties. It is inconceivable that on their own they could have maintained the peace in the counties; there were just not enough of them.

That said, JPs had considerable powers. A justice acting on his own could, *inter alia*, examine and imprison suspected felons, arrest vagabonds and rogues, stop affrays, arrest recusants (those refusing to attend their parish church normally because they were Catholics) and take recognizances for good behaviour from those accused of bad. Two justices together could, *inter alia*, fix the poor rate, grant alehouse licences, supervise the repair of roads and bridges, take bail and decide on paternity in cases of bastardy. But it was at the quarter sessions, so called because they were held four times a year, that the justices exercised most power. In these courts they sat as judges, assisted in criminal trials by both a grand jury and trial juries. Once an individual had been convicted it was the justices who determined within the law what punishment should be imposed.

Quarter sessions were normally held in county towns, but not always. In Cheshire the court was held twice a year at Chester, once at Nantwich and once either at Northwich or Middlewich. These were great public events involving large numbers of people. First, there were the magistrates, the justices's clerk and his under-clerks, the sheriff, under-sheriffs and coroners. Then there was a grand jury for the whole county. In some counties, for example Kent, each hundred would send its own grand jury drawn from a selection of villages. These juries were never less than twelve in size. In Kent, according to William Lambarde, a JP, "the common order with us is to have them of an odd number as 17, 19, or 21 to the end that if they should dissent in opinion somewhat equally, yet there should be always one to weigh down the balance. But if 12 of them do agree, the gain-saying of the residue cannot hinder the presentment." This suggests majority verdicts were acceptable from the grand juries. The grand jury decided whether or not there was a case to answer. In that event, a trial jury was summoned to try it. According to Lambarde these juries always consisted of twelve men, no more and no less. By implication their verdicts had to be unanimous. In addition to the justices, county officers and jurors, every village constable was required to attend, as were the hundredal constables. There were many lawyers representing complainants. Last but not least there were the defendants and witnesses.

At the Staffordshire Trinity Sessions of 1602, 35 of the 63 officers summoned (justices, coroners, chief constables, bailiffs, escheator, sheriff and clerk) attended. Jury lists for the same court reveal the attendance of 23 out of 30 grand jurymen, 35 out of 46 petty jurymen and 19 out of 36 special (liberty) jurymen. In all 112 (64 per cent) of the 175 summoned appeared. To this figure we must then add defendants, complainants, lawyers and possibly some of the village constables. There were perhaps between 150 and 200 people at any one meeting of the court. These were great public events.

The business of the court was largely regulatory; it pronounced on such matters as wage rates, alehouses and, from 1597 onwards, the Poor Law. From *c.* 1590 its criminal jurisdiction became limited to dealing mainly with misdemeanours (i.e. offences not warranting the death penalty). But this trend of remitting serious cases to the assizes should not be exaggerated. In the Devon Quarter Sessions over the 28 years between 1598 and 1639 for which evidence survives, an average of just under four people a year were executed for felony. This compares with just under 40 whippings a year. That said, the tendency for felonies (offences warranting the death penalty) to be tried in a higher court is clear, and the most important of these higher courts was the assizes.

Assizes

The assizes were the successors of the medieval eyre, which brought Westminster judges to the shires to hear Crown pleas both civil and criminal. By 1337 England was divided into six circuits. Each circuit, consisting of a number of contiguous counties, was visited by two Westminster justices. Assizes were held twice yearly (in the Lent vacation – late February to early March; in the Trinity vacation – July to August). They were normally held in the county towns but again not always. In Staffordshire, most were held at Stafford but some at Lichfield and Wolverhampton. They were presided over by two Westminster judges or by a judge and a serjeant (a common serjeant was roughly the equivalent of a modern QC). They normally sat with the county's JPs in attendance. They were assisted by a clerk and his staff.

The court was a grand and public affair, opening with the formal entry of the judges, then a sermon. The grand jury, numbering 13 to 23, was sworn. It consisted of freeholders and minor gentry. The judges began by reading a charge to the jury, drawing their attention to their duties and often raising matters of concern to the government in Westminster.

One judge heard the civil pleas while the other heard the criminal cases. They were empowered to hear cases of treason, felony and misdemeanours and to try all prisoners in gaol at the time of their arrival. The local constable made the presentments, that is to say he made the accusations on behalf of the community. The prisoner was then required to enter a plea of guilty or not guilty. Those refusing to plead were subject to be pressed to death in a procedure called *peine forte et dure*. The individual was stripped, placed naked on a pile of rocks and soaked with cold water. Then a board was placed on top of him and rocks placed on the board. The number and weight of rocks were increased until the prisoner either entered a plea or died. Since it was certainly more painful than hanging why might an individual opt for such a painful death? If you did not plead, you could not be convicted. If unconvicted a suspect's lands did not escheat to the Crown, that is the Crown could not seize the lands of a suspect, only of a convicted felon.

Once a prisoner had entered a plea of not guilty, the grand jury then decided whether or not there was a case to answer. Pressure of business meant that prisoners could be arraigned three or four at a time.

If there was a case to answer then a trial jury consisting of freeholders from the defendant's area was sworn. Crown witnesses were sworn and gave evidence; defence witnesses gave unsworn evidence. Those charged with treason or felonies were not allowed to be legally represented. All they could do was question witnesses and make what answer they could to the charges brought against them. The trial jury then retired to consider its verdict. The verdicts were then given in open court. Sentence was pronounced by the judge at the end of the day.

Table 2.1, giving figures for Elizabethan Essex, offers a rough indication of the serious offences, that is felonies, that predominated – whether heard at the assizes or quarter sessions.

Table 2.1 Kinds of felonies in Essex 1559–1602 (ten sample years – data mainly from assize records).

Offences	Number	
Against the person		
Rape and buggery	19	(2%)
Witchcraft	71	(7%)
Murder and homicide	71	(7%)
Sub-total	161	
Against property		
Burglary, robbery and forcible entry	170	(18%)
Theft	637	(66%)
Sub-total	807	
Total	968	

We can see from these figures that crimes against property predominated. Property indictments at the Sussex and Hertfordshire Assizes 1559–1625 accounted respectively for 74 and 86 per cent of the totals. Of offences against the person, the number and percentage of witchcraft cases in Elizabethan Essex was atypically high. Most counties had fewer prosecutions for that felony, only 1 per cent in Sussex and 2 per cent in Hertfordshire; the percentage figures for murder in those two counties were respectively 10 and 5. The proportions of the types of offences did not change much up to the 1640s; on the other hand there does seem to have been an increase in serious crime over this period (see Table 2.2).

Table 2.2 Number of felonies in Essex 1559–1602 (ten sample years – data mainly from assize records).

	1559–60	1570–71	1580–81	1588–9	1601–2
Number of felonies	88	155	162	261	302

We can see from these figures that the number of felonies in Essex increased throughout Elizabeth's reign. Now, although the population was rising during this period, it was not at the rate reflected in these figures. There does therefore seem to have been an increase in serious crime in Elizabethan Essex that continued into the 1620s. In the county palatine of Chester, indictments for felony at the court of great sessions rose from 350 in the decade beginning 1580 to over 650 in the decade beginning 1620, then fell sharply to under 200 in the decade beginning 1640.

Does the increase in recorded felonies mean there was an increase in serious crime up to the Civil War? Maybe, but the figures may reflect greater efficiency in bringing cases to court, or a redesignation of serious crime, leading to more cases being heard. We can say with reasonable confidence that assizes were busier in 1630 than they had been in 1500.

Serious crime and the Westminster courts

So far we appear to have a fairly simple criminal justice system, at least outside London. There was a hierarchy of peace-keeping officers: bailiffs and high constables of the hundreds reported to the sheriff; coroners reported to justices of assize; village constables reported to the justices of the peace; justices of the peace reported to the justices of assize, who were ultimately responsible to the Privy Council. There was too a hierarchy of courts in each county, quarter sessions meeting four times a year and dealing mainly with minor offences and regulatory acts and assizes dealing with the more serious criminal cases. In reality, the situation was more complex.

First of all, there were in parts of the country exempt or independent jurisdictions. For example, in the county palatinate of Chester nearly all cases were heard in the palatinate courts at Chester. A similar situation applied in Durham. If one lived on a Duchy of Lancaster manor one was more likely to appear before the Chancellor of the Duchy than before a local JP in quarter sessions. Other exempt jurisdictions included the Cinque Ports, the Council of the North, the Council of Wales and the Duchy of Cornwall.

Secondly, it was always possible that a local case could be transferred to a Westminster court. The most important in the criminal justice system were King's Bench, Requests and Star Chamber. King's Bench dealt with serious criminal cases, Requests (the poor man's court) with appeals against corrupt officials and similar matters, and Star Chamber with riots and the like. Serious crimes such as suspected treason might go before the Privy Council.

What proportion of criminal cases outside London went through these Westminster courts we do not know. It probably varied according to the defendant's closeness to London and for important cases whether or not there was a powerful local court ready and able to hear them. To complicate matters further, a single case could go through a number of courts. A series of riots on Cannock Chase in the early 1580s led to a case that went through the following courts: the local manor court, quarter sessions in Stafford, King's Bench, Star Chamber, the Privy Council, and then back to King's Bench.

There was then no single universal criminal justice system in early modern England. Similar cases might be dealt with differently in different courts, according to who one was and where one lived. A gentleman accused of murder was more likely to appear in a Westminster court than in a county court. All this should make us very cautious in attributing too much weight to assize and quarter sessions data. However, we can say that there was a plethora of courts dealing with criminal cases and that most of these seem to have enjoyed an increase in business in the latter half of the sixteenth century.

Conclusion

The following conclusions emerge. Contemporary myths about crime and criminals do not reflect the realities as revealed through court records. Secondly, London had a unique criminal problem. Thirdly, there was an increase in prosecution of serious crime up to the 1620s and that increase was greater than the increase in population. Fourthly, the assizes and to a lesser extent quarter sessions dealt with most serious crime outside London, although in some areas special jurisdictions were more important. Fifthly, the criminal justice system favoured the accused; however, the minority who were both convicted and punished were dealt with severely. Finally, the severity of the punishments had no observable effect on rates of offending.

Chapter 3
Church courts and manor courts

As we have seen, in early modern England a variety of royal courts dealt with crime and criminals, at county, regional and national levels. But these courts did not deal with all criminal cases; indeed, the bulk of petty crime was dealt with elsewhere. It is to these jurisdictions of the Church, the manor and the borough that we must now turn.

Church courts

In the late twelfth century, the English Church established its independent jurisdiction over both clerics and laity. Thenceforward certain types of case were to be tried not in secular courts but in church courts. By the end of the Middle Ages, the Church's legal system was well established. The Reformation ended appeals to Rome, but otherwise the system remained intact until the 1640s, indeed its business grew. In 1575 the Archbishop of York's visitations to his provinces generated 1,200 defendants, his successor's in 1636 over 5,000. This was no moribund jurisdiction.

England was divided into two provinces, York and Canterbury, each presided over by an archbishop. Each archbishop had his provincial court or courts that had jurisdiction over the whole province. Each province was divided into dioceses. Each diocese was headed by a bishop who had his own court, called a consistory court. Each diocese (except Chichester) was subdivided into archdeaconries headed by an archdeacon who held his own court, called unsurprisingly an archdeacon's court. Archdeaconries could be large. The archdeaconry of Stafford, part of the diocese of Coventry and Lichfield, was coterminous with the political county of Stafford. In addition, all dioceses had some parishes that lay outside the direct control of bishop and archdeacon; these exempt jurisdictions were called peculiars. So, for example, the parishes of Cannock and Rugeley (Staffordshire) were part of the peculiar of the dean and chapter of Lichfield Cathedral, so people who lived there went before the court of the dean and chapter for ecclesiastical causes, not the standard church courts.

Ecclesiastical courts had three basic jurisdictions: (1) record, which dealt with the granting of marriage licences and the proving of wills; (2) instance, which dealt with disputes between parties and (3) office, which dealt with disciplinary matters. This third category produced most of the "criminal" cases.

How were cases brought before the church courts? They could come through disputes between parishioners or through complaints from individuals, particularly a parish priest, but most cases were referred to the courts by churchwardens. The churchwardens, normally two in number, were elected annually at a meeting of the vestry. They were usually the more substantial landholders in a village or the richer tradesmen or merchants in a town. They were assisted by sidesmen or questmen (also from the parish). One of their many duties was to report any ecclesiastical offences to the bishop or archdeacon at their "visitations". These can best be thought of as judicial inquiries. A bishop visited his diocese every three years, an archdeacon normally twice a year, so there was plenty of opportunity to make presentments. If the accusations were thought reasonable, the defendants were then summoned to appear before the appropriate court, where they were tried before lay judges who acted on behalf of their ecclesiastical masters.

The role of the church courts was primarily not to punish but to reform people and reconcile them with God and their neighbours. This aim of reform was reflected in the punishments open to the court. Those found guilty could be admonished or sentenced to a public penance, which could be commuted in some cases into a money payment to some charitable cause; or they could be excommunicated. Excommunication carried with it not only ecclesiastical but also secular disadvantages. An excommunicate lost significant rights, for example, he could not hold public office, swear an oath, or be buried in consecrated ground. This said and in comparison with the secular courts, church courts had limited powers of punishment and had difficulty in enforcing even these judgments.

What sorts of case came before these courts? In 1585 the Bishop of Salisbury made a visitation of his diocese. In Wiltshire alone there were 685 presentments of which 214 (31 per cent) were for sexual offences, 178 (26 per cent) for matters relating to the repair of the church and maintenance of its fittings, and 147 (21 per cent) for failing to attend church or to take Communion.

Church courts have been called the "Bawdy Courts". In Elizabethan Essex, of some 20,000 church court cases 2,000 related to sexual delinquency. In the diocese of York, presentments of sexual immorality formed the largest single category. And as we have seen, nearly a third of church court cases in Elizabethan Wiltshire were for sex offences. We shall return to the issue of sexual regulation below, but it is important first to assess the role of church courts overall and not concentrate on one important yet minor part of their activity. They dealt with a great deal more than illicit sex.

The following are representative lists of non-sexual cases brought before the Essex church courts in the later sixteenth century:

Non-sexual offences by clerics:
- incompetence and failing to say the services;
- unlicensed preaching;
- failing to visit the sick;
- leaving the dead unburied;
- continuing to administer the sacraments although excommunicated;
- refusing to use the Book of Common Prayer;
- failing to keep the parish register;
- theft of parish documents;
- usury;
- stirring up vexatious lawsuits;
- scandalous behaviour by acting as the Lord of Misrule during the Christmas festivities;
- drunkenness;
- swearing and blasphemous speech;
- being a suspected papist;
- sheltering sheep in the church.

Non-sexual offences by churchwardens:
- failing to maintain the church fabric;
- permitting plays in church during Lent;
- bribing a court official;
- making false presentments.

Non-sexual offences by lay men and women:
- slander;
- tale-bearing;
- attacking the parson and the sexton;
- failing to pay the Easter offering;
- refusing to say the Ten Commandments;
- secreting the Communion bread;
- dancing on a Sunday;
- fighting during the sermon;
- playing football during service time;
- conducting a mock funeral;
- heresy;
- refusing to attend church;
- playing musical instruments on a Sunday;
- seeking the aid of a witch;
- witchcraft;
- wife-beating;
- vandalism;
- drunkenness;
- throwing stones at the church;
- morris dancing.

These may not sound much like criminal offences to our modern ears, but they were serious in their own day. (One must never forget that each age and society defines what is and is not a crime.) Is there a common theme running through these cases? Contemporaries would probably have justified them as the imposition of God's law as incorporated in the Ten Commandments. It is no accident that from 1559 onwards these were read to every congregation every Sunday, and that they were written up on boards at the front of a church so that everyone could see them. The Ten Commandments formed the theoretical benchmark against which all laws were to be judged. In retrospect, the business of church courts looks more like the desire of authority to regulate every aspect of human activity. A few case studies from Elizabethan Essex illustrate the point.

Case 1 (1599)

The church wardens of Chipping Ongar alleged that: William Farrington clerk, liveth idly in our town without serving any cure, contrary to the articles & laws ecclesiastical.

Item, we present him for not receiving the sacrament in our church for three quarters of this year, of purpose going out of the town every communion to avoid it.

Item, we present him to be a malicious, contentious & uncharitable person, & a railer of our minister & of most of the inhabitants that profess religion, calling them all heretics, hypocrites such as he hath ever & in every place detested, clowns etc.

Item, we present him for his open absence from prayers on the Sabbath days, in contempt of our minister, & for his usual departure out of the church, at such time as he cometh before the people be dismissed, contrary to the articles.

Here we see the community trying to control the activity of an unemployed and disruptive cleric. Note the mixture of ecclesiastical and secular malpractices alleged. Perhaps Farrington prompted this complaint by openly calling the good people of Chipping Ongar hypocrites and heretics.

Case 2 (1598)

Upon Sunday before Michaelmas in the time of afternoon service William Haynes of Sowthbemflete was dancing with minstrels on a green by Thomas Harris his howse.

Here we see the godly attempting to coerce the ungodly into seemly behaviour on Sundays. Is it dancing during the service or dancing in general to which they objected? Perhaps a modern equivalent would be middle-aged and middle-class objections to raves.

Case 3 (1600)

William Wallis and wife of Stanford Rivers reported for that they have made their habitation in the south porch of the parish church, & therwithall he doth not otherwise provide, but hath suffereth his wife to travail in childbirth therein & to continue there her whole month.

Here we see objection to the scandal of a man not providing adequately for his wife and child. Who wants to stumble across a poor couple and their baby every time one goes to church?

Case 4 (1592)

William Hylls, of Sandon was reported to be a very lewd and uncharitable man with his wife, and hath used her most ungodly, not only by refusing her company, but also by beating her most cruelly, without any pity or compassion.

Hylls came on that day and confessed that he upon occasion that his wife had beated and misused his sister and some fatherless children, whom he keepeth in his house, he gave her eight strokes with a wand: for the which he is sorry for now, and promiseth never to use himself in like sort hereafter.

It is worth noting that the church courts were very keen on protecting women and that proportionately more women appear as complainants in church courts than in other jurisdictions. At first sight this looks like a simple case of wife-beating. But why did Hylls beat his wife? Was it because she objected to his having his sister and her bastard children living with them? We can see here how the court penetrated into the very heart of home life.

Case 5 (1599)

Thomas Ward, of Purleigh was presented, as by report, to seek help at sorcerer's hands.

He confessed that he having lost certain cattle & suspecting that they were bewitched, he went to one Tailer in Thaxted, a wizard to know whether they were bewitched or not, and to have his help.

We see here the conflict between two belief systems, Christianity and natural religion, and the attempt by the court to regulate the latter. Ward, having lost his cattle, turns to magic to try to recover them. The Church's response is to summon him before its court. Magic was not to be tolerated.

Case 6 (1600)

Thomas Peryn of Rayleighe reported for a common drunkard &
railer and chider to the grief of the Godly & great danger of his soul.

The fate of his soul or the inconvenience of having a drunk in the parish
may have provoked this presentment.

We may infer from these cases that there was no room for unseemliness or
deviation from the norm in early modern England. No court so penetrated
the home and the mundane activities of ordinary people as the church
courts. There appear to be no activities the church court could not consider. But at whose insistence, the Church's or the people's? Most of these
cases began as complaints from neighbours; it was not so much the Church
hierarchy as the laity who demanded conformity. But we cannot say for
certain whether it was the people in general or just the "godly" who were
demanding these higher standards of conduct, but we can say that the
church courts were attempting to impose high Christian standards of
personal conduct on people at large. With what success is another matter.
No court had such a high proportion of defendants ignoring its jurisdiction
as the church courts. Church courts had high aims but displayed poor
performance. That said, the church court represented a more humane
approach to human frailty than the secular courts and had at its heart the
aim not so much of punishing as of reforming the criminal.

Manor courts

Where did the majority of Tudor Englishmen go to get justice in both civil
and criminal causes? Which court most impinged on their everyday lives?
The answer in many villages and towns was their local manor court or
borough court.

In origin, manor courts predate the Conquest. When their records
emerge in the mid-thirteenth century, it is clear that a fully developed legal
system was already in operation. In lay terms, manor courts were private
courts, that is they were the courts of a particular lord, rather than of the
Crown. However, the Crown ceded public functions to some of these private courts; that is these manor courts could and in some cases did administer royal justice. These were called courts leet. A similar process took place
with boroughs. In their criminal jurisdiction, borough courts and manor
courts were very similar. It is the criminal jurisdiction of these courts with
which we are concerned, but a vast number of civil and administrative
actions were also undertaken at these courts. In this they replicated the
business of quarter sessions and assizes. The sharp divisions between civil,
criminal and administrative law had yet to be made.

In the fourteenth century the peasants rebelled against excessive seigneurial demands, demands that were enforced in the manor courts. After the Great Revolt of 1381 the manorial lords conceded legal and economic freedoms to the peasantry (because they had to). However, the manor courts survived. The lord had an obvious vested interest in maintaining his courts; they gave him power and money. And the peasants got cheap, convenient and quite efficient justice. The courts were also necessary for the regulation of common rights and the organization of the common fields, which even in pastoral villages survived in some measure in most parts of England. Above all, they were crucial in the conveyance of land. So manor courts survived because they met a need; in the sixteenth century they went through something of a revival.

Courts leet normally met twice a year, once around Michaelmas and once around Easter. In general, all adult males (i.e. all males over 12) were required to attend. Numbers attending manor courts could be considerable. At the 1578 Michaelmas leet of the joint manor court of Cannock and Rugeley 265 suitors were summoned, of whom 190 attended. To them should be added the court's officers. The business of this court was in no way odd, so a figure of about 200 at any one meeting of the court seems likely. At the 1591 Michaelmas leet of Alstonfield (also Staffordshire) 340 suitors were summoned, of whom 237 (70 per cent) attended. Again we must add the officials, say a total of *c.* 250. The Elizabethan Manchester leets had in attendance 78 officeholders plus the jurymen, about 100 officials in all; then there were the suitors. In comparison, the numbers attending the Elizabethan Staffordshire Quarter Sessions were about 150 to 200, and the numbers attending the Chester palatinate courts at this time between 400 and 450. The very number attending courts leet indicates their importance.

At Cannock the court was held at the market cross, a simple open-sided structure; when at Rugeley it was held in the "corte house". Neither was large enough to hold 200 people. It may be that the jury and the officers of the court sat in the court-house or market cross, under shelter, behind opened shutters, where they could be seen and heard. Maybe the suitors milled around outside, pressing forward when their particular villages or hamlets were being dealt with. A meeting of such a court should be thought of as much more mobile than that of present-day courts with constant comings and goings of defendants and suitors.

The judge of a manor court was the steward; in borough courts it was usually the mayor. Stewards of manors on large estates were often gentlemen, even knights, but regardless of status all stewards required a considerable knowledge of the law since manorial law was quite complex. The steward sat with a clerk, who kept a record of the court in Latin. The steward was assisted by a bailiff, a paid official whose duty was to summon the jury and collect all fines and amercements. (Amercements were non-fixed fines.) The other chief court official was the reeve. He was elected annually from among the more substantial peasant landowners.

The jury consisted of local peasant landholders. In theory they should have been freeholders, but in reality they were often copyholders, even cottagers. The jury never changed completely from court to court so there was always some continuity. The numbers on manorial juries varied enormously but was never less than twelve. The surveyor John Norden argued for odd-numbered juries to prevent a hung jury, which suggests that such juries operated on majority verdicts.

How were cases brought before the court? Except for the smallest, each manor was divided into a number of tithings – groups of neighbours responsible for each other's behaviour. Each year one or more of these neighbours were elected tithingmen. They were responsible for presenting all offences in their tithings. On many manors there were also ale-tasters. Their job was to report any offences against the assize of bread and ale. In some manors offences were also presented by the village constable. He too was elected annually at the manor courts.

So ale-tasters, tithingmen and/or a constable presented offenders to the court. A jury decided on guilt or innocence and added presentments of offences omitted by the lesser officers. The jury also laid down standard punishments for common offences in intermittently issued by-laws. Finally, two or more additional elected officers, called affeerers, decided on the level of punishment, nearly always a fine or amercement. Corporal punishment was rare save in the case of common scolds (nearly always women) for whom a ducking in the village ducking stool could be ordered.

There are two things to notice about this process: first, a large number of villagers were involved as officials of the court – it was an atypically democratic court in this sense; and secondly its penalties was enforceable. If a defendant failed to pay a fine, the bailiff attached goods to the value of the unpaid fine. The final sanction of the court was to dispossess the peasant of his land.

The sort of criminal case that came before these courts varied widely. At Cannock and Rugeley the number of presentments for theft at any one court was low; they consisted of allegations of theft of small domestic or farming items and stock. However, some serious thefts do appear on the record; for example four horses in 1551 and a gelding worth £4 in 1583. And in 1554 a local was convicted of robbing a lone woman on Cannock Chase of over ten shillings. He fled the area and his lands and goods were seized by the lord. But few cases of theft were dealt with in this court. Perhaps this means the people of Cannock and Rugeley were basically honest. Perhaps not, for many (perhaps most) cases of theft were dealt with not through the criminal process but through the civil process. If you stole from someone, he took a civil action against you for trespass or damage rather than a criminal action. The low number of presentments in the court leet for theft give a misleading notion of the general level of theft.

The great majority of criminal presentments in Cannock and Rugeley were for affrays. The villagers would fight anywhere, even in the graveyard and the parish church. Social status was no barrier as the occasional presentment of a gentleman or cleric shows. Nor was sex a bar, affrays between women and women and between men and women being regularly presented. The disputants used axes, browsing-hooks, pitchforks, hammers, candlesticks, knives, spades and their bare hands. There were seldom fewer than a dozen presentments at each court, and by the end of the sixteenth century the number had risen to well over twenty per court. Indeed so common was the offence that in 1560 the jury promulgated a new by-law laying down the level of amercements. Affrays of words cost a shilling, affrays leading to blows 1s 8d, affrays leading to blood-shedding 3s 4d, and affrays in someone's house 5 shillings. The "Saturday night punch-up" that today is tried in a magistrate's court was then more often than not tried in a manor court or borough court.

Another area in which the court was active was the alehouse, which was clearly seen as a place of disorder and criminality. In 1560 the Cannock jury ordered that no alehouse keeper was to accommodate vagrants, travelling men or women of evil fame (i.e. prostitutes) for more than one night under a penalty of 6s 8d. In 1592 a further by-law instructed alehouse keepers not to permit daughters or servants to stay after nine o'clock at night. The most regular presentments after affrays were for gambling: cards, dice, bowls and, above-all, shove-ha'penny. These offences were always associated with alehouses. For example, Tomkins of Cannock was amerced three times in the 1580s for permitting his alehouse to be used for gambling, and in April 1580 he was amerced the large sum of 6s 8d for permitting strangers suspected of being thieves to stay in his house. It is clear the court saw a link between gambling and thefts.

One atypical case illustrates the power of these minor courts. On 20 December 1586 the vicar of Rugeley attempted to rape Alice Parker, the wife of a Rugeley alehouse keeper. A rape was clearly beyond the jurisdiction of the court, yet the vicar was tried for that offence. First he was amerced 1s 8d for an affray (i.e. the rape), then 6s 8d for playing cards, then 6s 8d for playing shove-ha'penny. Finally, he was fined a massive £10 (twice his annual income) for wearing a velvet cap in church on Christmas Day, a breach of a law passed in Mary's reign. How did the jury recall this obsolete piece of legislation? Because the steward copied out the law and read it to them. Thus through this legal trick did the local people deal with this serious assault.

Between 1584 and 1602 the joint manor court of Cannock and Rugeley dealt with hundreds of criminal cases, mostly assaults. During the same period the Staffordshire justices of the peace dealt with only 9 cases of assault, 18 cases of theft and 7 cases of poaching from this area.

But was this peculiar to Cannock and Rugeley or to Staffordshire? Was it peculiar to the sixteenth century? Harland, writing of the Elizabethan court leet of Manchester said:

> Much of the ancient power of the lord of a manor was delegated to the steward, the boroughreeve and constables, the Court Leet juries, and the executive manorial officers under their direction and control. For an autocracy, was in fact substituted a sort of representative government, however imperfectly modelled or constituted.

Willcox, writing on the governance of Gloucestershire between 1590 and 1640 observed:

> While the court leet operated in a humbler sphere than the county courts, and by a law of its own, it was both a focus of community life and an active agency of government. The principle of authority was personified for the countryman in the manorial steward as much as in the village constable, and the law which affected him most nearly was the custom of the manor, as administered in its court, rather than the king's law of sessions and assizes. To him the manorial system was the government of his daily life.

On the Lancashire manor of Prescott (population *c.* 500), between 1615 and 1660, just under 4,800 cases were recorded at the court leet. Of these, 1,250 were for assaults. During the same period only 23 cases of assault were presented in the quarter sessions. King argues that "no study of nonfelonious crime can claim to be complete unless it includes leet data. Focusing upon only the higher courts misrepresents the nature and frequency of illegal activity." However, this frequency of criminal jurisdiction is not found at Wakefield (Yorkshire). This huge manor, which in 1583 required the court to meet on four separate days in four different places to do its business, still dealt with only about 40 affrays, which given the size of the manor and its population seems low. Wakefield was a Duchy of Lancaster manor, so perhaps serious cases went before the main Duchy courts. A similar absence of manorial criminal jurisdiction is to be found in early modern Kent.

So the question remains, just how widespread was the criminal jurisdiction of courts leet? Was it active in most villages and towns? We do not and will not know until more local studies are completed. We can say with reasonable certainty, however, that in many areas manor courts and borough courts were an integral part of the administration of criminal justice in Tudor and early Stuart England.

Sex and the courts in early modern England

Both church courts and manor courts were actively engaged in regulating sex and it is to criminal sexual activity that we now turn. Most societies have sexual taboos and punish those who break them. The Tudors were no exception; for them, vice was dangerous both to society and the individual, and its cure was punishment. As the Duke in Dekker's *Honest whore* put it: "vice, like a wound lanced, mends by punishment". (Why sexual deviance should be considered dangerous to society is an interesting question. That this view has a long history is well illustrated in this book.) However, along-side this official attitude towards illicit sex was another that indulged in hypocrisy, self-righteousness and a certain vicarious pleasure in the sexual offences of others. Thus Lear in his madness cries out:

Thou rascal beadle hold thy bloody hand!
Why does thou lash that whore? Strip thine own back;
Thou hotly lusts to use her in that kind
For which thou whipp'st her.

Traditionally, the regulation of sexual behaviour had been the responsi-bility of the Church. One of the practical consequences of the Reformation, with the decline of ecclesiastical authority and power, was the intervention of the secular arm in this area. There was some legislation. Thus acts against "the detestable vyce of Buggorie" were passed in 1533, 1549 and 1563. However, on the whole, legislative action was limited. The state intervened largely through administrative devices such as proclamations and Privy Council letters where and when it felt it necessary. Many city councils and manor courts also legislated on sexual matters.

The first responsibility for the regulation of sexuality remained, however, with the Church and its courts. As we have seen they dealt with a large number of cases, over 2,000 or about 50 a year in Elizabethan Essex alone. The range of sex cases coming before the church courts was impressive. Consider the following sexual offences taken from the Essex church court records: adultery; rape; bigamy; father/daughter incest; mother/son incest; woman dressed as a man; running a brothel; sex before marriage; cuckoldry (not intervening when one's wife openly commits adultery); having sex with an unmarried woman. (Note that some of these activities are still illegal, others not.) However, the percentage of contumacious persons, those who ignored the judgment of the court, in this category was higher than that for any other offence. That is to say, whilst the Anglican Church was active in enforcing puritan sexual morality, its authority was flouted.

No wonder. The standard punishment was public penance. A penitent was expected to stand in the parish church during morning prayer for three consecutive Sundays, bare-headed, bare-legged, dressed in a white sheet carrying a white rod. The priest was instructed to denounce the sinner, who in turn was to publicly confess to the fault. It is little wonder that most avoided this public humiliation by not attending. The Church's failure to impose these punishments is one of the reasons why church courts fell into disrepute.

In practical terms, the most serious sexual offence was to produce a bastard, because the unfortunate child was likely to become a charge on the parish. (The child also lost many legal rights, could neither inherit, hold nor bequeath land for example.) It was in this area, above all others, that the lay arm was most active. The main aim was to establish who the father was and force him to take financial responsibility for his child. Increasingly this became the task of the JPs and the local overseers of the poor.

Pre-marital sex was not in itself an offence. Betrothal gave a couple *de facto* rights to sexual intercourse. This accounts for the high proportion of women who were pregnant at the time of marriage. Marriage was only necessary when a union had proved fruitful.

In the first half of the century extra-marital sex in the form of prostitution was openly available to Londoners in the stews of Southwark. In 1546 the stews were closed permanently by royal proclamation. Between then and 1553 the city fathers were very active in putting down prostitution. In July 1548, Founsing Besse, a one-time whore of the stews was taken with one of the king's trumpeters *in flagrante delicto* in a garden by Finsbury Court. The unfortunate woman (note it was the woman who was punished not the man) was led "with bassons tynged afore her" to Cheap, where she was set on the pillory, her hair cut off and a paper set on her breast detailing her vicious life, "which punishment", said the chronicler, "hath been an old ancient law in this city of long time and now put in use again".

Other typical London sex offences were adultery, rape and incest. These seem to have been quite lightly dealt with. An adulterous butcher was led through the city facing the back end of a horse to be set in the pillory for three and a half hours. A woman who acted as bawd for her own daughter and a young maidservant did public penance and was then banished. A married priest taken in the act of adultery was carried by a mocking crowd to Bridewell, his breeches still hanging around his knees. Stowe commented that "they were greatly blamed that apprehended him and committed him". A man who lay with his own daughter who died during her subsequent pregnancy was pilloried. In comparison with non-sexual offences these punishments seem light.

It is perhaps worth noting the offences that seem not to have occurred. Printing had not yet led to the development of published pornography, although by the mid-seventeenth century doubtful books of a sexually titillating nature were widely available, not just in London but nationwide. There seems to have been no equivalent of the modern "strip-show"; perhaps it was just too cold before central heating! Indecent exposure either did not happen or was not punished. Abortion appears rarely, but infanticide more frequently. As to the socio-economic status of sex offenders, they were mainly common people.

> Through tatter'd clothes small vices do appear;
> Robes and furr'd gowns hide all. Plate sin with gold
> And the strong arm of justice hurtless breaks;
> Arm it in rags, a pigmy's straw does pierce it.

Shakespeare was right, nevertheless; not all the mighty escaped public punishment. Lady Margaret Bowmer was burnt to death in 1537 for being wife to one Cheney and allowing herself to be "sold" as "wife" to Sir John Bowmer. Lord Hungerford was beheaded in 1540 (with Cromwell) allegedly for having sodomized his own daughter. Hungerford came from an accident-prone family; perhaps they were recidivists? His father's second wife murdered her first husband in 1518 and was hanged at Tyburn in 1524.

Even the episcopal bench was not immune to scandal. Edward Sandys, Archbishop of York from 1577 to 1588 was enticed into the bed of the wife of a Doncaster innkeeper. He was then discovered by the husband, who blackmailed him. Eventually Sandys had to reveal all and throw himself on the mercy of the Privy Council to escape the blackmailer's demands. Nor were Oxford colleges without their scandals: a fellow of Magdalen and master of the college school who went on to become Bishop of Lincoln and then of Winchester had the misfortune to have a wife who slept with his brother.

London did not have a monopoly on sexual immorality. Prostitution was widespread in other towns and more surprisingly in the countryside. Despite public prohibition, prostitution was to a certain extent institutionalized. The link between drinking, gambling and sexual immorality, which London's city fathers strove so hard against in mid-century, was also evident in the country. In Cannock and Rugeley, the manor court was constantly attempting to put down disorderly alehouses because in them gambling and prostitution were rife. In 1573 the Rugeley jury ordered all "mysordered women of evill conversacion" to leave the village. In 1576 three local men including one of the village constables were amerced (fined) for keeping Mary Patriche, a whore, in their houses. The frequent references in the manor court to this sort of sexual immorality show that it was very common, and such names as Grett Jane and Mother Margaret amongst the defendants leaves us in no doubt that Rugeley, a village of about 200 adult males, supported a number of working prostitutes.

The same seems to have been true of Keele where in 1570 the manor court ordered that villagers were not to take into their houses "any great bellied women as strangers" for more than three days under the threat of a massive 10s 0d amercement for each offence. Two years later they were ordered not to lodge in their houses "any women of evil conversation or being with child & unmarried or being openly suspected to be kept as misswomen either with married men or single". This appears to be an attempt by the manor court both to keep out bastards, who would be a charge on the parish, and to prevent loose living, perhaps even prostitution, within the village. The scattered evidence suggests that professional sexual services were available not only in the towns but also in the villages.

Borough courts and manor courts supplemented the activities of the church courts and the quarter sessions in attempting to regulate deviant sexual activity. (Deviant in this context simply means sex outside marriage.) Why this desire to impose sexual conformity through criminal law? Was it primarily the desire to impose God's law as they saw it? Or was there something more deap-seated about it. Given the number of cases, one thing we can say is that it did not work. Does it ever?

Conclusion

Church courts and manor courts were an integral part of the criminal justice system until the Restoration. Many, perhaps most, petty cases were heard in these courts, which intervened at every level of human activity. Each jurisdiction had its limitations but offered systems of justice more humane and in some respects more effective than quarter sessions and assizes. The justices of the peace, important as they were, had not yet replaced the manorial steward and the archdeacon as the arbiters of criminality in early modern England.

Chapter 4
The machinery of law enforcement

We have seen something of the pattern of early modern crime and of the array of courts operating at the time. But what of the territory in between? Was there a satisfactory system of bringing people to court once a crime had been committed? And were there in place mechanisms to put the rulings of the court into effect once a decision had been made? It is the purpose of this chapter to suggest that by the close of the sixteenth century there was in existence a sophisticated and many-layered system of law enforcement and that, if anything, this system became more complex and effective as time went by.

The macro-level

Some law-enforcement agencies operated on a regional level. The Council of the North, based at York, whose jurisdiction covered Durham, Yorkshire, Northumberland, Cumberland and Westmorland, is an example. So too is the Council in the Marches of Wales, which had its headquarters at Ludlow and performed a similar function in Wales and along the borderland of the principality. However, the crucial large-scale unit of law enforcement was the county.

Arguably, the principal figure operating at county level was the justice of the peace. It is certainly beyond question that, as well as acting in the capacity of judges at quarter sessions and petty sessions and sometimes sitting singly in their own homes, the justices had a considerable hand in imposing the law. This involvement took several forms. One way the JPs played a part in law enforcement was as supervisors, keeping others up to the mark. It was the justices, for example, who generally oversaw the imposition of the Poor Law. They appointed officials such as parish overseers of the poor, they scrutinized Poor Law accounts, they approved parish poor rates, they adjudicated in disputes and they heard appeals against overseers' decisions. Frequently, lax officials were heavily reprimanded by the justices. In 1622, for instance, the overseers of Northallerton were peremptorily commanded by the assembled JPs at Richmond Quarter Sessions "to receive and provide for Jane Dawson al[ia]s Aselbie". The order was accompanied by the threat of a hefty £5 fine "for everie Overseer that shall refuse".

In another Yorkshire case in 1651 the justices imposed the huge fine of £20 on a group of overseers "for contemning an Order and not paying monies due".

As well as acting in a supervisory capacity, JPs performed a regulatory role – fixing wage rates, for instance, and licensing alehouses. The latter function was regarded as particularly important. Alehouses were looked on with apprehension for a whole variety of reasons. They were regarded by many in authority as a leading cause of poverty – places where working people frittered away their earnings on drink and gambling. Some observers also saw them as politically subversive. "Too many of them", declared Robert Harris in 1610, "are even the nurseries of all riot, excess and idleness." Many alehouse keepers were suspected of harbouring thieves and other criminals, a charge in which there was probably some substance. Certainly a surprising number of landlords were brought before the courts accused of receiving stolen goods. On top of all this many people had moral qualms about the rougher houses. Here drunkenness and brawling were commonplace, and sexual licence suspected. Many London premises were known to double as brothels. Some provincial establishments, too, had far from blameless reputations. Elizabeth Hodges, a lodger at one Worcestershire alehouse, was allowed by her landlord to have sex with her clients "upon his own bed and his wife put her apron before the window to shadow them". Their reward was a cut of the profits.

Still more important than his work as regulator and supervisor was the JP's direct involvement in imposing the law. His most significant contribution was the way he acted on receiving a complaint from a member of the public. It was the JP's duty, once an allegation of wrongdoing had been made, to take evidence from the aggrieved party and also from witnesses. Next, he would take the accused's statement. If the case was a trivial misdemeanour the justice might deal with it there and then. But if it was anything more serious the JP usually took all the necessary steps to bring the issue before the appropriate court – normally the quarter sessions or the assizes. In practice this meant either bailing or remanding the accused in custody and, in the fullness of time, ensuring that the defendant, plaintiff and prosecution witnesses turned up at the court hearing. At the same time, of course, the justice would hand on to the court officials the various statements and depositions he had taken. These documents would then form the basis of the court's examination.

Thus it can be seen that the JP's direct involvement in law enforcement was absolutely crucial. Most cases that came before the assizes and the quarter sessions were initiated by a member of the public, and, although a citizen could go direct to a court, the normal procedure was to take complaints to a JP. The reason for this was that courts assembled only intermittently and then often in a distant town. JPs, by contrast, were much nearer to hand: normally there was a justice resident in most villages of any size.

Further, as time went by, the JP's direct role increased in importance. Before the end of the seventeenth century it was the accepted view that, unless a case was a minor infringement, the JP had, once he had gathered evidence, to pass the matter on to the appropriate court. Even if the case seemed woefully weak, or the prosecution was simply malicious, the justice had no discretion. All cases, the flawed as well as those with some substance, had to be forwarded for trial. As the eighteenth century proceeded, however, JPs began to take more authority into their own hands.

The change came about in two ways. First, magistrates came to deal summarily with a growing range of matters. Wood theft, the embezzlement of materials by employees, game cases, vagrancy – all these were increasingly dealt with by justices sitting alone at home. This change is reflected in the increasing numbers of "idle and disorderly and pilfering persons" who begin to appear in local houses of correction from the reign of Queen Anne onwards, sent there on the order of a particular justice. But even more striking was the second development. By the middle years of the eighteenth century more and more magistrates were taking it upon themselves to throw out weak cases – even when accusations of felony were involved – at the preliminary fact-gathering stage. For instance, Richard Wyatt, the mid-eighteenth-century Surrey justice, dismissed a charge against two chimney-sweeps who had been working around the northern part of the county and sleeping in barns and who were suspected of burgling a yeoman's house at Egham. He did so when, after cross-examining the two men, he concluded that there was simply "insufficient evidence" to justify sending them to trial. Similarly, we know that on a number of occasions in 1752 Henry Fielding discharged people who had been brought before him at Bow Street accused of serious offences. On one occasion Fielding even set free a man implicated in a murder because he felt the accused "made his innocence appear so evident".

JPs, then, played a major role in the story of early modern law enforcement. They acted in a supervisory and a regulatory capacity, and above all they were heavily and directly involved in bringing people to justice. Even so, the JPs were by no means the only officers engaged in law enforcement at county level. Another crucial county figure was the sheriff.

For much of the Middle Ages the sheriff had been the dominating servant of the Crown in most English shires. During the course of the sixteenth century, however, a good deal of the sheriff's authority was stripped away. For example, much of the work of the sheriff's two courts – the tourn and the county court – was taken over by the court of quarter sessions, while the emergence of the lords lieutenant deprived sheriffs of most of their military importance. Despite this diminution in his stature, however, the sheriff retained important functions as a law-enforcement officer.

One of a sheriff's tasks in the law-enforcement field was to publicize the dates of the meetings of the quarter sessions and assize courts. He was, in addition, responsible for serving writs – not just writs issued by quarter sessions and assizes, but also writs from the Westminster courts. It also fell to the sheriff to ensure the presence of jurors at assizes and quarter sessions and also of others required to attend. In 1613 the high sheriff of the county of York was fined forty shillings "for his Bailiffes Generall Default in not returning sufficient Jurors for his Maties service" for the September quarter sessions at New Malton. And, once the courts had completed their business, the sheriff was called on to carry out the punishment of those found guilty and, in particular, to collect all the fines imposed.

Perhaps the most important legal function of the sheriff, however, arose from his control of the county gaol. As we shall see in the chapter on punishments, incarceration had, by the close of the eighteenth century, become an extremely important form of punishment. In consequence, many JPs at quarter sessions became increasingly concerned that the county gaols were under the jurisdiction of the sheriffs and therefore largely outside their own direct control. In the 1770s it was music to their ears to hear John Howard propose that the justices meeting at quarter sessions should be given the power to appoint the county gaoler and his warders as their salaried officials. But even before this, when prisons were used primarily as holding institutions for those awaiting trial, the magistrates were constantly intervening in an effort to keep the sheriffs up to the mark. In 1619, for example, the Yorkshire sheriff, Sir Robert Swift, was rapped over the knuckles for carelessly permitting a prisoner to break out of the county gaol. Thirty-eight years later one of his successors was ordered to take immediate steps to recapture two men who had escaped from his custody. He was threatened with a peremptory fine of £20 "unless they are apprehended and brought before a Justice of the Peace within twenty days".

The sheriff and the JPs were unquestionably the chief law-enforcement officers operating at county level. But they do not constitute the full range of county officials. The sheriff, for instance, had a number of subordinates. These included under sheriffs and bailiffs, both of whom served writs and carried out arrests. There were also other free-standing officials, such as coroners. The main brief of a coroner was to investigate suspicious deaths. He took depositions and could imprison those he suspected of homicide. He also had the power to require both witnesses and suspects to appear at subsequent assizes or quarter sessions. Viewed in the round, therefore, the machinery for enforcing the law on a macro scale was by no means simple or lacking in refinement.

The micro-level

At the other extreme, contrasting the region and the county, was small-scale law enforcement. Here, one unit of significance, certainly until well into the seventeenth century, was the manor (the role of the manor court and its officers was considered in Ch. 3). By the close of the sixteenth century, however, the manor was being challenged by the parish as an area of law enforcement at the local level. Despite the remoteness and the modest size of many villages, by the time the last Tudor departed the throne in 1603 they had all acquired a liberal sprinkling of parish officials, all of whom were engaged in one way or another in law enforcement. These included surveyors of the highway, who dealt with various infringements and wrongdoings connected with the upkeep of roads and the free flow of traffic, and overseers of the poor. (The Poor Law Act of 1601 stated that there should be two, three or four of these overseers for every parish.) The overseers had a hand in bringing to justice a variety of Poor Law cases. In particular, especially before the easing of population pressure in the 1660s, they were heavily involved in the disciplining of vagrants and other ne'er-do-wells. From the point of view of law enforcement, however, the two most significant parish officials were the churchwardens (two per parish) and, above all, the petty constables (in theory one per township but, by the late seventeenth century, often in practice one per parish).

The chief obligations of the churchwardens had nothing to do with the law and its enforcement but, as the name of the office implies, concerned the running and administration of the parish church. In particular, wardens were responsible for the upkeep of the fabric of their church and church-yard and for the church furniture. The latter included not only things like the Communion table and "a comely and honest pulpit" but also the parish registers and various doctrinal and devotional books. In 1579, for example, Ralph Wright, one of the churchwardens of the parish of Stockton in the North Riding of Yorkshire, was excommunicated for failing to ensure that the church contained a copy of "the Communion Boke". The wardens also made provision out of the parish funds for a supply of church plate, robes for the clergy, a surplice for the parish clerk and a dress for the beadle. In 1662 the churchwardens of the parish of Houghton-le-Spring laid in a stock of 17 gallons and 1 pint of Communion wine "against Easter" at a cost of £1 17s 6d. They also spent a further 1s 4d on bringing it home. Evidently, either the size of the Easter congregation at Houghton was expected to be exceptional or communicants in the parish were in the habit of taking a more than normally large swig of the healing fluid.

Even so, although the churchwardens' main interests lay outside the sphere of the law, they none the less formed an important component of the law-enforcement machine. For one thing, it became the accepted practice in many areas for the churchwardens to serve on the hundredal juries; and the job of these juries was to bring to the attention of the magistrates gathered at quarter sessions any crimes or misdemeanours that had occurred in the various parts of their counties. Indeed, in 1661 the Essex bench, meeting at Chelmsford, alarmed at the poor quality of the hundredal juries in the county, actually went so far as to order that "the Bayliffs of ev[er]y hundred doe for the future impagnell the Constables and Churchwardens of ev[er]y p[ar]ish, village and hamblett to serve upon the petty Juries". In this way, it was felt, there would be a reasonable chance that "all misdemeano[ur]s, nusances & breaches of the peace" would be punished since the wardens and constables were the "best accquainted wth the grievances, annoyances & distemp[er]s in this County".

Still more important than the churchwarden's contribution as a member of the hundredal jury was his role in relation to what today we would probably loosely classify as family law. The warden was recognized to have a special obligation to bring before the courts all moral offences that came to his attention within the parish. Normally the court in question would be one of the many ecclesiastical courts, but it could also on occasion – when sabbath breaking, for example, was involved or where there was an infringement of the law relating to alehouses – be the quarter sessions court. The variety of these moral offences was immense. They ranged from drunkenness, unruly behaviour and the singing of bawdy songs to homosexuality, rape and incest. Most cases, however, seem to have involved either adultery or pre-marital sex, which by the seventeenth century was becoming less acceptable. In 1608, in a typical case, the churchwardens of Thame in Oxfordshire reported to the archdeacon's court that "John Thomlinson and the wiffe of George Ellis were Lockt into a Rome togither very suspiciously by her husbands report". In another Oxfordshire case of the 1660s, John Applegarth and Katherine Baker were both sentenced to do penance in Benson church after being presented by the churchwardens "for lyinge in bed together three nights". Applegarth seems to have been quite smitten with the Baker family for five years later he was again hauled before the courts by the local wardens for "liveing together" with Joane Baker "haveing not showne any sufficient proofe that they are married". The result of this second liaison was an illegitimate child.

As well as being expected to act in cases of moral delinquency among parishioners the churchwardens were enjoined to keep a special eye on the behaviour of the parish priest. Sometimes the incumbent's failings mirrored those of his flock. For instance, in 1625 one curate of a village a dozen miles or so to the north of Henley-on-Thames was brought in shame before the church court when it was belatedly discovered that he was the father of a village child "unlawfully begotten" three years before. In a moment of weakness the curate had, it seems, lain with a comely maiden from his parish "by the fires syde att her mothers howse in the night tyme when her mother was gone to bed" and he had lived with this dark secret ever since. Usually, however, a vicar's crime was neglect rather than moral turpitude. In 1587, in an abnormally bitter dispute, the churchwardens of Barnard Castle in County Durham severely criticized their local priest, Thomas Clark, for his general inattention to duty. They accused him of not signing children on the forehead with a cross, of neglecting to perambulate the parish on Rogation Days, of refusing to administer Communion to a sick man despite the fact that he had obtained the necessary complement of people to receive the sacrament with him, of not being at home when needed to bury two corpses and of declining to christen a child on a working day unless its father swore that the child was going to die, "though he had christened wealthy men's children". This case, with its hint of class antagonism (one warden was a husbandman, the other a labourer, and both were illiterate) is a particularly fascinating one.

The churchwardens, the overseers of the poor and the surveyors of the highway all played their part in law enforcement. But the leading law-enforcement officer at parish level was, it is becoming increasingly clear, the petty or parish constable.

One clue to the constable's importance as a lawgiver is contained in the number of occasions on which he was called on to report to higher authority. Four times a year the constable had to attend on the justices at the court of quarter sessions. Four times also it was his duty to attend the petty sessions of the high constable. In addition, twice a year he was obliged to appear before the justices to give an account of all rogues and vagabonds found in his area of jurisdiction. Few local officials were so regularly on show, so frequently on the move or so carefully scrutinized.

A second tell-tale sign is the constable's social standing. In his memorable portrait of Dogberry in *Much ado about nothing* Shakespeare depicted the village constable as a figure of fun – lazy, ineffective and unlettered. But in her recent writings Joan Kent has taught us how misplaced this view really is. Real-life examples of Shakespeare's rustic buffoon no doubt existed, but they were far from being the norm. Most constables were men of wealth and authority within their communities. Typically they were substantial yeomen, just below the level of gentry. In the village of Pattingham in Staffordshire, for example, 63 of the 81 constables who held office between 1583 and 1642 were large or middling farmers. A further nine were either craftsmen or traders – men drawn from the more prosperous and stable element of the cottage population. Men like these were not village idiots. They were, on the contrary, numbered among the leaders of the parish. Many also served as churchwardens. They put their names to important decisions of the vestry, and they sat year after year on the leet jury. They were the salt of the village earth.

The real pointer to the constable's importance, however, is to be found in the nature of his work. By the close of the sixteenth century hardly any aspect of law enforcement at the local level lay outside his brief. He helped administer the vagrancy acts. He supervised all alehouses within his area of jurisdiction. It was his duty to apprehend anyone who had committed a felony. Also he could, if he saw a minor offence or a breach of the peace about to take place, seize and place the offender in the stocks or in some other secure place until justice could be done. In addition, the constable had to execute all warrants sent to him by a superior officer and obey all orders of the justices and the sheriff. It is perhaps not too extravagant to say that, at village level anyway, the constable represented the cutting edge of the law. He was a one-man police force, handling issues that today might command the attention of an army of officers or a fleet of panda cars. "The parish", wrote Eleanor Trotter three-quarters of a century ago, "might have existed without its surveyor, its overseer, or even its churchwardens, but assuredly not without its constable, since on him depended the continuance of order and stability in those restless and uncertain times." Her words cannot be bettered today.

The intermediate level

We have examined the law-enforcement machine at county and parish levels. But in between was a series of intermediate components whose area of authority was greater than that of the parish but less extensive than that of the county.

One intermediate division of the realm was the hundred. This was a sub-unit of the county, containing usually half a dozen or so parishes. And within a hundred the chief figure was the high constable. The high constable was a man of real social standing, in dignity only a little below the level of a JP. As far as rural England was concerned his essential function was to link up the large-scale with the small. Appointed by the bench of magistrates, he passed the instructions of quarter sessions down to the individual parishes, and he kept a beady eye on the performance of all local officers. In addition, the high constable performed the role of peace keeping in his hundred that the petty constable performed in the parish. In effect he was the Scotland Yard of the early modern policing world.

The other crucial middle-level division of the country was the borough. By contemporary reckoning early modern England and Wales contained six hundred or more towns and cities. In his *Index Villaris*, published in 1680, John Adams put the figure at 788, excluding London and Westminster. A decade or so later Gregory King revised the number upward to 794. Many of these settlements would, of course, have been very small, scarcely more than villages to modern eyes. But a good number of them were quite sizeable communities containing within their boundaries several parishes. For instance, in sixteenth-century Shrewsbury there were 5 parishes and no fewer than 19 in Exeter. Great cities like York and Norwich were positively bristling with parish churches.

These larger towns had often developed quite complex systems of government and law enforcement on the backs of the lesser parish officers. Normally one would have a governing council, consisting usually of an inner group of aldermen, and a larger common council. The corporation of Lincoln, for instance, comprised 13 aldermen and 26 common councillors. At Leicester the numbers were 24 and 48. In addition to the councils there would, too, be an array of town officials and also a number of town courts. A town court would often include a civil court, usually known as the "mayor's court" or the "court of record" (Ipswich had three such bodies), a court leet that handled petty police matters and perhaps a minor court or two, such as a court of the clerk of the market to sort out trading disputes on market days or a court of conservancy for enforcing customs relating to the local river. The most important towns even had their own courts of quarter sessions and their own JPs. One group of officials, not unknown at village level but particularly associated with towns, was especially concerned with enforcing law and order: the watch. The watch consisted of a number of officers known as watchmen who paraded the streets at night checking on prowlers and generally endeavouring to keep the peace. Often the watchmen were under the control of a town or ward sergeant. Sometimes the watch would be a salaried body, but in other places – at Hereford, for example – it was made up of volunteers.

The ladder of authority

One thing that added substance to the early modern law-enforcement mechanism was the fact that the various parts were not discrete elements separated one from another. On the contrary, the levels and units of enforcement were grouped together in a linked hierarchy, a ladder of authority. Information and orders were passed down from the apex of the system to the middle-rank officials and thence to the local level. Each layer in the hierarchy supervised and monitored the layer below it. Even within a level there was a good deal of cross-checking. We have already seen magistrates upbraiding sheriffs for allowing prisoners to escape and churchwardens hauling their vicars before the church court. The cross-disciplining was as likely to happen the other way round, a priest informing on his wardens or a sheriff admonishing the justices. All this meant that when the Crown or government wished to tighten up on the enforcement of a particular law their wishes carried real weight.

A classic example of such wish fulfilment occurred in the early 1630s when Charles I issued his celebrated "books of orders". The background to the production of the books was a major economic crisis. Successive harvest failures in 1629 and 1630 had resulted in soaring grain prices. At the same time the cloth industry was in deep trouble, and unemployment levels were climbing throughout East Anglia and much of the west of England. On top of all this came rumours of plague. In January 1631, fearing widespread disorder – there had already been food riots in the worst-hit areas of the

West Country – the Privy Council despatched 314 books of orders to the sheriffs for distribution among JPs and municipal authorities. The books comprised a series of instructions to the localities to tighten up on law enforcement generally and, in particular, to put into effect all the provisions of the Poor Law. JPs were to meet monthly in every hundred to supervise the work of the high and petty constables, the churchwardens and overseers of the poor. The justices were to send reports to the sheriffs, who were, in turn, to report to the assize judges, the direct agents of the Privy Council, on their six-monthly visits to each county.

The galvanizing effect of the books of orders appears to have been quite remarkable. Vagrants were vigorously suppressed, masters were forced to take apprentices whether they wished to or not (one JP, Thomas Coningsby of Herefordshire, protested vigorously about this) and the deserving poor were relieved as never before. Some of the remoter areas of the realm – Westmorland and parts of Wales, for example – set up systems of compulsory poor relief for the very first time, and elsewhere things were made much more thoroughgoing and inclusive. Although, not unnaturally, the whole movement began to run out of steam once the economic crisis that gave birth to it had passed, the effects of the campaign were perhaps never entirely lost. "It seems doubtful", writes Esther Moir, "how much of local government, and above all of the administration of poor relief, would have survived the dislocation of the Civil War without the Book of Orders. For nine years Justices and overseers had been drilled, parishioners had been compelled to pay rates, and the general population had become accustomed to the organization of poor relief."

One should not, of course, exaggerate. The ladder of authority had its limitations. For a council directive to succeed it was essential that the officials remote from the capital should be in broad sympathy with a policy being propounded. This is clearly demonstrated by the muted success that attended the campaigns against recusants launched from time to time during Elizabeth's long reign. In places like Lancashire, where many JPs and other officials remained loyal to the old faith, the anti-Catholic legislation made little headway. But where no such conflict of principle existed a royal drive to tighten up some aspect of law enforcement could be surprisingly successful.

Moving forward

One final aspect of the early modern system of law enforcement is perhaps worth stressing. As time went by the system became more and more effective. In a number of ways, for instance, the quality of the bench of magistrates was improving. One thing that helped to bring this about was the publication of simple legal textbooks to guide the faltering footsteps of the less educated JPs. Volumes by Marow (1503) and Fitzherbert (1538) had already appeared before the middle years of the sixteenth century, and these were followed by Lambarde's celebrated manual *Eirenarcha* in 1581. Finally, in 1754 came Richard Burn's classic four-volume study *The justice of the peace and the parish officer*, a book that went through edition after edition in the years that followed. Arranged alphabetically, Burn's invaluable guide took the uncertain justice through every conceivable variety of topic, defining terms with care and explaining the state of the law and the magistrate's powers on every issue. With Burn at his elbow not even the most inexperienced and ill-informed JP had cause to worry.

Another development that led to improvements in the magistracy was the increasing use of clerical justices. Occasionally clergy had found their way on to the bench in the seventeenth century, but it was only from the middle of the eighteenth century that they began to do so in significant numbers. By the close of the period clergy often accounted for a quarter or even a third of the magistrates in many counties. The significance of this remarkable move was that, with their university training and their sense of vocation, the clergy were often among the most active and effective of justices. They lent an altogether higher and more authoritative tone to the bench.

The growing effectiveness of the JPs constitutes just one aspect of improvement. Equally telling were changes lower down the scale. In many towns, for example, the watch threw off its dowdy image as the eighteenth century proceeded. One thing that led to improvement here was the spread of street lighting, a development that made it easier for the patrolling watchmen to spot potential criminals. Oil-lamps first began to appear in the streets of London in the 1680s, and by the 1690s they had spread to Bristol and Norwich. By 1713 word of the new-fangled lighting had reached as far north as Hull: in that year the city authorities instructed the local MPs to look out for a suitable set of lamps when they were in London on their parliamentary duties. From then on street-lighting schemes became a positive craze. At the same time a number of towns took steps to reorganize the structure of the watch. In parts of Westminster, for instance, greater attention was paid to the siting of watch-boxes, the hiring of suitable men and the laying out of patrol areas. The effect of such moves, combined with the more brightly lit streets, was to lend a new pride and professionalism to urban policing.

Better justices and better watchmen were accompanied by yet other changes. Not the least of these was the development of a system of petty sessions. Petty sessions were gatherings of justices that took place in the intervals between quarter sessions. Normally these meetings would be on a hundred or wapentake basis and they would involve the magistrates from that particular division. Before the close of the sixteenth century JPs from a number of regions had already begun to meet informally in this way. The real take-off point, however, seems to have come with the introduction of the books of orders in the 1630s. These books, demanding as they did regular monthly meetings of the justices within each hundred, ensured that petty sessions would henceforward become a more or less country-wide phenomenon. As a rule, the venue for the gatherings would be a prominent local inn, although, as the period wore on, purpose-built accommodation began to be provided in some places. In the 1780s, for instance, Gloucestershire designed and built a series of new houses of correction, and the plans for each building included a committee room for petty-session sittings. But, whatever the meeting place, the nature of the business transacted was the same. Matters relating to vagabonds, to alehouses, to wages, to the regulation of markets and to the Poor Law were all dealt with, as were cases of assault and petty larceny. All this meant that the burden on quarter sessions was eased, that justice was imposed in a more regular and more considered manner, and that local officials were monitored more closely. The efficiency of law enforcement was in consequence tightened and enhanced.

None of the changes we have so far noticed were specific to particular places. They could be found in all parts of the land. But there were, in addition to these broadly based developments, a number of changes that were more geographically concentrated. Normally these more localized advances were focused in and around the capital. Among the most notable was the introduction, from the 1730s, of what were to become known as "rotation offices". One of the problems with the traditional system of JPs was that, with the best will in the world, part-time, amateur justices could not always be on call. This meant that when an aggrieved person endeavoured to lay a complaint before a magistrate the JP was often not immediately to hand. Not infrequently the complainant, busy with other things, would not bother to return, so the crime would go unreported. Even if the justice was at home he might have other private business to detain him, so there would be a delay before the complaint could be properly dealt with. Inevitably this often gave criminals time to escape.

The rotation offices were designed to eliminate these shortcomings. The offices were special rooms set aside for the purpose where JPs, sitting in sequence (hence the word "rotation"), would be available for consultation at specific times each day. The first such office was in all probability that established by the corporation of London in 1737. Here the mayor and aldermen, who acted as magistrates for the city, took turns sitting daily at Guildhall between the hours of 11 am and 2 pm to transact judicial business. A couple of years later a similar office was organized in Westminster by the Bow Street justice Thomas de Veil. In the 1750s and 1760s others followed, including, in 1763, the first office south of the river, at St Margaret's Hill in Southwark. The whole process was brought to a climax with the Middlesex Justice Act of 1792 – a theme that is taken up in Chapter 10.

An interesting feature of the new rotation offices was that most of them appear to have had attached to them a small force of constables. Most of the income of these constables came from the rewards they received when they apprehended criminals. This seems to have encouraged at least some of them to be overzealous in their activities and even to rig evidence against suspects. In addition to the reward money, however, constables received a small regular wage plus a sum to cover expenses. This was a development full of implications for the future. In the past some historians have tended to see our modern salaried police force as a creation of the nineteenth-century reformers. Such a view oversimplifies what happened. The faint outlines of the Victorian police station, with its blue lamp shining palely through the mist, can, in fact, already be discerned in the rotation offices of the eighteenth-century capital.

The establishment of the rotation offices was only one of the notable London-based developments in law enforcement that took place during the course of the early modern period. Just as significant was the work of the Westminster justice Sir John Fielding in the 1770s. He established a national information network co-ordinated from the Bow Street office and encouraged justices of the peace, mayors, innkeepers, stable managers and others to furnish him with details of criminals and unsolved crimes. The Bow Street magistrate then published this material in a sheet called the *General Hue and Cry* (later retitled the *Hue and Cry and Police Gazette*) that was distributed widely across the country. As a result, criminals who had hitherto slipped easily and unnoticed from one area of jurisdiction to another began to find it more difficult to escape detection. A typical case was that of Richard Myett. In July 1773 Myett stole a quantity of silver from a silversmith's shop in Wallingford. Details of the theft were put in the *Hue and Cry*, and a fortnight later the offender was successfully picked up 130 miles away from the scene of the crime.

Conclusion

Our examination of the law-enforcement mechanisms of early modern England has revealed a tale of some complexity and not a little sophistication. By the end of the sixteenth century the country had acquired an elaborate and many-layered system for tackling crime and pursuing criminals. It was a system made all the more effective by its being hierarchical, and it was a system that, in a number of ways, improved over time. The view, still current in many quarters, that sees the policing and law-enforcing institutions of the three centuries of the early modern era as both primitive and ossified, staggering ineffectually along until mercifully reformed by Sir Robert Peel and his successors, is, it would appear, a view that is somewhat overstated. Certainly, as we shall see in the next chapter, the old system was not without its faults. But it was by no means the ramshackle and unchanging affair it is sometimes portrayed as.

Chapter 5
Imposing the law

In the previous chapter we saw that, by the end of the sixteenth century, England had acquired a dense and complex system of law enforcement. But how adequately was this machinery utilized? Was the law rigorously applied? Were offenders, as one might reasonably expect, routinely brought to justice? If not why, given the quite sophisticated mechanism of law enforcement, were criminals not regularly hounded down? These are the questions that will concern us in this chapter.

The pattern of law enforcement

It is, perhaps, unreasonable to expect an entirely uniform pattern of law enforcement over the whole span of the early modern period, a period that lasted for some three hundred years from the beginning of the sixteenth century to the end of the eighteenth. Not surprisingly, therefore, it is possible to detect fluctuations in the rigour with which the law was imposed. One thing that seems to have goaded the authorities into especially brisk activity was economic pressure. In towns in particular crime levels shot up when there was a dip in the trade cycle and hence a growth in unemployment. The courts responded with increased levels of indictments. A similar pattern occurred when wheat prices rose, though on these occasions the change was felt more sharply in the countryside than in the towns. All this suggests, argues Professor Beattie, "that a large number of people were close enough to the subsistence line for changes in prices to register immediately in their fortunes and for them to turn to theft to fill the gap". He might have added that it also suggests a certain degree of panic on the part of the public and of the powers that be, alarmed by the rising level of crime.

Even more marked than the upward trend in crimes and indictments in periods of economic difficulty was the contrast between peacetime and wartime. Almost without exception the courts swung into a phase of brisk activity whenever a major war came to an end. Douglas Hay has shown how in Staffordshire with the ending of hostilities in 1748 and again in 1763, and after the American war in 1783, "an immediate increase in committals for theft followed and was usually sustained until the year in which war was resumed". As was the case with the economy, this peacetime jump in the number of indictments was partly a question of soaring crime levels and also partly a product of an alarmed reaction on the part of society at large. One reason for the surge in criminality with the onset of peace was the unemployment created by the release of thousands of demobbed soldiers on to the labour market. Another was the effect on the economy when orders for uniforms, ammunition, ships' stores and the like dried up. But perhaps more significant than any of these reasons was the age profile of the returning soldiers. Mainly adolescent and young unmarried males were recruited into the army in wartime and it was this same group that formed the backbone of the criminal fraternity in early modern England. In the peacetime years of the mid-1780s, for example, about half of all those indicted on the home circuit were aged between 18 and 26. The reintroduction of so many young men into society with the signing of peace, therefore, provided a sure recipe for increased levels of crime.

There were, then, a series of short-term undulations in the pattern of law enforcement during the early modern period, and this situation was brought about in part by fluctuations in the economy and in part by the sequence of war and peace. But, over and above these short-term movements, it is possible to isolate two clear, long-term features of the law-enforcement pattern. The first of these is that, except in London, levels of prosecution and conviction fell away startlingly after the middle years of the seventeenth century. Gaol delivery records for Devon indicate that between 1598 and 1640 some two hundred and fifty cases were tried at the county assizes every year. By the first decade of the eighteenth century this figure had slumped to 38. The statistics for both the home circuit and the palatinate of Chester show a similar trend, while in Essex in the 1660s indictments in property cases were only at about a third of what they had been in the decade from 1625 to 1634. True, in the second half of the eighteenth century numbers coming before the courts began to climb once more. But in the main this reflects the rise in population and is, to some extent, an optical illusion. Certainly this is the case for homicide. In Surrey at the time of the Stuart restoration, for example, six people in every thousand were indicted for homicide each year. By the early years of the eighteenth century numbers had fallen to less than four per thousand per year; by the close of the century they were down to fewer than one per thousand. Moreover, in some areas declining indictments were matched by falling conviction rates. By 1734–7 no fewer than 40 per cent of felony cases tried at the Norfolk and Suffolk Assizes ended in dismissal or acquittal.

Over time an apparent decline in the rigour with which the law was enforced is one of the features of the early modern English legal system. Equally striking is another long-term characteristic, the patchy enforcement of the law, even early on when judges, juries and magistrates were seemingly at their keenest and most diligent. The thing that reveals this most clearly is the so-called "dark figure". The dark figure represents those crimes committed but never brought before the courts. By the very nature of things it is impossible to deploy precise data on the full extent of such unrecorded criminal activity. It is clear, however, that throughout the three centuries of the early modern era the size of the dark figure was considerable indeed. Writing in the 1790s Patrick Colquhoun reckoned that 90 per cent of London's crime went unreported. But even in the 1590s, when law enforcement was apparently much more vigorous and extensive, a man like the Somerset JP Edward Hext could express the opinion that only about one in five criminals in his native county had the misfortune to be hauled before the courts.

But why was this so? Why was crime, despite the existence of a many-layered law-enforcement system, apparently so laxly treated? And how do we explain the dwindling number of prosecutions and convictions in the years that followed the Civil War? Let us turn first to the broader problem of the patchy enforcement of the law over the period as a whole.

The limitations of the system

One of the chief factors underlying the patchy imposition of the law in the years after 1500 was a series of shortcomings in the machinery of enforcement. Sophisticated though the mechanism was in many ways there were also gaps and weaknesses. Some of these faults and failings concerned the justices of the peace themselves, the central figures in the drama of law enforcement. In the first place there were often simply too few justices around for the law to be effectively administered. At any one time the numbers of JPs varied from county to county. A list of 1580 gives a total of 1,738 justices for England as a whole. At the bottom of the league stood Rutland with 13, while Kent was the leading shire with no fewer than 83. Thirteen JPs was perhaps not an unreasonable number for a tiny county but many other shires were clearly understaffed. Throughout most of Elizabeth's reign, for example, the extensive county of Staffordshire usually had twenty justices, a number patently too few to control such a wide area. As for the 13 Welsh shires, the Act of Union of 1536 specified a maximum of eight JPs per county, and while this figure was not rigidly adhered to in all cases it is clear that Wales hardly had too many justices.

Perhaps even more important than the small numbers was the calibre of many JPs. Unquestionably, throughout the period there were, in almost every county, dedicated and gifted men on the bench. Typical of these activists was the Elizabethan squire George Owen of Henllys in Pembrokeshire. He attended quarter sessions with meticulous regularity and was endlessly resourceful in devising schemes to cope with the various problems thrown up by his office. One of his projects was to establish a county armoury to house the weapons and armour of the local militia and thus to circumvent the pilfering of armour and the deterioration of weaponry through poor storage. Another idea to issue from his fertile brain was the practice of tagging the ears of sheep and cattle. Cattle-rustling was a major problem in much of Wales and the borderland, and Owen's scheme was one of the first practical steps taken to combat it.

On a par with George Owen were men like the eighteenth-century Yorkshire justice Samuel Lister. Just how much time and effort Lister was prepared to put into his job is shown by the way he tracked down one particular felon in 1756. The man – who claimed his name was William Wilkins – had been detained in Bradford for failing to pay several inn bills. In Wilkins's pocket were bills of exchange and a promissory note adding up to the huge sum of £1,200. Suspecting that Wilkins had been up to something shady, Lister decided to pull out all the stops in investigating his case. He wrote for information to a number of people in the West Country, from where Wilkins claimed to come, and he also placed an advertisement in the *Evening Post* asking for help and information. Replies poured in, and eventually Lister was able to establish that Wilkins was a man called Edward Wilson who had participated in a major forgery in Gloucestershire. Accordingly, the prisoner was despatched southwards, where he stood trial at Gloucester Assizes and was sentenced to death. The whole investigation had taken Lister three months of painstaking work.

But for every George Owen and Samuel Lister there were a dozen men of less energy. Some JPs were little better than the criminals they were meant to pursue. In Elizabeth's reign Sir Thomas Jones of Carmarthenshire became notorious for his misuse of funds gathered for the purpose of equipping the county militia. He ordered parishes to buy armour from him and charged more than the cost price. He then proceeded to supply them with old armour, claiming it was new. It was reckoned that he cleared around £2,000 in this way. Another Welsh justice, Richard Price, head of the powerful Gogerddan family of Cardiganshire, ordered all the people of the locality to attend divine service at Tregaron church one Sunday in 1599. When the congregation emerged they found Tregaron market place full of Price's retainers. A wooden platter had been placed on the stile leading from the churchyard, and grouped around it were Price and three other JPs. In a short speech the squire informed the churchgoers that he had organized a comortha or voluntary gift and that he hoped people would find it in their hearts to be generous. He also informed the listeners that he and his fellow JPs were empowered to enlist people for service in the army in Ireland if they saw fit. By the time the last desolate country dweller had filed out of the churchyard Price and his cronies were richer by a hundred pounds.

Most of the less exemplary JPs, however, were neither crooks nor tyrants. They were simply not very committed to the job. The title justice of the peace carried with it considerable cachet. No-one who was anyone wanted to be left out of the commission. Hence, many justices in any given county at any one time were simply there for the prestige the office brought. They had no intention of attending boring meetings or working into the small hours. Thus, even in counties that at first glance might seem to be quite generously supplied with justices, those who were active JPs could be alarmingly few. Lord Hardwicke put the situation succinctly in 1754. "Gentlemen", he wrote, "are apt to be very pressing to get into the Commission of the Peace, and when they are appointed, to be very backward in acting. Tis a common complaint in many counties, that, tho great numbers are in the Commission, yet there are not acting justices enough to do the ordinary business of the county." Hardwicke urged the judges, as they went on circuit, to do all in their power to end this "great abuse" and to "exhort and encourage" the inactive to bestir themselves. His words, however, fell on deaf ears. Indeed, if anything the situation got worse as time went by. In Kent, according to Norma Landau, about two-thirds of the commission attended quarter sessions and assizes or involved themselves in criminal and administrative matters in their own parishes at the time of Queen Anne's death in 1714. By 1760 only some forty per cent did so.

It was not, however, just their inactivity or the questionable character of so many magistrates that blunted their effectiveness. The job JPs were called on to do was simply too vast. Not only did the justices have a role in law enforcement. They stood in as judges at quarter sessions and petty sessions and even acted singly in their own parlours. They were, too, the chief administrative officers of their own counties, supervising the implementation of such diverse subjects as road repairs, poor relief, recusancy legislation, alehouse licensing, apprenticeship indentures and wage regulation. Practically all the matters taken over in the nineteenth century by the county councils, with their specialist committees and salaried officials, were in the eighteenth century and earlier handled by these part-time, unpaid, amateur justices of the peace. Small wonder that even the most active and committed of them were not always entirely successful in imposing the law.

The JPs were not the only law-enforcement officials who left something to be desired. Town watchmen had their failings also. True, from the late seventeenth century, there were, as we have seen, improvements in the watch, but even in the eighteenth century few watchmen were shining examples of skill and rectitude. Henry Fielding, the celebrated Westminster magistrate, was scathing about the London variety. They were, he averred, chosen "out of those poor, old decrepit people who are for want of bodily strength rendered incapable of getting a livelihood by work". Frequently they passed their time chatting to each other or going on errands for various citizens rather than patrolling the streets. There was a suspicion, too, that some of the night watchmen were not above turning a blind eye if their palms were well enough oiled. Certainly one eighteenth-century Lord Mayor of London, Matthew Wood, was of this view. "From their practice of being fixed in their stations and boxes for many years", he wrote, "there is no doubt that some of them receive bribes from persons who commit robberies in the streets as well as in houses." As proof of his suspicions Wood cited the fact that "notorious characters" who "must be well known to the watchmen" were permitted to "attend Fleet Street and other public streets every night" unchallenged and to engage freely "in constant conversations with prostitutes".

Problems were not limited to JPs and watchmen. Even the parish constables, who were not, as we have seen, the bumbling halfwits of Shakespearian legend, had their failings. One difficulty was the constable's brief tenure of office: he was appointed for only a year, then the post was rotated. Each incumbent had therefore only just got to grips with the intricacies of office when he had to hand the torch on. Another limiting factor was the lack of backup. The constable had no assistants and certainly no formal protection. In consequence threats and other forms of intimidation by the general public were far from uncommon if a constable proved too insistent or too heavy-handed. Typical was the case of the Shrewsbury cooper John Morgan, who in 1707 was fined 20 shillings and ordered "to stand comitted to the Comon Serjt. till he pay the same with the ffees" for "Assaulting George Clarke One of the Constables for the Stone Ward Within the Walls in the Execucon his sd. Office". The stiffness of the fine, despite the fact that Morgan voluntarily appeared before the court and was not backward in "submitting to the same", is perhaps an indication of how difficult it was to curb such violent behaviour.

The chief trouble with the constables, however, arose from their dual role. Both Keith Wrightson and Joan Kent have pointed out that the constable was as much a representative of his community as an officer of the Crown. In most places, certainly in the first half of the period, the constable was not, like the JP, chosen by the central government or, like the high constable, appointed by his administrative superiors. He was, rather, elected by the people of the locality, usually in the court leet. Indeed, in a case that came before the King's Bench in 1612 the judges made the limits of the justices' power crystal clear. They ruled that a group of London magistrates who had taken it upon themselves to remove a constable at Stepney and replace him with someone of their own choice had acted outside the law. Moreover, not only was the constable chosen by the local community but he saw it as part of his task to serve his electorate in a variety of ways. The constable's accounts for the villages of Branston and Waltham-on-the-Wolds in Leicestershire are a revelation here. They show the man participating in various communal rituals, maintaining village gates and hedges, taking custody of the communal bull, guarding crops from straying animals, eradicating vermin and even thatching the herdsman's house. In an illuminating parallel Professor Kent has likened the constable's position to that of the village headman in colonial Africa: he had certain responsibilities to the ruling powers but he was also the spokesman of his village. And if a clash of interests occurred the constable was as likely to come down on the side of the locality as he was to back the government. Apart from anything else he was constable for only a year, while he had to live with his friends and neighbours all his life.

Magistrates, watchmen and petty constables could all fail the system from time to time. But the most serious brake on the whole process was the fact that, ultimately, law enforcement depended on private initiative. In nearly all cases the victim had to take on the burden of prosecution. It was the victim who reported the crime to the authorities and, in the absence of a trained police force and a Crown prosecution service, it was up to the victim to pursue the matter to a satisfactory conclusion. In practice this usually meant identifying the criminal, gathering relevant evidence, assembling witnesses and taking the lead in laying the facts before the court. For many ordinary, unlettered people all this was a daunting prospect. It could be cripplingly expensive too. Fees had to be paid to a medley of officials, travel undertaken, witnesses' expenses met and, often, accommodation hired in the town where the assizes or quarter sessions were being held. Professor Beattie has calculated that in the eighteenth century the fees alone probably ran to ten shillings or a pound. For a labouring man this could mean more than a fortnight's wages. One begins to understand why Henry Fielding felt that the average victim of crime "already plundered by the Thief" must be "a Miracle of Public Spirit" if he chose to prosecute rather than "conceal the Felony".

Alternatives to court

There were then a number of weaknesses that served to undermine the efficiency of the law-enforcement machinery during the early modern period, and these shortcomings go a long way towards accounting for the patchy imposition of the law at this time. In addition to these failings, however, it is possible to point to another broad set of reasons for the apparent restraint of the authorities. Appearance before a court was only the last in a long line of possible alternatives for the criminal who could be dealt with in a variety of other and less formal ways.

One such alternative to prosecution was a reprimand from a local notable. Many a minor offender was carpeted in this way by the local squire or the village priest. Often the dressing-down would be accompanied by a threat that if the delinquent did not reform rougher treatment could be expected in the future. When, for instance, George Ritschel, curate of Hexham in the early years of the eighteenth century, reproved one of his parishioners, a drunkard, who should by rights have come before the ecclesiastical courts, he warned the man that if he did not mend his ways he would not only find himself facing a church-court appearance but also a gaol sentence for a debt he owed.

Another possibility was arbitration. Here the good offices of a respected local figure would be sought to bring about an accommodation between two contending parties. Sometimes a magistrate assumed the role of mediator. When, for instance, early in George III's reign, a widow complained to the Surrey justice Richard Wyatt that she had been assaulted and beaten by a blacksmith in a local public house the JP was able to bring the two parties together and to reconcile them. Having taken depositions from both of them, Wyatt ruled that the blacksmith should pay the complainant the sum of eight shillings, "the assault being proved". Not infrequently out-of-court settlements like this were arrived at even without the presence of an arbitrator. The victim would agree to accept an offer of compensation from the guilty party or, in the case of theft, would receive back the stolen goods together with an apology.

Just as important as the out-of-court settlement or the lecture from on high was community action. Perhaps the most celebrated form of communal disciplining was the practice known in France as the "charivari" and in England often described as "rough music". An offender would be surrounded, either at home or elsewhere, by neighbours who would then proceed to show their disapproval of the delinquent's conduct by noisily banging pots and pans. To be so treated by one's fellow villagers or townsfolk was regarded as a sign of much shame and dishonour, and it was a punishment that was greatly feared. The practice has been immortalized in Thomas Hardy's novel *The mayor of Casterbridge*, but there are many real-life parallels to the treatment there meted out to Michael Henchard. In one early seventeenth-century case in Burton-on-Trent a group of about forty townspeople broke into the house of an unmarried couple who were living in sin together. The hapless pair were dragged from the dwelling and paraded through the streets to the accompaniment of cries of "A Whore and a Knave" and the "ringing of cow bells, basons, candlesticks, frying pannes and the sounde of a drumme".

Rough music was usually reserved for people who had in some way infringed the moral norms of a community. But similar direct justice was inflicted on those who had offended in other ways. Sometimes the punishment would be almost a knee-jerk reaction. The *Gentleman's Magazine* carried a report of one such case in 1784. A pickpocket, who had stolen a man's purse while the latter was gazing into the window of a print shop, was seized by bystanders and "rolled in the kennel" and in other ways subjected to "the discipline of the mob" before being allowed to make good his escape. At other times careful planning would be involved. A superb example of this more contrived justice is given by Richard Gough in his account of life in the Shropshire village of Myddle at the close of the Stuart period. Word circulated that one of the village's petty criminals, Reece Wenlocke, a man notorious for stripping wood from his neighbours' hedges, had built a new oven and was about to give it a test firing. On hearing the news, the servant of one of the long-suffering neighbours decided to take matters into his own hands. As he walked by a hedge near Wenlocke's house, Gough informs us, he noticed "a great dry stick of wood". This the servant took home and he then proceeded to bore a hole in the end of it with an auger. After putting "a good quantity of gun powder" into the stick and sealing it with a peg the man carefully replaced it in the hedge. True to form, Wenlocke collected the stick "among other hedgewood". The result was a not inconsiderable explosion that blew the top off the new oven and set the end of Wenlocke's house ablaze.

Long-term changes

So shortcomings in the law-enforcement system and a range of alternatives to the court option explain why the law was so patchily imposed during the early modern era. But why did the rigour of the authorities apparently decline further over time? How do we account for dwindling case loads and falling conviction rates?

One factor seems to have been the changing demographic pattern. Throughout the sixteenth century the population rose inexorably, so that by 1600 there were probably about twice as many mouths to feed as there had been a hundred years before – four and a half million as against two and a quarter million. This upward surge continued well into the seventeenth century. By 1660 the number of inhabitants had probably reached the five and a half million mark. Poverty and unemployment became pressing problems, and gangs of vagrants began to stalk the land. Matters were made worse by a series of poor harvests in the 1590s and by problems with England's main export industry – cloth manufacture – in the 1620s. Inevitably, faced with difficulties like these, the authorities became jumpy and the courts were kept on their toes. One sign of official concern was the development of the Tudor Poor Law. This process reached its culmination in the great Poor Law Statute of 1601, which set out to provide relief for the impotent, work for the able-bodied unemployed and punishment for the malingerer.

After 1660, however, all this changed. Population pressure eased. If anything England and Wales contained fewer people in the 1690s than thirty years earlier. At the same time prices began to fall and wages rise. A series of good harvests in the early years of the eighteenth century only added to the happy picture. Even quite ordinary people began to indulge in luxuries like sugar, tea and chocolate. The records for the assize of bread in Shrewsbury show that by the 1760s the town's bakers had ceased to sell maslin – a rough, peasant bread of mixed grains. There was no longer any market for it. Even the poorest inhabitants of the town were now eating wheat loaves. Hence the sense of crisis and panic lifted and the courts were able to relax and to view wrongdoing with a more indulgent eye.

Accompanying the improvement in living standards was an ideological change – the decline of puritanism. This too helps to explain the fading rigour of law enforcement. What brought about the change in attitude is not entirely clear. Obviously politics played a part. The collapse of the Cromwellian regime and the triumphant return of Charles II inevitably brought in their wake a less austere climate. But the easing of demographic pressure, alluded to above, probably also had an influence. The spread of puritan values from the reign of Elizabeth onwards had been as much a part of the economic difficulties confronting society as it had been a product of high politics. The puritans were always at their strongest in the towns where the demographic and social pressures were at their worst. Naturally, therefore, as the various social and economic problems receded in the second half of the seventeenth century, the harsh, unbending outlook of the puritans also lost some of its lustre and appeal. At all events, whatever the cause of puritan decline, the result is incontestable. Society became less censorious and less moralizing. A more sympathetic attitude to the delinquent and to the victim of temptation slowly spread.

Thus the easing of demographic pressures and the attendant tempering of puritan values after 1660 both contributed to the decline in indictments and convictions in the latter part of the early modern period. Even more important were certain legal changes that were taking place at this time. After 1688 judges became less biased. A crucial step here was the Act of Settlement of 1701, which laid down that judges should henceforward be appointed during good behaviour and not at the king's pleasure. Rules about what constituted proof were also tightened. The Treason Trials Bill of 1696, for instance, declared that the Crown would now need two witnesses to obtain a conviction, not one as before. The Bill also allowed those accused, for the first time, to swear witnesses in their defence and to have notice of charges against them at least a week before their trial. A later act, which reached the statute book in 1708, specified that in cases of felony defence witnesses would in future be able to give evidence on oath. The introduction of counsel from the 1730s onwards also stiffened the legal process. In particular, courts became increasingly reluctant to accept hearsay evidence. The net result of all these changes was to discourage frivolous or ill-founded prosecutions on the one hand and to make convictions harder to obtain on the other. Indeed, in the wake of the changes, whole categories of crime all but disappeared. It is, for example, becoming increasingly fashionable to argue that the precipitate decline in witchcraft prosecutions as the seventeenth century wore on was as much a consequence of legal reform as it was a product of shifting beliefs.

Conclusion

The story of the imposition of the law in the early modern era is a curious tale. The complex system of law enforcement that was unquestionably in place by the end of the sixteenth century would, at first sight, suggest that the law should have been imposed with stern rigour. In fact, reality was very different. The number of wrongdoers who escaped the clutches of the law was always large, and this number was expanding as the years passed.

A closer examination of the problem, however, solves many of the puzzles. The patchy enforcement of the law, even in the sixteenth and early seventeenth centuries, when the authorities acted with energy and purpose, was almost inevitable when one bears two factors in mind. The first of these is the flawed character of the legal machine, notwithstanding its apparent sophistication. The second is the existence of a panoply of alternative ways of dealing with offenders outside the official court system. As for the declining levels of indictment and conviction, these too, when scrutinized with care, become readily explicable. Declining economic pressure played a part. Ideological change was also important. But perhaps most significant of all were changes to the legal system, in particular the tightening of the rules of evidence. Convictions might have been fewer in 1800 than in 1500, but verdicts were safer and justice more secure.

Chapter 6
Punishment

At first glance it may well seem that the penal regime that obtained during the pre-industrial period was monochrome in character, that it was a regime based almost exclusively on a single form of punishment – the death penalty. Indeed, it has long been the custom for general historians to describe the penal system of the eighteenth century in particular as "the bloody code". Such a belief, however, is a gross oversimplification. Although, as we shall see, the death penalty was a leading feature of penal thinking and practice throughout the early modern period, the most striking feature about the pre-modern system of punishment was its complexity. Variety not monotony was its keynote. Some of the punishments that were characteristic of the period are still very much part of modern penal practice. Imprisonment and the levying of fines are examples. Other punishments – whipping and the use of the stocks, for instance – have long since vanished. It is the purpose of this chapter to describe the various punishments that were in operation before 1800 and to suggest how and why the balance between them was changing.

Capital punishment

Although the death penalty was only one of a whole range of punishments meted out by the courts of early modern England, it occupied a central place in the penal system. Not just treason and murder carried the death penalty, but a variety of other offences also. Moreover, the number of crimes punishable by death rose inexorably throughout the period. Growth was particularly rapid during the eighteenth century. At the time of the accession of James I in 1603, some fifty different crimes were classified as capital offences. By the time of Napoleon's defeat in 1815, the figure had risen to more than two hundred. Stealing property worth a shilling or more, setting fire to a heap of hay, breaking down the head of a fish pond so that the fish might escape, defacing Westminster Bridge, cutting a hop-bind in a hop plantation – all these crimes were, at least in theory, hanging offences. Seventy-four people in Devon alone were condemned to death in 1598. Every year hundreds of English men and women met their end on the gallows.

Thus the death penalty was a central feature of the pre-modern penal regime. Even so, it is easy to exaggerate. Capital punishment was never as extensive as, in theory, it should have been. For instance only about a quarter of those accused of felony before the assize courts in Elizabethan England were eventually hanged. Why was this so? How do we account for the discrepancy between theory and practice?

Some of the factors adduced in the previous chapter to explain the patchy enforcement of the law in general also help to account for the unexpectedly low number of capital convictions. But it is clear that other more specific influences were also at work. One of the most significant was the practice known as "benefit of clergy". This practice had grown up during the Middle Ages as a by-product of the medieval dispute between Church and king. The Church claimed that its own courts – which did not have the power to impose the death penalty – and not the lay courts had sole jurisdiction over the clergy. Since the term clergy encompassed not just bishops and parish priests but practically every minor officer associated with the Church, huge numbers of people were involved. In effect most educated men were, in one way or another, covered by the term. Indeed, by the close of the medieval period, it had become the custom to accept that every literate adult male could claim benefit of clergy. All an accused man had to do was prove that he could read a passage from the Bible – normally the opening verse of Psalm 51. If he could do this he would be granted benefit of clergy. In practice, this meant that instead of being sentenced to death a prisoner would have the letters M (for murderer) or T (for thief) branded on his thumb and would then be set free. Only if the man came before the courts a second time accused of murder or grand larceny could he be executed. The fiction behind this was that the punishment exacted by the ecclesiastical courts for the first offence had been defrocking, and that the accused, being no longer a clergyman, was now free to be dealt with in the normal way by the lay courts.

In the years after 1500, benefit of clergy was modified in a number of ways. In some respects things were tightened up. During the course of the sixteenth century, for example, a number of offences were made "non clergyable". Among these were robbery, burglary, rape, murder, witchcraft, horse stealing and theft from churches. In the eighteenth century sheep stealing; theft from a ship, in a navigable river or from a wharf, of goods valued at thirty shillings or more; stealing mail and other crimes were added to the list. In other respects benefit of clergy was granted more freely as the years went by. It is clear, for instance, that by the reign of Elizabeth the rule forbidding benefit of clergy to second offenders was not being applied with any consistency. Two statutes of 1623 and 1692 extended benefit of clergy to women, while a further act of 1706 removed the literacy test. But all this tinkering and adjustment did not alter the fact that between 1500 and 1800 thousands of convicted felons escaped hanging by pleading benefit of clergy.

The system of benefit of clergy was one reason for the partial enforcement of the death sentence. But there was, too, a range of other mitigating factors at work. Cases were dismissed; judges handed down lesser sentences; pardons and reprieves were common. Reprieves were, in the words of Blackstone, "the withdrawal of the sentence for an interval of time" and they often led to a full pardon. A sixteenth-century Staffordshire case uncovered by Dr Harrison gives us a rare glimpse of the mechanism at work. In December 1576 two local men, Mitchel and Snape, were arrested at Burton market for passing counterfeit coin. Their houses were searched and counterfeiting equipment discovered. Snape then confessed. The two men were subsequently arraigned, tried and convicted at the following assizes. Both were sentenced to death, but the judge reprieved Snape because he was so impressed with his remorse. A local lord then personally appealed to Queen Elizabeth for a pardon for Snape. This she granted subject to the trial judge's concurrence. This he gave.

On top of all this came the behaviour of juries. Frequently juries would find defendants guilty of lesser crimes than those they had been charged with. Professor Beattie has calculated that in Surrey juries reduced the charges in about a quarter of the non-clergyable cases that came before them in the years 1660–1800. The classic move was to substitute petty larceny (stealing goods worth less than a shilling) for grand larceny (the theft of goods to the value of a shilling or more), since grand larceny attracted the death sentence while petty larceny involved a lesser punishment. Sometimes this sleight of hand was achieved by finding a prisoner guilty of stealing only one of a package of goods. At other times a jury would deliberately undervalue the goods involved. An example is the case of Eleanor Hughes who, in 1579, was indicted before Shrewsbury Sessions for stealing a coverlet and canvas sheet worth 2s 6d in all. The jury found her guilty but reduced the value of the goods to 11½d. Sometimes such undervaluation by the jury was blatant and ludicrously obvious. In 1751, for instance, a jury from the Home Counties found a defendant guilty of stealing 11 half crowns (27s 6d) to the value of 10d!

One of the most interesting devices used to circumvent the death penalty was the so-called "benefit of the belly". A woman would claim to be pregnant so the sentence of death would be respited until after the innocent child had been born. In theory, the woman should then have been hanged, but such records as we have suggest that, in most cases, the respite was treated as tantamount to a pardon and no execution would take place. Moreover, although a woman's claim to pregnancy was supposed to be verified by a midwife it is clear that this process was often little more than a fiction. J. S. Cockburn, for instance, found that 38 per cent of the women capitally convicted on the Home Circuit between 1559 and 1625 successfully claimed pregnancy – a pregnancy figure that demographers would argue to be most unlikely, if not downright impossible, even in a period of expanding population.

Throughout the early modern period, therefore, a motley collection of devices and subterfuges was employed to save people from the gallows. Further, more often than not, these devices were deployed with the blessing and even the active co-operation of the authorities. We shall now consider what ultimately lay behind all this, why recourse to benefit of clergy and benefit of the belly was so frequent and why juries and judges were induced to seek out mechanisms to enable them to avoid imposing the death sentence.

The answer seems to be that no-one had ever intended that the death penalty should be rigorously applied in all cases and at all times. Most of those convicted of murder were hanged. Where property crimes were involved, however, it was a different story. In his study of crime in and around eighteenth-century Southwark, J. M. Beattie found that whereas murderers were rarely reprieved by the assize judges the same judges recommended nearly three-quarters of sheep stealers and horse thieves for pardon. The thinking that underlay such action was the notion that, for most offences, capital punishment was there primarily to serve as a deterrent and that only a limited number of executions were necessary to bring this point home to the public. The link with deterrence is perhaps most clearly shown when, for one reason or another, crime figures rose. Then, in order to arrest the upward trend in numbers, the proportion of executions sanctioned by the courts also increased. When, for instance, the signing of peace in 1748 disgorged large numbers of former soldiers on to the labour market and unemployment and property crime shot up, the authorities responded by stepping up both prosecutions and capital convictions. By contrast, when the country went to war again in 1757 and there was less unemployment, and hence less property crime, the number of executions dropped. Surrey is typical of the country as a whole. Executions in the county in the eight years of peace between 1749 and 1756 averaged 6.25 per year; in the seven years of war that followed the average fell to 1.4 per year. Over the same period the proportion of convicted felons executed fell from over a half to under a quarter.

What sort of people were selected by judges and juries as examples? Was it just a random sample of offenders? Or were particular types of criminal targeted? The answer seems to be that the most hardened criminals were those most likely to suffer the ultimate penalty – members of gangs, for example, or those unable to produce character witnesses of repute and standing. By contrast, an offender of good character or one who could point to the existence of extenuating circumstances was likely to receive a pardon or a lesser sentence. The case of the Londoner Ann Flynn shows the thinking at work. In 1743 Flynn stole a shoulder of mutton from a Whitechapel butcher, who then prosecuted her. In court it emerged that her husband was ill and her children starving when she committed the offence. The jurors pronounced their verdict of guilty in a mumbling tone – a sign that they thought the defendant, though guilty, was worthy of compassion. The judge said "Gentlemen, I hear you." He then fined Flynn the token sum of one shilling – a fine that the jury promptly proceeded to pay.

One further feature of capital punishment in these years is perhaps worth stressing: the trend over time. Not only was the death penalty not always employed; its use was declining. In Essex in the last decade of the sixteenth century 26 per cent of felons were hanged, in Middlesex 19 per cent, in Cheshire 22 per cent. By the first decade of the eighteenth century the figures were quite different. In Norfolk and Suffolk 12 per cent were executed, in Cheshire 10 per cent, in Devon a mere 8 per cent. Roughly speaking, the execution rate had dropped from a quarter to one in ten.

The factors underlying this dramatic shift are not altogether clear. One influence that seems to have played a part is the changing climate of public opinion – a change best encapsulated in the term "the Enlightenment". Among other things the Enlightenment led to the spread of more humane attitudes and to more civilized and less violent behaviour. The founding of municipal hospitals, the establishment of charity schools, the more sensitive treatment of unmarried mothers, the hostility to violent sports like bull baiting and cock throwing, the opposition to the slave trade – all these illustrate the new outlook. The increasing reluctance to send people to the gallows probably also reflects the growing humanitarianism. However, the main development facilitating the downward trend was undoubtedly the emergence of alternative forms of punishment. To these, as well as other sorts of punishment, we must now turn.

Shaming punishments

Throughout the pre-modern period the courts had a range of shaming punishments at their disposal. One of the most characteristic of these was the pillory. The pillory was a device in which an offender stood with head and hands pinioned between two planks of wood. Sometimes it would be at ground level. Not infrequently, however, especially in the larger towns, it would be raised on a platform and hence would be more visible to the crowds milling around it. Pillorying usually took place at midday and often on market day, when a good number of people could be expected to be abroad to witness the victim's humiliation. Normally the pillory seems to have been used for fairly minor offences such as cheating at cards, selling defective goods and uttering seditious words. However, it was also customary for people convicted of sexual offences to be pilloried, particularly those found guilty of homosexual acts or of molesting children. For instance, a man convicted of "a fowle and great trespass in attempting an Act of uncleanness with a girl about eight years old" was set in the pillory at Southwark in 1663. In cases like this the consequences for the offender

Engraved for The Malefactor's Register.

The punishment formerly inflicted on those who REFUSED PLEADING *to an Indictment.*

Figure 6.1 From *The Malefactor's register.*

could be very serious. Often an angry crowd would turn on the prisoner and beat and abuse him. It was not unknown for pilloried homosexuals or those found guilty of child rape to be stoned to death.

The pillory was by no means the only form of shaming punishment employed by the courts in the years after 1500. Women accused of being scolds were sometimes strapped in a ducking stool and plunged into the local river or pond with friends and neighbours looking on. Other offenders were sentenced to sit in the stocks. This involved being placed on a bench in full public view with feet clamped between two boards. Carting was yet another common form of shaming punishment, used particularly for sexual offences such as adultery or running a brothel. In 1579, for example, John Bellman of St John Street in Clerkenwell was put in a cart and paraded around the local streets because he had "lodged lewde persons in his house" and had also allowed "lewde women" to be "delyverd of chylde" there. Occasionally a person would just be ordered to stand in a public place for a given time with a paper attached reciting the offence. In 1751 a woman who had stolen a sheet from the workhouse in St Saviour's parish in Southwark was made to stand in the workhouse yard once every week for a month. Another woman convicted of stealing a turnip was ordered to stand on a stool for an hour in a public street in Wandsworth.

All these punishments were inflicted by the secular courts. However, the church courts above all specialized in shaming punishments. These courts, which remained vigorously active in many areas for much of the period, dealt not just with theological concerns but also with moral issues and matters of family law such as drunkenness and adultery. The most serious sanction the ecclesiastical courts could impose was excommunication – the casting out of an individual from the fellowship of the Church. But they also frequently inflicted public penance on church members. When this happened the offender would have to stand before the congregation during divine service on the Lord's Day clad in a white sheet and with head bowed. Sometimes the convicted person would carry a placard denoting the offence. Alternatively the penitent would be compelled to make a declaration of sorrow to the listening audience. Either way it was a humbling experience.

To us, shaming punishments may well seem strange. What made them so effective and so important in early modern times was the different character of society. Communities were smaller and more stable. Values were shared by all. In this more intimate world, to be paraded in the streets or in church before one's neighbours, men and women with whom one rubbed shoulders day in and day out, whom one may well have known all one's life, was no mean ordeal.

Corporal punishment

From Tudor times until the era of the French Revolution corporal punishment in the form of whipping figured prominently in the repertoire of punishments inflicted by the courts. Whipping was often used in vagrancy cases and it was in many ways the standard punishment for petty larceny – the theft of goods worth less than a shilling. Typical was the case of Sarah

Blanley of Shrewsbury. In 1721 she was found guilty of stealing a duck from William Nicholas. The court ordered her to be "stripped naked to the waist and taken to the whipping post on Saturday next at full markett between the hours of twelve and one and there whipped until her body be bloody".

Details on the actual mechanics of whipping are few and far between. The number of strokes to be applied was rarely specified, for instance, nor was the exact character of the whipping instrument. We do know, however, that until the middle years of the eighteenth century, when a more humane atmosphere developed, it was normal for a whipping to take place in public. Humiliation was thus added to the pain suffered. Usually public whippings took place in one of two places. Either the punishment would be inflicted "at the cart's tail" – that is, the prisoner's hands would be tied to the rear of a cart and the vehicle would be drawn through the streets while the whipping took place – or it would be administered at the community whipping-post – a structure normally situated in a main street or market place. It was normal, too, for the court to specify the precise time and date of the whipping. Typically this would be on a market day when trade was at its busiest. Finally, it was the rule for the court to insist that the offender, man or woman, should be naked from the waist upward during the flogging, and also that blood should be drawn from the sufferer's back.

From the late seventeenth century onwards whipping underwent something of a renaissance. This was because the courts began to use it with increasing frequency for those accused of grand larceny. J. M. Beattie found that in a sample of 470 cases of men and women indicted for grand larceny before the assize court in Surrey between 1660 and 1715, 40 per cent were whipped. The change was brought about because juries chose more and more to reduce verdicts from grand to petty larceny. In the third quarter of the eighteenth century a further – and quite dramatic – development took place, when the courts suddenly and mysteriously began to sentence people convicted of grand larceny to whipping. The subterfuge of reducing a charge from grand to petty larceny was apparently no longer deemed necessary. Whipping, therefore, became one of the substitute punishments for the death penalty that resulted in the decline in the number of capital convictions already noted. Much more significant, however, was the spread of two other forms of punishment – transportation and imprisonment.

Transportation

The transportation of convicted felons to the colonies in the West Indies and North America had occurred from time to time in the seventeenth century – particularly after the Restoration in 1660. But, for a variety of reasons, the practice faltered in the 1670s. For one thing the merchants engaged in the trade became increasingly choosy about which convicts they would take.

They tended to select for passage only the strongest and fittest, and hence the most saleable, individuals and to baulk at carrying undesirables. Colonies like Virginia, anxious not to become flooded with the dregs of English society, also began to cause trouble. On top of this there was a widespread feeling in England in the late seventeenth century that the country was underpopulated and could ill afford to lose able-bodied people. It was therefore only with the passing of the Transportation Act in 1718 that a new impetus was given to the transportation of offenders and that it became a regular and routine practice.

The 1718 act made it possible for the courts to sentence non-capital felons (those who could claim benefit of clergy) to seven years' transportation. It also established a term of fourteen years' transportation for capital felons (people not eligible for benefit of clergy) who had received a royal pardon. The act thus brought about a real change in the penal regime. Benefit of clergy had long been under attack by thinking people as unacceptably lenient. Many, indeed, pointed out that a person convicted of grand larceny and granted benefit of clergy was more lightly punished by merely being branded in the hand than a person found guilty of the lesser crime of petty larceny and sentenced to be whipped before neighbours on market day. In consequence, after 1718 the courts seized on the provision allowing them to consign non-capital felons to the colonies. Of the 27 people convicted of clergyable offences at the Old Bailey in 1719, 25 were transported; only two were allowed benefit of clergy. In the 52 years from 1663 to 1715 57.8 per cent of those convicted of non-capital property offences in Surrey were given benefit of clergy. For the 27-year period 1722–49 the figure fell to 8.7 per cent. It would be wrong to say that the Transportation Act ended the age-old system of benefit of clergy. But certainly it was granted far less freely after 1718 than before. It became the exception rather than the norm.

But if the 1718 act transformed the clergy system it also radically changed attitudes to capital punishment. The fact that a pardoned felon would now normally be transported for 14 years rather than go scot-free greatly increased the number of pardons granted. Again, the Surrey evidence is revealing. In the early 1720s 78.9 per cent of felons sentenced to death in the county were actually hanged. Ten years later the figure had fallen to 38.1 per cent. In other words, pardons were now allowed in 61.9 per cent of cases compared with 21.1 per cent previously. Thus the development of transportation is one of the pivotal factors accounting for the decline of the death sentence.

Imprisonment

Traditionally, except in the rather specialized case of debtors, prison had rarely been used as a form of punishment. Gaols were places where the accused were held pending trial; they were not institutions where the convicted served their sentences. From the late seventeenth century onwards, however, increasing numbers of petty offenders were sent for a spell of hard labour to the various houses of correction around the country. When they were first established in the reign of Elizabeth the houses of correction had been specifically designed to discipline the able-bodied poor who stubbornly refused to work. But from the 1690s a medley of minor offenders, ranging from poachers and runaway apprentices to petty thieves, cheats and utterers of seditious words, began to find themselves rubbing shoulders in the houses of correction with the vagrants and the idle poor, consigned there by the justices of the peace. After 1706 more serious criminals were imprisoned. This came as a consequence of a particular clause in the act of that year which ended the literacy test in the granting of benefit of clergy. This clause gave assize judges the right to commit a clergied offender to a house of correction for a period of hard labour. In some parts of the country at least, this new power was extensively used by the judges. Joanna Innes, for example, has calculated that in Devon almost a quarter of those accused of felonies at the assizes between 1707 and 1717 were sentenced to hard labour in a house of correction.

For the rest of the eighteenth century minor offenders continued to be imprisoned either in a house of correction or in the county gaol. However, after the passage of the Transportation Act in 1718, and with the consequent growing popularity of transportation, fewer and fewer felons seem to have found their way to prison. But the popularity of the hard labour option for felons revived permanently in the 1770s when the trouble with the American colonies made transportation increasingly difficult. Even the founding of the penal colony at Botany Bay in New South Wales in 1786 made little difference. As a result, by 1800 imprisonment had become the standard punishment for offences against property that did not involve some specially heinous aggravation. Thus incarceration took its place alongside transportation as an alternative to capital punishment.

Fines

Fining was, throughout the early modern period, a leading form of punishment. Borough courts, quarter sessions, petty sessions, assize courts and, above all, manor courts all regularly imposed fines. Usually a fine was a punishment for a minor offence, such as petty fraud, contempt of an official, the flouting of a regulation and, especially, assault. Some fines were fixed. Legislation passed in James I's reign, for example, made drunkards subject to a 5s fine. Other fines varied. But fixed or variable, most fines were quite small, ranging from a few pence to a few shillings. J. A. Sharpe has shown in his analysis of assault charges tried at the Essex assizes and quarter sessions courts between 1620 and 1680 that in 81 out of the 123 cases in which the values of the fines are known the sums levied were between one and ten shillings. The median fine for assault in 93 quarter sessions cases in late-seventeenth-century Surrey was 2s 6d. Over a third of the fines were between 6d and 1s.

One reason why fines were so low was that they were imposed mainly on ordinary working people, people whose incomes and resources were minimal. It is instructive to note that often when men and women of more exalted status were fined the penalty exacted was far heavier: in 1687 William Cavendish, Duke of Devonshire, was fined the enormous sum of £30,000 for striking a man within the verge of the king's palace. But a second reason for the lightness of some fines appears to be that fines were not always what they seem. The fine in this second case appears to have been a token and symbolic payment after a defendant had reached a settlement with a prosecutor. The Recorder of London explained the connection between a small public fine and a prior settlement between the parties in dispute when discussing a case of assault and battery in 1729. It was, he said, "usual in these cases for the Defendant to make satisfaction to the Prosecutor for his wounds and costs and charges – before the Court sets the fine which is usually greater if a Defendant won't make a Prosecutor easy as the Court directs". Professor Beattie believes that most of the fines of 6d or 1s levied by the Surrey quarter sessions court in the latter part of the seventeenth century were of this token kind.

The logic of punishment

The pattern of punishment between 1500 and 1800 was, we have seen, a complex one. But perhaps there is a unifying theme. Perhaps early modern punishments, however much they might differ individually, all had a common purpose.

The rationale of pre-modern punishment seems essentially to have been fourfold. One of the central aims of the early modern penal system was unquestionably deterrence. This is seen at its starkest in capital punishment. Hangings were not carried out in private but before large crowds and with great theatre. The condemned person would process ceremonially to the place of execution in a cart which threaded its way slowly between rows of awestruck spectators. The platform on which the gallows were erected, set high above the mob, would be the scene of a dying speech. The prisoner, having first knelt before the gallows in the company of a priest, would have the noose fitted. Then the ladder would be kicked away. Before the nine-teenth century the drop was not used, so the neck would often not be broken. Instead, the victim would be strangled to death in a slow agony. Frequently friends or relatives would rush forward in an endeavour to pull the prisoner's legs or to beat him or her on the chest so as to end the torment more quickly. The effect all this had – and was intended to have – on the spectators was often shattering. John Wesley recalled how, as a small child, he was taken by his mother to witness such an execution as a dire warning of the consequences of sin. The spectacle haunted him for the rest of his life.

If deterrence was one of the purposes of the early modern penal regime, another was retribution. Crime, it was felt, merited punishment, and ter-rible crime merited terrible punishment. This notion of retribution and proportionality is well illustrated by the different types of capital punish-ment in vogue in the years after 1500. A serious but straightforward crime such as rape or murder, people believed, was expiated by hanging. On the other hand, if a wife murdered her husband this was regarded as more serious than straightforward murder. Wives in the early modern period were considered subject to their husbands. Hence, for a wife to turn on her husband was to go against the natural order of things, to challenge the very structure of God's universe. It was to commit an act of petty treason. In consequence, hanging was not seen as punishment enough for such a heinous offence. Husband murderers were, therefore, not just strung up on the gallows: they were burnt alive. Even more serious than this sort of petty treason, of course, was full-blown high treason. The terrible fate of those guilty of this offence was to be hung, drawn and quartered. The convicted prisoner would first be drawn through the streets on a hurdle. He – it was usually a man – was then hung from the gallows. Before he expired, however, the traitor would be cut down, disembowelled while still alive and chopped into four pieces.

A third aim of early modern punishment was ritual cleansing. By flouting the laws and rules of society criminals were regarded as having cut them-selves off from the community at large. For their crimes to be set aside, therefore, it was deemed necessary for wrongdoers to be cleansed of their iniquities before being readmitted to the body of society. This function of the penal system is clearly evident in many shaming punishments. A penitent standing meekly before the church congregation on a Sunday morning, clad in white, expressing sorrow and begging forgiveness, illustrates the theme. The expression of remorse customarily made by condemned felons and murderers before they met their final end fulfilled the same reintegrating function. Dr Sharpe has drawn attention to the consternation caused in the 1580s by one young felon who, as he stood on the gallows, refused to believe that he had been readmitted to the fellowship of God's people. The chaplain present at the execution, the celebrated puritan divine William Perkins, called the man down from the ladder; together the two knelt side by side and prayed until Perkins succeeded in convincing the youth that God had forgiven him his sins. The lad then mounted the gallows once more with tears of joy in his eyes, "as if he actually saw himself delivered from the hell which he feared before, and heaven opened for receiving his soul".

Deterrence, retribution, ritual cleansing – these were all built into the pre-modern penal system. But, certainly by the close of the period, it is possible to discern a fourth strand in the philosophy of early modern punishment. This was the endeavour to reform the wrongdoer. One of the main drives leading to the development of imprisonment as a form of punishment in the eighteenth century was the belief that in gaol offenders might be brought to see the error of their ways. When, in 1753, Henry Fielding proposed the establishment of a county house of correction in Middlesex where petty offenders might be incarcerated rather than be transported, he did so with the idea of rehabilitation firmly in mind. He envisaged malefactors being subjected to a strict regime of training while imprisoned. Such training, he argued, should involve periods of solitude, a structured work programme and careful and pointed religious instruction. With luck, the offender would then emerge corrected both in body and in mind. Even earlier, in 1730, Sollom Emlyn had maintained that, in his view, imprisonment with hard labour would "reclaim" as well as "deter". Similarly, a Bill – eventually lost – that was introduced into the Commons in May 1776 by William Eden for the enlargement of houses of correction expressed the hope that hard labour in the houses would not simply act as a deterrent but "might also be the means of reforming many offenders, and of rendering them useful members of the community". In like manner, the celebrated Penitentiary Act of 1779, which sought to set up penitentiary houses around London where the convicted would labour, be subjected to religious indoctrination and be kept in separate cells, had a reforming purpose. Incarceration in the houses, it was hoped, would not simply be a form of punishment but would also succeed in "reforming the individuals, and inuring them to habits of industry". The spirit was to be transformed as well as the body chastised.

Conclusion

The idea that the penal regime of early modern England was a regime animated by the death sentence is, we have seen, in many ways misleading. Variety of punishment was the dominating note throughout these three centuries or so. Indeed, despite talk of the eighteenth-century "bloody code", capital punishment became less important as time went by. Primarily this was because punishments like transportation and imprisonment came increasingly to be seen as viable alternatives to the death sentence in all but the most serious and the most savage of capital cases. In all this – as well as in the gradual abandonment of the age-old custom of benefit of clergy – England may well seem a more modern country in 1800 than it had been in 1500. While there is unquestionably a degree of truth in such a view, we should be wary of applying the notion of modernity too freely. Reformers like John Howard were not struck by the advanced character of the late-eighteenth-century English penal system. Punishments like transportation have strong traditional elements. Consigning criminals to the colonies was as much a revival of the medieval notion of banishment as a new departure. The England of 1800 was different from the England of 1500, but it was also different from modern England.

Chapter 7
Socio-political crime

In a previous chapter we saw how the bulk of crime committed in Tudor and Stuart England was small-scale in character, involving, as it did, things like brawling, petty theft and drunkenness. This continued to be the pattern throughout the rest of the early modern period. The cases that came before the Wiltshire courts in 1736 illustrate the point. Things stolen included cheese, butter and bread. A sow had also gone astray, "a piece of old blanket", a knife and "a shift worth 5/-". The woman who stole the last item was publicly whipped and sentenced to three months hard labour. The Wiltshire affrays in 1736 were equally unremarkable. Typical here was the offence of the brickmaker John Watkins who, while in the local alehouse one day, got carried away and called his neighbour and fellow building worker Thomas Hopkins a "rogue and son of a whore" and "pulled the said Hopkins by the nose". Indeed, many of the crimes brought before the courts in these years were not only minor but victimless. A farmer would be reprimanded for failing to scour a ditch, a housewife for selling ale without a licence, a cottager for letting his geese wander the common unyoked. Between 1560 and 1699 no fewer than two-thirds of all the charges that went forward to the assizes and the quarter sessions from the Essex parish of Terling were of this regulatory, non-personal kind.

Even so, although petty crime remained very much centre-stage for the whole of the pre-modern era, another and quite distinct form of criminal activity began to assume increasing prominence as the period progressed. This was a form of lawbreaking that was considered crime only by one section of society – normally the landed classes, who both dominated the courts and controlled parliament. By other sections of society, and in particular by the poorer cottagers and craftsmen, such lawbreaking was not considered crime at all. Since crime of this kind represented a clash between two social groupings, it is usually labelled "social crime" by historians. We, however, will call it "socio-political crime" because, as well as involving social conflict, the lawbreaking carried with it political overtones. When flouting the law, the perpetrators of this kind of offence were making political statements. Either they were attacking a particular law or set of laws as irrational or unjust, or they were criticizing the policy or the behaviour of the ruling elite.

Long-term disputes

What was the nature of socio-political crime? Three distinct categories of socio-political conflict can perhaps be discerned. First, there were those offences that were classified as illegal throughout the period. In the second place, there were activities and customs that were criminalized during the course of the early modern era itself. Thirdly, there was conduct on the part of the elite that was opposed by ordinary people as being immoral and contrary to natural justice. It is with the first, long-term class of socio-political crime that this particular section is concerned.

Among the most prominent of this first category of socio-political crimes was smuggling. By the eighteenth century smuggling had in many areas assumed enormous proportions. In 1745 Abraham Walter, a dealer in tea who had himself dabbled in the illicit importing of goods, told the parliamentary committee set up to investigate the problem that he reckoned there were more than 20,000 smugglers by trade. Other witnesses to the committee estimated that over three million pounds of tea alone were imported illegally every year. Smuggling in spirits and other commodities, they felt, was equally extensive.

Many of the people engaged in this huge illicit trade were no doubt common criminals. To run a successful smuggling enterprise a considerable investment of capital was needed. Ships had to be fitted out, warehouses constructed and gangs of men, fifty, sixty or even a hundred strong, employed to unload and transport cargoes. People with this sort of money to spare were unlikely to be in it simply to make a political point. They were more akin to modern drugs barons than to freedom fighters. Nevertheless, a good many of the ordinary inhabitants of coastal towns and villages who became mixed up in smuggling or who refused to inform on neighbours engaged in the trade seem to have been politically motivated. Ordinary people of this sort were quite willing to pay a fair price for foreign goods and also to cover the costs of their transport. But they felt that the government's attempt to charge an extra, and often quite prohibitive, duty on top of these legitimate costs was wrong. Hence, in their view, smuggling was not a crime but a perfectly legitimate activity.

One thing that hints at this more political attitude is the bitterness with which both revenue officers and those who told tales to the authorities were viewed. This hostility went far beyond normal limits. A terrible incident took place in 1748 involving a gang from West Sussex; it reveals the depth of the smugglers' loathing for those who opposed them. The gang seized a revenue officer, William Galley, and another man, Daniel Chater, who they thought was about to inform on them, and brutally murdered them. The two men were first whipped and then tied under their horses' bellies and dragged along. The gang then buried Galley, possibly while he was still alive, having first of all "cut off his nose and privities, [and] broke every bone in his body". Chater was similarly disfigured with a knife before being cast into a well, where he was stoned to death.

In some ways, of course, the Galley–Chater case is exceptional. Examples of such extreme barbarity are few and far between. But the festering hatreds that gave rise to the incident were widespread. In the very same year Richard Patrick, a minor customs clerk, came across similar hostility in Kent. When a man called Harrison informed on a number of smugglers from the Hastings area almost the whole town was seized with fury. The incident, Patrick reported, "has put the inhabitants in the greatest flame imaginable". "I am really of the opinion", he continued, "that nine parts in ten thereof would as freely murder Harrison as they would eat or drink when hungry or dry."

It is not, however, simply the extraordinary intensity of the distaste felt for revenue officials and informers which indicates that smuggling had a political dimension. Contemporaries said as much themselves. The Duke of Richmond, for example, who spent much of his life endeavouring to combat smuggling along the south coast, was in no doubt about the socio-political motivation of many smugglers. "I have often heard you say", he wrote to Sir Cecil Bishop in 1749, "and with great truth, that the common people of this country have no notion that smuggling is a crime." John Taylor, the chaplain at Newgate prison, had, after talking with many smugglers in the condemned cells, formed a similar view. "The common people of England in general", he averred, "fancy there is nothing in the crime of smuggling." The poor, he was convinced, felt they had "a right to shun paying any duty on their goods". The views of Taylor and Richmond are strikingly corroborated by the behaviour of one West Country dweller, Jack Rattenbury. Imprisoned in Exeter for smuggling, Rattenbury complained of being "most unpleasantly associated" with those guilty of "every description of crime". When some of these "criminals" tried to escape by knocking out a warder, Rattenbury, together with a number of other incarcerated smugglers, prevented their breaking out. To Rattenbury, smuggling was a legitimate activity engaged in by upright citizens. "Crime" was not.

Smuggling constitutes one important example of socio-political crime in evidence throughout the whole length of the early modern period. A still more significant instance is poaching. Smuggling was largely confined to the coastal regions – though , of course, the goods imported were distributed widely inland. Poaching, by contrast, was not chained to the sea. In almost every part of England the poacher and his gun could be found. The significance of poaching was further enhanced by the fact that the practice was by no means confined to the poorer elements in society. Even to kill a hare on his own land, a man had to enjoy a substantial income from landed property. "The basic game qualification", writes Douglas Hay of the eighteenth century, "was an income of £100 yearly from a freehold estate, which in 1750 was between five and ten times the income of a labourer, and fifty times the property qualification to vote for a knight of the shire." Thus substantial farmers as well as cottagers and labourers were excluded by law from pursuing game, and they could in consequence be found among the poachers. Indeed, even men of the cloth were by no means whiter than white where poaching was concerned. In 1754, when his house was raided by keepers, the curate of Longdon in Staffordshire was found to be in possession of a pointer, a gun and a net – all contrary to the law.

As with smuggling, so also with poaching there is no doubt that one can find straightforward criminality at work. Fashionable poulterers in London and elsewhere had a ready market for game even though, strictly speaking, its sale was illegal. The smarter inns also liked to serve hare, grouse and pheasant, not to mention the odd haunch of venison. Money could thereby be made and this attracted the professional criminal. One Staffordshire labourer, John Lightwood, killed nearly eighty hares in 1764 alone, selling them in Lichfield for 3s apiece. He probably made more on these deals than he could earn in an entire year at his job. And Lightfoot was merely a petty criminal, working independently of the organized gangs.

Again, however, as was the case with smugglers, most of the people engaged in poaching seem to have been of a different stamp. Wild life they regarded as a gift of God and open for all to pursue. The game laws were therefore seen as an affront and a flagrant denial of natural justice. In this respect it is interesting to note that most poachers viewed officialdom with the same loathing that most smugglers did. Estate gamekeepers in particular were deeply despised by the average villager. They were ostracized and vilified by their neighbours at every turn. No-one would tell a gamekeeper anything if it could be avoided. Not infrequently, gamekeepers suffered the same kind of physical abuse that customs officers were forced to endure. In 1780, for instance, a Staffordshire farmer snatched back the hare taken from him by a keeper and then proceeded to horsewhip the man. The farmer was prepared to risk a heavy fine rather than submit to what he considered tyranny. Twelve years later two Rugeley farmers entered the grounds of Lord Paget's gamekeeper, killed his horse by shooting it in the head, then waited with the gun pointing menacingly at the bedroom window. Fortunately, perhaps, the keeper did not waken and look out. Hundreds of similar incidents could be listed, all of them illustrating the point that, for most of those engaged in the practice, poaching was not considered a crime but was seen rather as an assertion of an immemorial and inalienable right.

Smuggling and poaching constitute just two examples of our first class of socio-political crime. They do not form a complete listing. John Styles, for example, has shown how in Yorkshire coining was viewed in the same way. Provided the fake coins were manufactured from the clippings of genuine gold coins and not from base metal, people could see nothing wrong in fashioning their own money. After all, the value lay in the gold not in who struck the coin. Similarly, throughout most of the coastal regions of the country "wrecking" – the purloining of materials and cargo from ships that had foundered – was regarded by many as a legitimate practice. Early in the eighteenth century, for instance, when a customs officer in Anglesey tried to restrain a group of wreckers, he was curtly informed by them that they had as much right to be there as he had. Throughout the period the people of Cornwall claimed the right to anything that the sea might cast up. When he visited East Anglia in Queen Anne's reign, Daniel Defoe was astonished at the extent of wrecking there. Travelling from Great Yarmouth to Cromer along the coast road, he confessed himself "surprized to see in all the way from Winterton, that the farmers and the country people had scarce a barn, or a shed, or a stable; nay not the pales of their yards and gardens, not a hogstye, not a necessary-house, but what was built of old planks, beams, wales and timbers, etc. – the wrecks of ships and ruins of mariners' and merchants' fortunes". Clearly whole villages along the east coast – men, women and children – were engaging in the practice, convinced that there was no impropriety in such activity. But there is perhaps no need to labour the point. Enough has been said to show that there were certain socio-political crimes that were present throughout the span of the early modern era.

Custom criminalized

Some socio-political crimes were already in evidence in 1500. Others were added to the list in the years that followed as the law was tightened and extended. One of these new crimes was wood theft. For much of the early modern period the gathering of "snapping wood" from royal forests and other woodland was a widespread custom. According to Charles Vancouver, writing of the practice in Hampshire, snapping wood consisted not just of fallen branches but also of "such as they can snap off by hand, or break down with a hook fixed in the end of a long pole". The wood, it seems, was used mainly as fuel, but sometimes it was used in fencing and even to repair houses. Often the right was enshrined in charters and other manorial records. The wood collecting was not random but systematic, and it formed a vital part of the economy of many country dwellers.

From the early eighteenth century onward, however, the custom came under increasing attack, and legal sanctions against it were progressively introduced. Finally in 1766 came a statute that, in the words of R. W. Bushaway, "aimed to remove all possible equivocation and establish firmly the criminality of wood gathering". The act made it an offence "to wilfully cut or break down, bark, burn, pluck up, lop, top, crop, or otherwise deface, damage, spoil, or destroy, or carry away any Timber tree". Similar clauses were included banning the taking of underwood. Backed by these sanctions, landowners all over the country began to suppress wood gathering, and in places like Alice Holt Forest and Eling Manor in Hampshire bitter conflict ensued. The landed men did not always triumph. In Grovely Forest to the west of Salisbury, the villagers of Great Wishford and Barford St Martin, aided by two charters that spelt out the legitimacy of their claims, successfully resisted the Earl of Pembroke's efforts to end their wood-collecting rights. But elsewhere country people were less fortunate and were increasingly subjected to the rigours of the law. Especially was this so during the French wars, when timber became a much valued commodity. The rising population at the end of the eighteenth century and the consequent increase in the numbers denuding the woodlands also propelled landlords in the same direction. In village after village, God-fearing, law-abiding men and women were subjected to summary trial and conviction for simply behaving as their ancestors had done time out of mind. As a result, by 1800 wood theft had become the most common form of crime in the countryside.

Wood rights were the particular concern of the peasant and the rural labourer. But there was also a custom associated with the industrial worker that came under increasing attack as the years went by. This was the right enjoyed by many workers to keep the waste and surplus materials left over after manufacture. Shipwrights took home "chips" – the odds and ends of wood that were an inevitable by-product of boat building. Tailors clung on to the remaining material after cutting out cloth already bespoken to customers. In many areas weavers had the right to "thrums". These were the weft ends left on the loom after a length of cloth had been removed. Framework knitters gathered up waste yarn, sawyers carted away their bags of sawdust, and so on. By most workers such perquisites were not regarded as extras but as an integral part of their remuneration. They were payments in kind that supplemented low money wages. Thomas Campbell, writing in 1747, made this point specifically about cutting-out tailors.

More and more, however, as the early modern period progressed, employers and manufacturers began to take action to try to limit and even stamp out such practices. In Essex, for example, there was a bitter and drawn out dispute in 1757 and 1758 about weavers' thrums. It began in Colchester in the winter of 1757 and quickly spread to Braintree, Bocking and other cloth-producing centres. Eventually, after a lengthy strike, the weavers were defeated. They were forced to surrender their claim to thrums, though to sweeten the pill the masters offered a small sum to compensate the workers for their loss.

The reason why, with the passage of time, the right to industrial perquisites became such a battleground in this way is the subject of some debate. John Rule and others have suggested that it may well have had something to do with the decline of independent craftsmen and the consequent spread of the putting-out system. John Styles, on the other hand, thinks that the various dips in the trade cycle during the course of the early modern era may have been more important. It is clear, too, that a number of manufacturers were alarmed at the rather liberal interpretation of their customary rights that some workers and craftsmen were making. In 1762 the house of a labourer working at a gunpowder mill on Hounslow Heath was searched. The dwelling was found to contain two bushels of nails, 70 bottles of lamp oil, over a hundred bags of saltpetre and close on a cartload of matches. In addition, secreted away were large quantities of candles and deal boards as well as £100 in cash. In powder mills, workers did have the right to supplement their wages by making matches for sale. They did this by splitting pieces of deal and dipping the resulting slivers of wood into the brimstone they were using to make their gunpowder. Even so, the contents of the house on Hounslow Heath do suggest that at least some employees were apt to take custom a little too far.

However, whatever the reason for the hardening attitudes of employers, the fact remains that, as time went by, the traditional rights of industrial workers to leftover materials came under growing pressure. As was the case with wood gathering the claim to remuneration in kind was subjected to legal challenge. Custom was criminalized.

Protest

So far we have been considering customs that were regarded by ordinary people as rights but that were looked on, or came to be looked on, by the courts and by parliament as illegal and unacceptable. But there was, in addition, another class of socio-political crime. An act that broke the criminal law could win popular acclaim and backing not because of the inherent nature of the crime itself but because of the protest context in which the offence occurred. Most ordinary men and women, for instance, would not have considered acts such as assault, threats of violence, the killing of livestock, arson, the tearing down of fences and hedgerows or breaking and entering as acceptable behaviour in normal circumstances. But there were certain occasions when actions of this sort were viewed with more sympathy.

One such context was often provided by enclosure. Enclosure was the process which saw the breaking up of the wide common fields and wastelands that surrounded many English villages into smaller enclosures that were privately farmed and managed. It was a process that went on throughout the early modern period and in many parishes enclosure was accomplished with little opposition or ill feeling. At times, however, trouble ensued. For instance, if cottagers felt they had been deprived of their right to gather fuel or to graze stock on the commons without adequate compensation, stiff opposition could follow. Sometimes, notably in the fifteenth and early sixteenth centuries, enclosure was accompanied by a switch from arable to pasture farming. Villagers might take the law into their own hands because, since the keeping of animals was less labour intensive than the raising of crops, the job market often shrank. Another major source of tension occurred when, as a consequence of enclosure, land was taken out of production and converted to parkland. On occasions like this, normally law-abiding citizens would often engage in an orgy of violence and destruction. In 1607, for instance, there was serious rioting in parts of the Midlands and dozens of new fences and hedges were destroyed. In the 1630s there was a further outbreak of violence. On this occasion the Archbishop of Canterbury reproved one of the enclosing landowners, Lord Brudenell, for "devouring the people with a shepherd and a dog" by turning their common land over to sheep pasture.

Closely related to enclosure riots were disagreements about agrarian improvement. Sometimes when an owner decided to improve his land this would have unfortunate economic implications for those living in the area. Often when this happened local farmers and cottagers, stung by the threat to their livelihood, would rise up in protest. For instance, the endeavours of the Dukes of Bedford and other magnates from the 1620s onwards to drain large areas of the Fens and thereby increase the agricultural yield of the region produced widespread disaffection in parts of Lincolnshire. Villagers who depended on the flora and fauna of the marshland environment – the fish, the wildfowl and the lush summer grazing – were incensed. Normally the most docile and reasonable of people they turned out in their hundreds to demolish the drainage works and to destroy houses, mills and barns. Similar scenes followed the Earl of Uxbridge's efforts to extend his rabbit warrens on Cannock Chase in the 1750s. Armed with spades and clubs, two hundred men from the parishes around the Chase, fearing that the rabbits would consume the grass they needed for their sheep, marched on the warrens determined to destroy them. One farmer, Charles Marshall, killed an ox and he and other farmers brought bread, cheese and ale to the diggers every day. Only some two weeks later when they had reduced the earl's warren to its original size did the diggers rest contented.

Another circumstance that could trigger protest and disorder was dearth. When the harvest failed or when, for some other reason, the price of foodstuffs rose people would often take to the streets in droves, determined to right the situation by means of direct action. Not infrequently this would involve stopping the movement of grain out of the district. In 1762, for example, the inhabitants of Newcastle under Lyme blocked roads leading out of the town when rumours spread that there were plans to transport quantities of foodstuffs north to Chester and Liverpool. At Tewkesbury in 1795 a mob of women unloaded barges bound for Birmingham, while at Burford carts heading in the same direction were also forced to disgorge their sacks of provisions. Five years later a crowd sank a boat laden with coal to block the canal near Wolverhampton in an effort to foil wheat shipments. Movement of corn out of the country was even more vigorously opposed than transporting it from region to region. Ports like Plymouth,

Southampton and Liverpool were the frequent target of food rioters, while at Dover in 1740 a group of women "rose in a tumultuous manner, cut the sacks, and took away the grain that some farmers were bringing to the Ports for shipping".

Blockage riots of this sort, however, were only one reaction to soaring food prices. Sometimes a crowd set about middlemen such as millers or merchants whom it suspected of hoarding or profiteering. In 1766, in a typical instance, an infuriated mob in Norwich destroyed a mill, threw the flour it contained into the river and carried off the miller's accounts. And even more common than personal or property attack was the price-setting riot. The crowd would intervene to ensure that grain was sold at what it considered to be a just rather than an inflated price. This might mean badgering farmers and dealers to lower their prices, or the mob might seize the corn itself and resell it at what it deemed an appropriate figure. In 1742 the Cornish tinners even went out into the countryside carrying sacks to search for supplies. They rifled stocks of cereals they found in barns, cellars and malt-houses and then returned to town to sell their booty at a shilling a sack – well below the current price. Normally in cases like this the proceeds of the sale would be scrupulously guarded and the money eventually handed back to the owners of the grain.

Enclosure, agrarian improvement and shortage of corn – all these at times resulted in communal protest and lawbreaking. They were, however, by no means the only divisive issues of the early modern era. An unpopular tax could produce a similar reaction, as could the use of deceit or strong-arm tactics in military recruiting. From the late seventeenth century turnpike riots became quite common. These usually involved the tearing down of the gates across the roads where tolls were collected on the new turnpike routes. These tolls, it was feared, would drive up the cost of goods coming into the area. There was also a widespread concern that the better surfaces of the turnpiked roads might facilitate the flow of food and other essential commodities out of the vicinity. But, whatever the occasion for the protest, the reaction of the local inhabitants was always very much the same. People were willing to do whatever was necessary to defend what they believed in, even if this involved flouting the law. In these circumstances what would at other times have been viewed by people as criminal behaviour was not seen by them as crime at all.

The psychology of opposition

There was, we have seen, a wide range of differing socio-political crimes in early modern England. All the offences carried with them an implicit criticism of the conduct and policy of the ruling elite. Yet curiously those in rebellion – whom we might term the sub-political nation – were not prepared to take matters further than this. People were more than ready to censure their rulers over particular issues when the need arose, but that is as far as opposition went. There was rarely any suggestion that the political system itself should be changed, that the man – let alone the woman – in the street should be given the vote and thereby a voice in the formal machinery of government. On the contrary, those guilty of socio-political crime seem to have gone out of their way to stress their loyalty to the constitution as it stood.

Perhaps the thing which above all others demonstrates the reluctance of those in revolt to be seen as revolutionaries is the peculiar ritual that accompanied much socio-political crime. When, in the winter of 1753, the commoners of Cannock Chase descended on the rabbit warrens of the Earl of Uxbridge they called themselves "dragoons" and marched in strict formation. A trumpeter blew his horn, a hat was hoisted on a stick for colours, and the marchers wore badges of broom and rushes. The co-ordinator of the enclosure riots in the Midlands in 1607 called himself "Captain Pouch", and the rioters themselves wore feathers and other insignia. In the West Fen near Boston in November 1757, two hundred people assembled with "drums beating and colours flying" to destroy some newly erected drainage works. By taking on a military persona like this the protestors were endeavouring to show that they were not a lawless rabble, that they were disciplined and loyal citizens intent only on righting a wrong. They were not trying to overthrow rank and order or to turn the world upside down.

So popular opposition was muted and restricted. One reason for this is unquestionably the prevailing ideology of early modern England. Most people believed that God had constructed the world according to a hierarchical plan. According to this view, each person had been selected by the Almighty to fulfil a particular role in life. Some were to be hewers of wood and drawers of water while others were to be the rulers of the Earth. The Reverend Isaac Watts captured the outlook succinctly in his *Essay towards the encouragement of charity schools* published in 1728:

> The Great God has wisely ordained in the course of His Providence in all ages, that among mankind there should be some rich and some poor. And the same Providence hath allotted to the poor the meaner services, and hath given to the rich the superior and more honourable business of life. Nor is it possible according to the present course of nature and human affairs to alter this constitution of things, nor is it our design to attempt anything so unreasonable.

This hierarchical view was taught in the schools, it was preached from the pulpit and it was acted out in everyday life. Hence, it must have been very difficult for men and women, confronted at every turn by such a powerful and intrusive ideology, to think in terms of votes for all and parliament for the people.

A second reason why the common man's political horizons were so circumscribed revolves around the power balance of the early modern era. Ordinary townspeople and country dwellers just did not possess the know-how or the mental furniture to be able to take on the ruling elite on anything approaching equal terms. Even as late as the 1750s half the bridegrooms who married in the village church of Keele were too illiterate even to sign their own names. In the case of brides less than one in seven was able to accomplish this simple task. Moreover, the power of the gentry and of the other social leaders must have seemed to contemporaries all but limitless. As judges and lawgivers these people dispensed huge political authority; as employers and landlords they also exercised economic control. Just what this could mean in practice was demonstrated by the behaviour of the Earl of Uxbridge in 1754 after his rabbit warrens on Cannock Chase had been attacked. Not only did Uxbridge pursue the culprits relentlessly through the courts but he also took steps to evict as many people as he could from their cottages. He embarked on the mass ejection in July, before the crops were all in, so that the punishment of the villagers would be, in the words of his steward, "the better proportioned to their offence". Among those who suffered were Ralph Walker, an elderly day labourer with a large family, one of whose sons had participated in the dig at the warren, and Walter Elliots, a yeoman, whose mother had testified in court on behalf of the commoners. Faced with such awesome opposition it is little wonder that the common man had limited political aims.

The hierarchical ideology of the early modern period plus the unequal distribution of power in society go a long way to explain the restrained political ambitions of ordinary citizens. But there was also a third issue at stake. The ruling classes did not ignore the worries and concerns of those engaged in socio-political crime. On the contrary, all the evidence suggests that the elite listened with care to the voices that were raised. One clue to this, notwithstanding the example of the Earl of Uxbridge, is the lightness of the punishments meted out to socio-political criminals compared with those for other lawbreakers. As a rule, poachers and smugglers were shown little consideration. But elsewhere it was a different tale. Many who transgressed were not arrested and even those brought before the courts were not severely treated. Of the 12 men charged in connection with food rioting at the Staffordshire Quarter Sessions between 1733 and 1743 two were discharged, five were fined, one was whipped and only four were imprisoned – and all four of those gaoled had been involved in theft as well as riot. Of the ten women charged over the same period not a single one was incarcerated. Nobody, male or female, was sentenced to death.

Even more telling than the light punishment is the effort that was made by those in authority to remedy situations. The government responded to the midland enclosure riots of 1607 by sending down a commission to investigate the justice of the rioters' claims. It decided broadly in their favour and, as a result, a number of powerful landed men, including the Earl of Lincoln, were reprimanded and fined. The disturbances in the Fens from the 1620s onwards resulted in the abandonment of many drainage schemes, and by the close of the seventeenth century crumbling dykes and rusting equipment were a common sight. In 1741, after a major outbreak of grain rioting in Staffordshire, a group of gentlemen in the Cheadle area took up a collection for the poor and agreed to make, every Monday, regular deliveries of cheap food to those in need. People in the scheme were charged 6d a peck for oatmeal – oatbread was the staple food of the area – and this was a full 6d below the market price. Fifteen years later, in another period of dearth, Liverpool corporation borrowed £2,000 to buy corn, which they rationed and sold to poor people at cost price. In the bleak year of 1795 the city fathers of Norwich called together all the local millers and made them agree not to send any wheat or flour out of the country.

Time and again, therefore, the elite listened with sympathy and understanding to those engaged in socio-political disorder. The common people thus had no need to demand drastic change in the political system. They got their message across anyway. Their voice was heard.

Conclusion

Small-scale, mundane offences continued to flood the courts throughout the pre-industrial period. Another sort of lawbreaking, however, socio-political crime, became more prominent. Although the variety of socio-political crimes was considerable, it is possible to split offences into three broad categories: practices viewed as illegitimate by the authorities right from the outset; practices that increasingly became criminalized as the years went by; finally, the behaviour of the powerful that the common man and woman regarded as immoral and unacceptable and that they were determined to oppose and protest about whatever the consequence might be.

Though people were, in these various ways, prepared to make a stand, the degree of popular disenchantment was limited. Early modern men and women were not the stuff of which revolutions are made. An inhibiting ideology and an unequal distribution of power help to explain this reticence. But just as crucial is the fact that socio-political crime was treated differently from other sorts of criminality. Those in authority listened to the criticisms being made and, not infrequently, responded with surprising sensitivity. It is still a widely held view among historians that the common people only found their voice in the wake of the Industrial Revolution and that it was only during the nineteenth and twentieth centuries that democracy took root. The story of early modern socio-political crime suggests that this perspective may well be in need of some revision. Ordinary men and women were already politically articulate in 1500, and there was a democratic element in English politics from that time.

Part II
Crime, police and punishment in England after the Industrial Revolution, 1800–75

Chapter 8
The ordering of society

Informal disciplines

A. J. P. Taylor argues that one of the impacts of the demands of the First World War on civilian society was that "The history of the state and of the English people merged for the first time." The proposal is that until then the state and Britain's citizens inhabited separate spheres. This means that any exploration of the way in which society was ordered at the beginning of the nineteenth century cannot confine itself to a study of legal codes and the actions of officers of the law. It has to go beyond that and undertake the more subtle task of understanding how the much less easily defined forces of opinion, habit and aspiration affected people's behaviour in a society that existed long before the emergence of the omni-competent state. W. L. Burn expresses it in these terms:

> As its far-ranging missionaries of social discipline and progress [individualistic England] took the individual man and woman, impelled by their desire to better their condition in this world and to secure a crown of glory in the next. Behind them were the powerful voluntary agencies, the religious and philanthropic associations, the schools and universities, the hospitals, the innumerable societies for inducing people to do something or refrain from doing something else. In the third line was the State. That was the usual order but it was capable of alteration and on occasions the State moved into first place.

Society, then, was in normal times essentially ordered by individual motivation, the desire to stand well with your peers and with your God, and by the informal disciplines of family, factory, congregation and the great estate. This was a society in large measure confined within parochial boundaries. Within such confines, informal disciplines – defined as the disciplines of publicity, respectability, dependency, religion and of work and play – were for the most part tolerably efficient, especially when it is remembered that the shadow of the workhouse, the only formal provision for the poor, was cast across all working-class homes in the kingdom. An absence of formal constraints does not, therefore, mean that society was threateningly anarchic, for although legal constraints may have been few, social disciplines were well entrenched and respected. Landlordism, employer–employee relationships, tied cottages, different forms of patronage, all were part of the woof and warp of everyday life.

> A labourer earning fifteen shillings a week, whose wife made a little extra by sewing at the Big House and who was trying to get his daughters into service there, was not in a position to dispute the standards which the Big House stood for. If it was determined to maintain and inculcate Anglicanism, chastity, sobriety, cleanliness and thrift, then it behoved him, if he wanted help in bad times, to be or affect to be a chaste, sober, clean and thrifty Anglican. (W. L. Burn)

With the growth of industry, moreover, the influence of the large manufacturer upon his workforce could easily aspire to the totalitarianism of the great estate. The building of industrial tied cottages and industrial suburbs is testimony to that. Indentures of apprenticeships similarly show the masters' intent to govern not just the working lives of their employees but their leisure activities and their domestic relationships as well. Josiah Wedgwood's indenture to his brother contained the following prescriptions: "at Cards, Dice, or any other unlawful games he shall not play; Taverns or Ale Houses he shall not frequent, Fornication he shall not commit, Matrimony he shall not contract". This kind of control continued: the new professional bodies of the nineteenth century, which guaranteed a certain level of service to the public, also disciplined the lives of their members. The new factory employment, or for that matter employment by one of the new corporations such as the post office or a large railway company, added another disciplinary agency to the tendency of the times through the demands it made for punctuality, regularity and dutiful care.

Social control

The concept of social control must not be reduced to too crude a form of manipulation, questioning the altruism of all philanthropists, doubting the humanitarianism of all humanitarians and seeing clergy, social workers and educators as merely "policeman without boots" (Donajgrodzki). Moreover, to suggest that certain institutions and individuals had a social-control function is not to deny other relationships; thus Donajgrodzki appositely remarks, "Parents undertake control functions with regard to their children, and vice versa, but it would be a cynic indeed who saw this as the true and only meaning of family life." But the control function was nevertheless powerful: W. E. Houghton asserts, with pardonable exaggeration, "Every young Victorian heard his father's voice sounding in his conscience,

'Remember your dear, good mother, and never do anything, think anything, imagine anything she would be ashamed of.' " Thus filial respect was
made the engine of "moral censorship and control", essentially within the
middle class. F. M. L. Thompson has questioned whether socialization is
not the better description of the process when it occurs within a class,
reserving social control for inter-class proclivities to exercise a moral discipline over others. In practice, however, the two expressions seem to be
used interchangeably.

Arguably religion, with its ability to judge motive as well as action and to
pursue beyond the grave, with eternal not just temporal sanctions, those
who escaped the law in this life, was the most effective policeman of all.
That is as long as its ministrations were heeded, and that was why the
revelation of the Religious Census of 1851 of poor church attendance in the
new industrial areas of the Midlands and the North threatened society as
much as the Church. This estrangement of the populace from the established church explains why parliament was prepared to grant a million
pounds in 1818 for the building of new churches in such areas and half a
million pounds in additional funds six years later. Publicly this might be
declared a thanksgiving for delivery from the tyranny of Napoleon; at the
same time these were properly regarded as sensible premiums to ensure that
such destructive revolutionary forces did not trouble British shores.

For the aspiring middle classes, notions such as gentility, propriety,
respectability and conformism all determined behaviour: "The proper
thing to do is not only what the individual *wants* to do in order to belong to
a good society, or what he *does* do out of ingrained habit; it is also what he
must do if he is to avoid social stigma" argues Houghton, relating this to
Mill's comment that in the mid-nineteenth century "everyone lives as under
the eye of a hostile and dreaded censorship", that all-seeing eye that has
everybody scrutinized, as for example in Dickens's *Bleak House*. Provocative
of much hypocrisy as it undoubtedly was, respectability also had its positive
values, for people of all classes. In a drink-sodden society, the sobriety for
which the drunkard's wife craved also served his employer's interests well,
as it also made for peace in the community within which he lived.

Historians should not therefore too readily accept the view that social
control was all of middle-class making and all of working-class receiving, as
if the lower classes were "so much putty in the hands of a masterful and
scheming bourgeoisie" (F. M. L. Thompson). That is to say that some
writers in their enthusiasm for social-control explanations have placed
insufficient emphasis on value systems and institutions generated by the
working classes themselves as representing the best way of coping with the
new capitalistic society: for example, it has long been argued that self-help
was a working-class method of seeking to secure or better themselves long
before it became canonized as a great middle-class virtue. Again it has been
queried whether "education from above", as provided by the two large

voluntary societies, the National Society, which believed that education should be based on the foundations of the Church of England, and the British and Foreign Schools Society, which eschewed denominational tests, ever did act as an effective agency of social control as many of its promoters clearly intended. The working classes for their part abstracted from it the literacy that was useful to them, while giving short shrift to the moralizing intentions of middle-class educators. Of football, the people's game, it has been argued that the working classes accepted its outward form as a participant sport that may have been intended by certain reformers as a mechanism for social control but, by filling it with their own lively, colourful and unrestrained content and switching the emphasis from players to spectators, made it into something very different from what had originally been intended.

Social change

English society in 1800 was still predominantly rural, but already towns and cities had developed a reputation for being havens where criminals might hide themselves in safe anonymity beyond the reaches of such agents of the law as then existed. Nevertheless, in this kind of world the informal system worked reasonably well, although there were exceptions seen in riots provoked by enclosure, by food shortages and inflation, or in resentment at the actions of the army press-gang. Society, however, was changing: a static, isolated, restricted, small-scale rural society was giving way to the new dynamic experience of a mass urban industrial world. The population was expanding rapidly: there were more and more people and more of them were town-dwellers. Significantly, too, for the incidence of crime, the proportion of young people was increasing, because men in their teens and twenties supplied a very high percentage of the total criminal cohort. Some doomsday pedlars were of the persuasion that society was almost immediately about to disintegrate into anarchy, although in the event it did not prove so fragile.

Such changes put the old informal mechanisms of keeping the peace under pressure. Not only that. The requirements of the new industry were quite different from those of agriculture. Whereas the old world essentially demanded brute strength and endurance and could tolerate bursts of energy alternating with periods of play and leisure, capitalist industry demanded good time-keeping, regularity in employment, predictable and reliable application of energy and precision in operating skills. To these tasks the men of the fields had to be schooled by new disciplines both formal and informal. Thus R. J. White affirms, "It required many schools, and particularly Sunday schools, with their lessoning in the industrial virtues of diligence, thrift, and especially 'regularity', to turn the people of the fields and the cottages into the people of the factories and the back-streets." New disciplines, new institutions and new codes of practice were required to fulfil this task. In part they were informal but the long-term recipient of the legacy of these changes was increasing state intervention. Samuel Smiles's secularized gospel of self-help set up the pulpit in the midst of everyday life when the pews in church were increasingly unoccupied; it became the positive inducement, the carrot, to attract the working classes to solid application to employment in a world where work was readily valued for its own sake and apart from its content, a philosophy reckoned to possess clear biblical warrant. But the confidence in the Smilesian gospel was never such as to dispense with the negative deterrent of the Poor Law embodied in the workhouse, the necessary stick underlining the continuing need for that resolute search for gainful employment that ensured Victorian industry never lacked a suitable supply of labour. It is in such a framework of social discipline that the actions of state and society in the face of the anti-state and anti-social behaviour of the criminal has to be set.

Political change

The changes of the late eighteenth and early nineteenth centuries were not only social but also political, for the Hammonds were right to see two revolutions converging: "The French Revolution had transformed the minds of the ruling classes and the Industrial Revolution had convulsed the world of the working classes." At the same time, some of the disturbances of these years reflected older divisions within society that seemed to take on new significance in the light of events in France. It was, for example, a sermon preached by the Unitarian divine, the Revd Dr Richard Price, in which he argued for both the ending of dissenting disabilities and a reform of the franchise, that provoked the writing of Edmund Burke's *Reflections on the French Revolution*, in 1790. Against this background, "constitutional" forces assembled in "Church and King" mobs, which assaulted dissenting property, most famously in Birmingham in 1791 when they took action against Joseph Priestley, a chemist and Unitarian minister and member of the innovative Lunar Society. In three days of rioting, 20 buildings were damaged or destroyed, including three Unitarian and one Baptist meeting-house, for which the law, which executed two of the rioters, offered compensation in a sum of little less than £24,000. Reactionary mobs also operated in Nottingham, Manchester, Exeter and Coventry, with deep suspicions in a number of cases that the magistracy was complicit with the rioters' intentions, either conveniently absenting themselves at the crucial moment or failing to act early enough. Mob, gentry and magistracy all represented the old order and reacted violently against every process they perceived to threaten the security of that order: dissenters, industrialists and reformers.

Events in France inevitably posed questions about the political situation in Britain and set the piecemeal proposals of the younger Pitt to deal with electoral unfairnesses in a wholly new direction. At the same time, legislation such as the Corn Laws of 1815, which guaranteed to British agriculture the protected home market that had come about through the French wars and the Napoleonic blockade, showed that parliament still over-represented the static land-based part of the nation and not the new dynamic capital and labour-based industrial sector of the entrepreneur and the workers, who thus had common cause in seeking reform. Reform represented a more constructive response to the problems of the post-war years, for machine-breaking and riot only served to justify the government in repression. But to convert economic grievance into political agitation required much patient education and equally patient strategizing as to action.

Popular disturbances

In this uncertain world, Viscount Sidmouth as home secretary operated the technique of repression known as "alarm". Minions, and most notoriously W. J. Richards, alias "Oliver the Spy", are supposed to have acted as *agents provocateurs*, provoking local revolt in order to tempt the disaffected into indictable action. One of the many weaknesses of the system, the extent of which is much debated, was that the government's secret agents were paid by results, which encouraged their conspiratorial suspicions for no more sophisticated purpose than personal financial gain. Government's normal response to periods of alarm was to suspend the Habeas Corpus Act, the British citizen's guarantee, originally passed in 1679, against arbitrary arrest and detention. The suspension of Habeas Corpus in 1817 together with legislation prohibiting seditious meetings and requiring prior permission from the magistrates for meetings in excess of fifty persons were readily nicknamed by the popular mind, with obvious perception, the "gagging acts"; their main effect was to drive even moderate reformers into illegal action. In the courts, full evidence was never produced because it was argued that, the nation being in a state of alarm, the rehearsing of the same could endanger the peace of the realm. In due time, Richards's actions became clear, and arrangements had to be made for him to emigrate to South Africa. Government spies seemed to be omni-present, whilst local postmasters, anticipating the phone-tapping of our own age, were required to test the posts for signs of sedition, and factory inspectors, in addition to their stated duties, were required to report upon the political temperature in the manufacturing regions. Such policies were, of course, developed in the absence of any effective local police force: spies and volunteers were in part a substitute for such more accountable agents for securing public order.

The three decades from 1815 to 1845 probably represent the most menacing years in modern British history. Peace, after more than two decades of war, saw the military released on to a satiated labour market that was further narrowed by the reduced demands upon the munitions industry, while peacetime patterns of exchange were yet to be re-established. Moreover, to the particularities of the moment had to be added all the long-term problems of urban and industrial change. These had been neglected for the duration of the wars, which, especially when combined with threats of French invasion, provided the government with an excuse for doing nothing. At the same time, the shadow of Bonaparte, it was argued, served to bind the nation together with bonds of national unity. That machine-breaking and hostility to industrial change which took on the name of Luddism after General Ned Lud, and which was particularly strong in the hosiery areas of the East Midlands, antedates the peace by several years. E. P. Thompson argues that this was not just a blind and unthinking rejection of all technical progress: it was in Hobsbawm's words an aspect of "collective bargaining by riot".

This points to the ambiguity of a number of the volunteer forces recruited at this time, which, although full of rhetoric about defending British liberties, were often extremely parochial, for the distances that local forces were prepared to travel in defending their interests were extremely limited. Quite frequently their constitutions overtly spelt out their concern to protect society as much from a fifth column of disaffected workers at home as from invading Frenchmen. For example, an open letter addressed to the Right Honourable the Lord Gower, Colonel of the Staffordshire Cavalry, by F. P. Eliot, a major in that force, was printed by the desire of a committee of subscribers concerned for "the internal defence of the county". Dated October 1794, it refers to alarms in the area arising not only from the action of enemies abroad, but from the discovery of an extensive conspiracy "fomented by disaffected subjects" at home. These agents were alleged to be "corresponding not only with other illegal societies in different parts of the kingdom but even with the avowed enemies of their country". This they did to the discomfiture not only of "the wealthy trader", "the man of landed property", but also of "the independent and respectable yeoman, cultivating and improving his paternal fields; enjoying in the bosom of domestic peace all that can endear or render life desirable".

Government's immediate response, alike to disaffection at home and threat from abroad, was to clamp down on any possibility that popular discontent would express itself. This it did by a series of repressive measures starting with the Combination Acts of 1799, which forbade the association of working men in common purpose. But such repression was counterproductive, for out of it emerged a radical championing of popular aspirations, even though the manifestation of this radicalism in due turn provoked further repressive measures.

In London, an intelligent radicalism enjoyed politically literate leadership: Sir Francis Burdett was elected Radical MP for Westminster in 1807 by popular vote. A determined advocate of parliamentary reform, he campaigned in favour of all those locked up in "English Bastilles", and in 1810 was committed to the Tower of London for his labours in the Radical cause. The popular support he enjoyed made this no easy task. Twenty thousand troops were deployed in the capital, the Tower moat was filled with water, and its canons were primed. National government was further embarrassed by the support afforded to Burdett by the authorities in the City of London, underlining the fact that local authorities could as easily side with popular causes against the administration of the day as become the agents for carrying out central government's policies. By dint of an early morning arrest Burdett was secured within the Tower, which was immediately surrounded by a mob who vented their ill-feeling on the soldiers, provoking a riot in which two people were killed and a dozen wounded. But the government's problems were not over, for they only had sanction to hold Burdett for a limited period of time and, having got him into the Tower, were almost immediately faced with as large a problem with regard to his discharge. This again offered the occasion for unwieldy popular demonstrations, which were only thwarted by Burdett's loss of nerve and quiet departure by river for his country residence at Wimbledon.

In the northwest in March 1817, without the patronage of men of the calibre of Burdett, the Manchester Blanketeers, hungry weavers marching in groups of ten, each with a blanket on his back, set out from Manchester in the drizzling rain to petition the Prince Regent to remedy the wretched plight of those who worked in the cotton trade. Such protests represented the politics of hunger, and yet not politics at all in so far as the men had no idea of any well-defined political remedy for their woes. The leaders were arrested even before they left Manchester, few got beyond the Staffordshire Moorlands, and only one man reached London. "Our first great absurdity" Samuel Bamford called it, but others have argued that it was a clever plan to make a protest while keeping within the boundaries of the law.

The so-called Pentrich Revolution of June 1817, "an affair of pistols, pikes, bill-hooks and bludgeons, parading and marching with great force and violence in and through divers villages and highways", was the work of the destitute farm labourers, quarrymen and iron-founders of southeast Derbyshire, men far removed from the intellectual revolution of these years that was producing a new view of political participation. Planned as part of a general insurrection of the North of England, it was pitiful in its isolation. Search for the language of franchise, manhood suffrage and annual parliaments in the talk of this group and you will search in vain. When one of its leaders, Jeremiah Brandreth, was heckled by "a practically-minded female" who insistently asked what kind of government should supersede that of the borough mongers, he replied "a provisional government", and it has been commented, "it is plain that he and his followers thought that a provisional government had something to do with provisions". This is the protest of the have-nots, not a programme for political change. But that did not lighten the sentence. Brandreth and three other ringleaders were sentenced to death and 23 others to transportation or imprisonment after the presiding judge pronounced that "economic distress was not to be corrected by political activity".

Behind these particulars, the basic problem of Radical reformers can be identified: how to foster popular opinion, apply pressure and deploy demonstrations without your followers drifting over the line separating moral from physical force, for the immediate consequence of that would be the forfeit of respectable sympathies and the affording to the government of a perfect justification for repressive action. This was a methodological difficulty that served to split Chartism as late as 1848. Thus, in contrast with constitutional reformers, the impatient men of violence, small in number but larger in reputation, planned conspiracies large and small, talking wildly about attacking the Bank of England, the Tower and other prisons – about doing in London what the French had done in Paris. It is difficult to estimate how much a threat such groups really were because it was generally in the government's interests to exaggerate it. Moreover, official spying and surveillance meant that much of the planning was revealed in advance and that, therefore, such action as took place occurred within the general framework of the government's knowledge. One of the more violent threats to political stability was the ill-organized Spencean march upon the Tower of London on 2 December 1816. Following on that, Arthur Thistlewood and his fellow Cato Street conspirators spent two and a half years planning a conspiracy which eventually took the shape of attempting to assassinate the whole of the Cabinet while members were dining at Lord Harrowby's house in Grosvenor Square on 22 February 1820: Thistlewood and four colleagues were executed and a further five conspirators transported. This misadventure served the people of England not an iota, its only function being to justify the government in the repressive measures it had taken. The government may not have been really threatened by such actions and may even have used their occurrence to strengthen its own position, but such events indicate the excluded classes' increasing frustration with the British political system.

Peterloo and new directions in popular protest

More significant in changing the public mood were the events of 16 August 1819, when a crowd of at least sixty thousand, including women and children, assembled peacefully and unarmed in St Peter's Square in Manchester. The local magistrates misjudged the situation, panicked and ordered in the local yeomanry. In Manchester and Salford this meant "the butcher, the baker and the candlestick-maker on horseback". Subsequently the magistrates ordered the hussars, who were wearing their Waterloo medals, to enter the fray to aid the yeomanry and disperse the crowd, with force if necessary. In the savage action that followed 11 people were killed and 400 wounded, a number suffering from trampling and suffocation from a too rapid retreat of so large a number of persons. Dubbed Peterloo by the Radical press in ironic comparison with the victory of British soldiers over the French some four years earlier, the Manchester event "was the climax of the prolonged post-war contest between governors and governed, when it seemed to many that English politics were fast becoming undistinguishable from the politics of continental countries, with their tendency to oscillate perilously between reaction and revolution" (R. J. White). It was this threat of the bogey of military rule that stirred the Whigs to champion the cause of reform, to broaden their base of support, converting middle-class wealth to the view that some form of reform was now unavoidable.

More important was the effect of the massacre in politicizing the nation, for it has been argued that Peterloo "marked the final conversion of provincial England to the doctrine of 'First Things First'". With Peterloo political reform came of age. All those years of meetings and conscience-forming had at last given birth to a forceful, coherent demand for political change. The demand for radical political reformation was seen now to be the precondition for any improvement in the condition of the people of England. The traditional governors of the nation, indicted for "committing high treason against the people", had in a moment lost the trust that the people had for so long willingly given to them. Popular protest was not going to go away while the army remained an over-blunt weapon for dealing with disturbances, at least in their early stages.

Once more the government replied with repressive measures in the form of the Six Acts of 1819. These made provision for the search of property without warrant, the prohibition of all private military training and the limitation of political meetings to the residents of the parish in which the meeting took place. This it was hoped would avert massive demonstrations such as had occurred at Peterloo. The Six Acts also required the immediate trial of those accused of political offences, by magistrates – not waiting for jury trial at the next assizes. They also increased stamp duty on pamphlets and periodicals in order to control their circulation. This was not just statute book activity; it heralded what has been called "the most sustained campaign of prosecutions in the courts in British history", with the summer of 1820 finding a large number of Radical leaders in prison (E. P. Thompson).

The struggle for reform

The 1820s were far from being years of stagnation. In 1824 Francis Place, the Radical tailor of Charing Cross, and Joseph Hume, Radical MP, secured the repeal of the Combination Acts of 1799 and the legitimization of early trade unions. A wave of strikes and other agitation broke out, taking advantage of the new legal situation, at a time when cotton weavers perceived an increasing threat to their labour from the spread of power looms. Such was the extent of these disturbances that the old acts were in danger of being brought back. Only with difficulty did Hume secure an Amending Act that secured the legality of the unions but proscribed any molesting or obstruction of individuals. Violent protest did not disappear, but as union organization improved so leaders emerged who were well aware that well-disciplined peaceful demonstrations were more persuasive than those which degenerated into exhibitions of uncontrolled violence.

In Ireland, then an integrated part of the United Kingdom, a virtual state of civil war followed the outcome of the by-election in the Clare constituency in 1828. The electorate returned Daniel O'Connell, the founder of the Catholic Association, although he was excluded by the Test Act from sitting at Westminister, as member for that constituency. The clear message was that at the forthcoming election the same pattern would be repeated in scores of constituencies with the inevitable consequence that Ireland would become ungovernable. The only solution seemed to be Catholic emancipation, which was duly granted in 1829. It had in fact been part of the original intention of the Act of Union in 1800 but had been omitted from the programme because the king believed that the granting of emancipation would compromise his coronation oath.

The repeal of the Test and Corporation Acts in order to provide full citizenship to Protestant dissenters in 1828, coupled with Catholic emancipation in the year following, demonstrated that the British constitution was not unalterable; taken together these two constitutional amendments gave hope to those seeking a more broadly based extension of the franchise. Moreover, 1830 witnessed the outbreak in rural England of riots of dramatic proportions. This was all the more significant for taking place at a time when industrial workers were beginning to question the tradition of "collective bargaining by riot". These "Captain Swing" disturbances, so named after the signature that appeared on many a threatening letter that preceded them, spread as far north as Carlisle and as far west as Hereford, but principally occurred in those counties where there was little employment other than agriculture and where living conditions had been deteriorating for many years. The spiralling resort to the Poor Law that ensued in turn made the local overseers increasingly mean when administering that instrument. It is interesting, however, that a very high proportion of those who were brought to trial represented the respectable labouring classes rather than the poorest. The grievances that provoked them were rarely political and almost entirely focused on local economic problems: enclosures, tithes, employment and wages. Their attitude was nearly always nostalgic and conservative, looking to past benefits and old securities, demanding the restitution of lost rights and customary wage levels. Rural aggression took the form of machine-breaking, rick-burning, animal-maiming, arson and the invasion of enclosed lands. It has further been suggested that the increased incidence of poaching, the stealing of stock and other rural crimes during the period also testifies to a breakdown in relationships in rural England. For their part the rioters were most often highly disciplined, only lightly armed, taking pains to avoid assault against the person. Although lacking any coherent rural police force the authorities were able to round up the miscreants without difficulty. Of these, 252 were sentenced to death, though only 19 suffered that fate. Nearly five hundred were transported, while over six hundred were imprisoned in England.

Elections in early-nineteenth-century England were frequently accompanied by disturbances; the reading of the Riot Act was a regular event to legitimize the actions of the army. The election following the fall of Wellington's Government in 1830 was particularly violent. This was followed by even more serious rioting when the House of Lords rejected Grey's second Bill proposing a reform of the franchise in October 1831. This provoked major disturbances in Nottingham and Bristol, where the damage done was calculated at some £300,000, together with 12 people killed, 94 wounded and 102 prisoners taken, of whom 31 received capital sentences: only four were carried out. This was not the extra-parliamentary pressure that Lord John Russell believed was so influential in securing the passing of the Reform Bill. That had rather to do with the creation of favourable public opinion and the ability to demonstrate its extent peacefully. John Stevenson argues, "Far from being evidence that reform would have to be passed at any cost, the lesson could be drawn that even the most flagrant obstruction of the people would only cause a reaction well within the capacities of the Government to cope with." That gets near to the heart of the problem of riot as an argument for political change, posing the question whether the people could ever amass enough force to secure the mastery of more highly trained and disciplined government forces.

The worst year for violence was 1831, 1832 was by contrast quiet: an effigy of the Archbishop of York was burnt in his cathedral city, while another of the Duke of Wellington suffered a similar fate in Worcester. There were large demonstrations in the great cities, but they were conducted in an orderly fashion and did not degenerate into riots. The Whigs, for their part, succeeded in passing a moderate reform measure that satisfied the interests of the new industrial and commercial interests without yielding anything substantial to popular forces. Therein lay the roots of Chartism.

Chartism and the debate about force

Disappointment with the partial nature of Whig reform was only one of the causes of the emergence of Chartism. The great economic transition of these years generated its own problems with the perpetuation of conditions of depression for the working classes in both the countryside and in the new towns, where the harnessing of mechanical power in aid of production seemed to put jobs under threat. In addition, expanded production had to contend with the unevenness of demand, so that over-production all too easily led to the economic slumps of a saturated market; these years proved to be peak years for Chartist activity. Meanwhile, the plight of groups like the hand-loom weavers of the northwest, the nail makers of the Black Country and the framework knitters of the East Midlands, no longer able to compete with factory production, became ever more desperate, their support of Chartism rather more constant than that of the factory workers. Part of this concern found form in the Anti-Truck movement, which protested against the payment of workers in truck, that is in commodities of little or no financial value that the employer wished to dispose of having previously purchased them cheaply. A monster Anti-Truck meeting convened at the Staffordshire Potteries Race Ground in October 1830 attracted an attendance of some 15,000, including "the manufacturer and the mechanic, the tradesman and the labourer" to attack a system that was no less than the "direct robbery and spoliation of the Working Classes".

In such a context widespread hostility to the introduction of the New Poor Law was understandable. Influenced by Bentham's concept of the pleasure–pain principle, the New Poor Law embraced the two principles of the Workhouse Test and Less Eligibility. The first meant, in theory, an end to all outdoor relief, the only relief offered being in the workhouse. The second required that conditions in the house should be less attractive than those enjoyed by the least well-off independent labourer. The law united the agricultural south and the industrial north in common opposition. Resistance in the north was more sustained and more inclined to violence, with the ugly image of the new "Poor Law Bastilles" powerfully reinforced by articles in the provincial press objecting to this new agency of centralizing government. The creation of the police forces, a further aspect of the intrusion of the new administrative state on the lives of ordinary citizens, also fed Chartism. John Stevenson writes that, "It was this regulatory and intrusive character of the police which probably led to more hostility than almost anything else, at a time when the authorities saw it as part of the police function to control an increasingly wide range of everyday activities." The regulatory aspirations of the new state were not to be accepted without resistance.

The People's Charter was first published by the largely artisan London Working Men's Association in May 1838; even as the impetus behind it was part economic, part political, so there were also divisions about its objectives. While the leadership was firm in perceiving that only a complete change in parliamentary representation would serve the long-term interests of the working classes, grass-roots supporters inclined more to the identification by the Revd J. Rayner Stephens (a former Wesleyan clergyman who had withdrawn from that body because of his desire to have more freedom to attack the established Church) of the suffrage with essentially economic concerns:

> Chartism is no political movement, where the main question is getting the ballot. The question of universal suffrage is a knife and fork question, after all, a bread and cheese question, notwithstanding all that has been said against it; and if any man asks me what I mean by universal suffrage, I would answer, that every working man in the land has the right to have a good coat to his back, a comfortable abode in which to shelter himself and his family, a good dinner upon his table, and no more work than is necessary for keeping him in good health and as much wages for that work as would keep him in plenty and afford him the enjoyment of all the blessings of life which a reasonable man could desire.

Most renownedly, Chartism was divided over whether its campaigning should be limited to moral force or whether it could legitimately embrace physical force. Quite where that divide came in the total story of Chartist activity is not clear since nearly all Chartists practised the rhetoric of violence, and there was in the early years a general backing for the politics of menace, that unless concessions were granted large peaceable demonstrations could turn to formidable riots. Just how far plans had been formulated for a nation-wide insurrection, as for example for late 1839, has been widely debated. The argument has also been offered that it was not the Chartists who brought violence to the situation but those authorities who did violence to the rights of free-born Englishmen with their new-fangled police and poor laws.

The summer of 1842 witnessed disturbances that combined elements of widespread riot affecting 23 counties with aspects of a general strike, "the first not only in Britain but any capitalist country". Lieutenant Colonel Maberley, Secretary of the Post Office and thereby equipped to know the breadth of sentiment in the country, described the events as "a commotion such as we have not witnessed for half a century". The starting point was a strike of colliers in north Staffordshire in response to wage reductions. The striking colliers drew the boiler plugs so that pit engines could not be restarted, thereby ensuring there could be no return to work and giving the disturbances their popular name, the Plug Plot Riots. Moreover, the dependence of the pottery industry on local coal meant that not only the

Figure 8.1   The police force on Bonner's Fields during the Chartist Disturbances in 1848. From the *Illustrated London News.*

pits but the pot-banks too were brought to a standstill. Within a few weeks there were also riots in the iron-making districts of the south of the county. Little wonder that the Staffordshire Quarter Sessions decided in 1842 in favour of a county police force, which was to have such a decisive influence in handling subsequent issues of public order.

Similar action by colliers took place in Lanarkshire, Lancashire and Cheshire. Not initially political in motivation, the disturbances only slowly became associated with Chartism. By the middle of August there was violence on both sides, violence to property and person by the rioters and retaliation by the military that resulted in some loss of life and considerable injury. In the ensuing months over a thousand arrests were made; three-quarters of those arrested were sentenced to imprisonment or transportation. Therefore the year of greatest Chartist threat to the stability of British society was 1842 rather than 1848. The analysis of committal statistics, although not without hazard, suggests that 1842 was unique, for only in that year did committals for riotous offences exceed 5 per cent of total committals; the quite exceptional figure of 19.46 per cent was recorded for Staffordshire, the epicentre of the disorders. In the seven years before 1842, the proportion had ranged from 1.8 per cent to 3.2 per cent. Over the next two decades the range declined from 2.24 per cent to 0.34 per cent, before increasing to as high as 1.63 per cent at the end of the 1860s. But the most important thing to note is how small a proportion of the whole these public-order offences are, even when admitting that some cases of contemporaneous assault should properly be included with them.

Towards an orderly society

Not until the industrial disputes of the twentieth century with their syndicalist association was anything like the threat of 1842 to be repeated. The third quarter of the nineteenth century was not to repeat the threats to public order that had characterized the first two. This was no small tribute to the effectiveness of the new police forces as they became less of a novelty and more acceptable in provincial society. That is not to say that the mid-century was riot-free but that the order of society was not significantly threatened. The incitement to riot was not necessarily to be found in major issues of reform. The provocation for the Hyde Park riots of June 1855 was Lord Grosvenor's Bill to suppress Sunday trading. On this occasion rioting was not confined to Hyde Park but also took place in Belgravia and in Hampstead and Tottenham Court Road. On the second Sunday of violence the police seemed to have got the better of the Hyde Park mob by driving a large part of it into the Serpentine, where police boats were already waiting to pick up the luckless amphibians. Some complained of police brutality, while the political right argued that the police had acted with great moderation and that Grosvenor's withdrawal of his bill was a dangerous yielding to "popular clamour".

The more famous Hyde Park riots took place during the debate on the Second Reform Bill in July 1866. The Reform League called a meeting in favour of reform but were denied permission to meet by Sir Richard Mayne, then Commissioner for the Metropolitan Police. The League, believing such prohibition to be without legal justification, decided to proceed with the demonstration, but they were refused entry to the park. Instead they had to meet in Trafalgar Square, where the passing of resolutions of gratitude to Gladstone and Bright was peacefully accomplished. Certain groups within the crowd who had come to watch the demonstration, not the demonstrators themselves, dislodged the park railings and took possession of the park, overcoming the capacities of a limited police force. A further demonstration was scheduled for the park for May 1867; this time it was forbidden by Spencer Walpole as home secretary but was nevertheless peacefully accomplished. While Royden Harrison argues that the riots persuaded men of property and power to offer timely concession in extending the franchise, Lord Blake argues that there is no evidence they influenced ministers in this way.

There was also a growing consciousness among at least some working-class leaders that the path of violent encounter with authority was unlikely to yield dividends. Rather the avenue of recognition and respectability was likely to be more profitable. For example, the securing of legal status by trade unions and the acceptance of their ability to discipline their own members were achieved in this way. The moderate leadership of the new model unions was able to exploit the royal commission set up to investigate trade union activities consequent upon the Sheffield "outrages". These included one case of murder, which the perpetrator claimed was "a shooting to wound which went wrong", and the blowing up of a non-member's house. These actions, though not unique for atrocities occurred in Manchester as well, were perpetrated by an untypical group of violent men in the cutlery trade. The leaders of new model union managed to secure out of the inquiry a recommendation to legalize trade unions, which was effected in the Trade Union Act of 1871. Industrial violence was not eliminated but it was so confined as to become remarkable for its rarity.

The coming of a quiet and orderly society should not be hurried. General elections were still frequently accompanied by violence. Legislation, including the introduction of the Secret Ballot in 1872 and the Corrupt Practices Act of 1883, did not end such blood-letting as quite literally occurred on such occasions. Local newspapers provide ample evidence of such events. For example, in the 1880 election in Stoke-on-Trent which, returned two Liberals with very large majorities, the "reds" (Tories) nevertheless came under heavy assault from local youths in the Longton part of the constituency; when no reds could be found, the police became targets for their missiles in their stead. The police, it was reported, were eventually compelled to draw their cutlasses, having secured the permission of the magistrates so to do. Although there was later doubt whether they had actually done so, clearly there had been sufficient violence in dispersing the crowd to provoke the calling of a protest meeting to denounce police behaviour. As late as 1910 Colonel "Jos" Wedgwood recalled that his first return to parliament for the borough of Newcastle under Lyme involved battles between schoolchildren painted in the rival colours of red and blue. His opponent was a high Tory of decidedly racist views, and both candidates needed bodyguards as they went around the borough: "From one meeting my football team threw his forty out after a long and bloody fight. Thereafter neither side was allowed to address anything but a sea of fists. Old men still tell with awe of that great free for all. It took the place of Agincourt."

Public order was equally challenged by Irish immigration and the belligerent anti-Catholicism that it provoked in so many places, but the riots that sometimes ensued, such as those in Stockport in 1852, in which one person was killed, and those at Wolverhampton in 1858 and 1867, did not pose a general threat to national composure. The lecture tours of the Protestant lecturer William Murphy, himself an ex-Catholic, were universally productive of disturbance until in 1871 he was attacked in Whitehaven, Cumberland, by a group of Irish miners and received injuries from which he died a year later. Anti-ritualist riots, fuelled by the energies of people like

John Kensit of the Protestant Truth Society, shared in that same popular Protestantism but were not fuelled by the ethnic hostility to the Irish that was inseparable from the anti-Catholic riots. A different kind of religious disturbance is to be seen in the Salvation Army riots of the 1880s, which came about with the organization of hostile Skeleton Armies, behind which lay the power of drink money: "in the early 1880s", according to Victor Bailey, "the brewers mobilized their lower-class 'rowdies' to silence a religion which challenged their profits and their prestige". Such groups sought to combat the aggressive military-style evangelism of General Booth and his troops, which also focused attention on the degrading effect of drink and a number of traditional popular amusements. It was this disturbance of traditional patterns of working-class behaviour that both provoked hostility and often found local authorities slow to defend the Salvationists, confident that they would secure community sanction for their inaction. That is a useful reminder that the securing of good order in society can never simply be confined to legislation and policing.

Conclusion

The purpose of this chapter has been to place issues of public order and of criminal behaviour more generally in the context of wider historical themes, and in particular to locate them in the framework of the repercussions of the growth of industry and of urbanization, with all that this involved in replacing old community values by new cash evaluations. At the same time, the development of towns and cities where a person could easily get lost in the mass brought into being vast areas where the criminal could easily find shelter. Instead of the intimacy and finite boundaries of a parish the new world was one of mobility and anonymity, with very obvious consequences for methods of social control. Such developments clearly challenged the effectiveness of old informal social disciplines and made necessary the development of more finite and formal mechanisms by defining legislation, developing, albeit on a pluralist model, a variety of forms of local policing. The government increasingly developed both the will and the capacity to intervene, and to intervene effectively, as it outgrew its *laissez-faire* adolescence. Nevertheless, effectiveness still depended on the ability of the police to secure the support and goodwill of the community. Where that was lacking, then even the best-trained police force could prove inadequate, as the breakdown of civil disciplines in England, no less than in Northern Ireland, was to demonstrate in the decade before the outbreak of the First World War, that great catalyst for the further growth of state power and the closer discipline of English domestic life. As at the beginning of the nineteenth century, this increase in central authority once more only came about through the manipulation of a foreign threat; only this made English citizens willing to cede greater powers to central government.

Chapter 9

The changing nature of crime in the nineteenth century

The classification of crime

Various ways of classifying crime have been suggested. For example, Rudé deduces a threefold categorization from the cases he studied. To basic acquisitive crime, the temptation of greed and avarice to take another person's possessions as your own, he adds survival crime, driven by the desperation of sheer need, and protest crime, the defiant act of breaching the law, not quietly and discreetly, but publicly and openly. More mundanely, the language of the lawyer differentiates the gravity of the offence committed, by distinguishing between misdemeanours and felonies. With the growth of an efficient police force, the very existence of law officers adds to the variety of offences: is it a crime "to resist and obstruct a constable in the execution of his duty"? Who is defining the concept, when even "acting suspiciously" could be seen as an offence? As late as 1869, the Habitual Criminals Act provided for a punishment of up to a year's imprisonment for those deemed to be "suspicious persons".

Not surprisingly the growth of the business of the state increased the regulatory aspirations of the law. With the extension of the state's involvement in education, for example, parents who failed to send their children to school and entrepreneurs who knowingly employed them under age were certainly guilty of offences. But were they criminals? The issue is at least debatable, but it is certain that such actions undoubtedly increased the crime statistics of the later decades of the nineteenth century. Other distinctions are helpful, such as that between crimes against the person and crimes against property. The first category would embrace all offences from simple assault to the various varieties of homicide. With offences against property it is wise to accept the broad distinction between crimes involving violence and those where violence is not involved. Thus robbery and burglary involve violence with a subspecies of malicious offences against property involving such actions as arson, machine-breaking and Luddism. Non-violent offences against property were generally regarded less seriously except for offences against the currency, which were seen as a grave challenge to the economic order of the nation.

At the beginning of the period grand larceny, a capital offence, was the appropriate charge when the property stolen was valued at more than one shilling, petty larceny pertaining to items of less value. The problem with petty theft, which in incidence overwhelmed all other offences throughout the period, lay just there, in its scale, and in the social awareness that it was taking place. Rarely were the sums of money or the amount of property at risk significant, and rarely was violence involved, but it was here that the limits were set between criminal and acceptable behaviour. This was the boundary above all that had to be policed, the place where human will unaided could not be trusted to resist temptation. It was here that English society chose to fight the battle for control of the new, traditionless, unpredictable urban communities emerging out of the Industrial Revolution. Public-order offences ranged from isolated incidents of disorderly behaviour through riot and sedition to high treason. By contrast a whole range of offences, such as those relating to drinking habits, Sunday observance and the promoting of illegal blood sports, have to be construed as essentially a defiance of the prevailing social code and of its desire to maintain a disciplined workforce within an ordered community.

Is the concept of social crime a useful analytical tool?

The question is also often raised as to whether the concept of social crime offers useful insights. Perhaps it helps to distinguish between those offences that secured the disapproval of the community and those that secured some measure of social consent. For example, was it acceptable in a deprived city slum to steal water from a street tap or pump? True, the water company had provided the facility, but there was a prevailing belief that water was a basic human resource which Almighty God provided freely through rain and rivers and to which, therefore, all should have gratuitous access. Similar arguments defended poaching against elitist game laws, which country opinion had long conceived of as offences against the birthright of every Englishman. Not without reason the villagers of England found it hard to see wild animals as the property of any individual. In 1819, Judge Edward Christian, reflecting on the many justifications offered in cases that came before him, observed, "Every magistrate knows that it is the common defence of a poacher, that it is very hard that he should be punished for taking what he has as good a right to as any other man." Or as one Berkshire JP put it in 1826, "The general opinion is that game is not private property. They say that God has made the game of the land free and left it free." But over against a village labourer taking a hare or two, there were gentleman poachers and, up to the legislation of 1831, armed gangs who made a business of taking game, hence the attempt to control poaching by restricting those allowed to sell game by licence. Elsewhere the problem was the illicit distilling of spirits in which the whole community could take a pride. Such behaviour was often differently perceived by lawbreakers and upholders.

Landless labourers and capitalist farmers would clearly regard the enclosure of the commons quite differently, as also the crops growing on newly enclosed land. As a consequence records of forcible entry and trespass may conceal as much as they reveal. There was more doubt about practices such as wrecking and smuggling. On the one hand there was an ancient right, as so many coastal communities perceived it, of garnering materials washed up on the foreshore. In 1842 Cyrus Redding claimed that the people of Cornwall had for generations past firmly believed that they had "a right to such spoils as the ocean may place within their reach". That the clergy and Methodist lay preachers readily engaged in such activities would suggest that no moral objection was entertained against these practices when the product was the result of an accident or act of God. It would be difficult to extend this argument either to occasioning a wreck deliberately or to smuggling, although the success of the latter very often depended upon the knowing connivance of many in the local community. On the other hand the armed revenue officers, who sought to control such illegalities, were construed as outsiders who unnecessarily brought violence into the situation. But small-scale country crime could, in times of restriction, become big business. Government saw the answer not so much in the development of more effective policing as in the application of the principles of *laissez-faire* so that, with a free open market, smuggling came to offer little advantage.

The concept of social crime helpfully draws attention to the limitation of powers embraced by laws and to the discretion afforded to the officers of the law. To pass a law through parliament was not of itself a sufficient action. Enforcement was the critical issue, and unless such laws could secure community consent their implementation would remain problematical. That is to say, certain patterns of behaviour, though deemed illegitimate by the law, could from time to time and in certain communities be legitimized by a local population. But E. P. Thompson is careful to issue the warning to take care not to cast the mantle of Robin Hood over too many lawbreakers: there is not "nice" social crime here and "nasty" anti-social crime there.

The concentration of crime

Criminal behaviour was not uniform throughout society. Geographically it seemed to be concentrated in London, other large towns and their surrounding suburban dependencies, where the scope was greatest and where anonymity gave maximum advantage to the criminal, although recent writers have commented upon the high incidence of crime in rural areas, especially where traditional methods of exploiting the land were changing. Enclosures, turnpike tolls and tithes were all equally unpopular while high bread prices always challenged rural peace. Chronologically, the pattern is of steady growth in crime from the mid-eighteenth century to a peak in the decade before the passing of the Reform Bill, with slower growth thereafter into the 1840s and a steady decline thereafter until the opening years of the twentieth century, when once more growth began to occur. This pattern is deduced from court statistics for committals for all indictable offences, but these have to be treated with very great caution, especially for the early part of the century, for they clearly cannot be equated with a barometer of actual crime in any very direct way. Crime committed, crime reported, persons brought to trial, convictions secured – all will obviously produce their own statistical series; reliable data is only available for the last two decades of the century.

Crime statistics are, however, helpful when measuring the seriousness with which similar actions were construed in different parts of the country. However, they have to embrace the willingness, or indeed the ability, of victims to prosecute, even with the support of a felons association or prosecution society if they belonged to such a body. As early as 1845 the criminal law commissioners were complaining of the "loose and unsatisfactory manner" in which many prosecutions were brought. Thereafter, because individuals were reluctant to prefer charges, or indeed to prefer them successfully, the new police began increasingly to bring prosecutions themselves, even though as a matter of strict law they brought such charges as private persons. The creation of the office of public prosecutor was frequently advocated by law reformers, and in 1879 the post of "director of public prosecutions" was brought into being: but initially the role of the incumbent was almost entirely advisory. The title of the office needs careful consideration: the person appointed was not a public prosecutor as such and did not so act even after the amending legislation of 1908, which defined the duties of the office in terms comparable with its present-day function.

Crime statistics must also be related first to the growth in population and secondly to the increasing effectiveness of the new police, who it may be presumed were capable of securing the committal to the courts of a higher proportion of criminals. "The pick-pocket who was formerly dragged to the village pump and half drowned by the mob", comments Royle, "was now arrested and became a criminal statistic." The other contextual factor is the growing wealth of society; this both raised people's aspirations and created a world in which there was more to steal, though it has been equally argued that fewer people were likely to find themselves in such distress as might drive them into criminal behaviour. Nevertheless it can properly be argued that acquisitive crime was a not unnatural function of the growth of an acquisitive, capitalist society, which is further evidenced by the special character of emerging middle-class crime.

The third point of concentration in criminal behaviour relates to age and gender. Three-quarters of offenders were young males in their teens and twenties. So there is a better case for arguing for the existence of a crime-prone generation than for suggesting the existence of some insidious criminal class with a subculture of villainous behaviour, although clearly there were cases of criminal parents training their offspring, Fagin-style, to the task. There also seems to have been a pattern of restraint of criminal action in time of war, with the suggestion that those most likely to act criminally had their energies diverted into an arena where bravado was to be praised rather than condemned. Indeed, some men apprehended for committing crimes were offered enlistment as an alternative to prosecution. If war otherwise occupies the criminal or potential criminal, then the consequence of peace is that this same person is discharged once more into civilian society, very often on to a saturated labour market, with not unexpected results. But there is once more a potential for exaggeration since the popular press, lacking war stories, has shown a tendency at such times to focus on crime instead.

The other pattern that has been discerned, even by those wary of lending support to any too crude a form of reductionism, is the correlation between a high number of committals and years of economic depression and political unrest, in terms not only of action committed but also of the greater readiness of victims, themselves under economic pressure or feeling the insecurity of the times, to prefer charges. Others have correlated an increase in the number of crimes of violence with buoyant periods in the business cycle, when greater prosperity occasioned higher wages, fuller employment and a larger consumption of alcohol, which in turn led to more violent crime. Members of the working class more often perpetrated such crimes within their class rather than on their social superiors.

Class and criminal behaviour

Douglas Hay has argued that the criminal law in the eighteenth century developed as a major part of the ideological weaponry for the defence of property, notwithstanding "the occasional victory of a cottager in the courts or the rare spectacle of a titled villain on the gallows". Property now included both old landed property and newer commercial and manufacturing property. This was soon reflected in the passing of new laws, often threatening capital punishment, to defend the new wealth which, being more portable, was also more vulnerable. Beyond that, Hay argues, "The criminal law was critically important in maintaining bonds of obedience and deference, in legitimizing the status quo, in constantly recreating the structure of authority which arose from property and in turn protected its interests."

Such a view has been questioned by others who have noted the infrequency of gentleman prosecutors and the discrepancy between prosecution

Figure 9.1   Types of male and female criminals. "The taint of crime is all the more potent in those whose parentage is evil." From A. Griffiths, *Mysteries of police and crime*, vol. 1 (1902), pp. 2–3, based upon photographs in the Black Museum, New Scotland Yard.

and conviction and between prescribed sentences and punishments actually suffered: thus Emsley argues, "The simple division which posits a ruling class making and administering the law, and a ruled class on the receiving end, obscures the often marked differences between the agents of the law and prosecutors." The concentration of the law on petty theft necessarily gave a class orientation to the work of the courts since inevitably its perpetrators came, for the most part, from the poorer sectors of society. The explanations offered for this concentration were rarely in terms of poverty or distress but rather in terms of greed, poor parenting and drink, with a heavy concentration on the last in the middle years of the nineteenth century: the belief was that a more temperate society would necessarily be a more law-abiding society. Such views readily supported the notion that there existed a criminal class, habitually given to living by crime, rather than subscribing to the belief that crime was committed by those who strove to live a moral life but who in a particular crisis succumbed to temptation. Thus the Royal Commission on the Rural Constabulary (1836–9) rejected poverty and indigence as causes of crime, rather directing attention to "indolence or the pursuit of easy excitement" and "the temptation of the profit of a career of depredation as compared with the profits of honest and even well paid labour".

The identification of a criminal class within the working class was all too easily made to serve a greater argument concerning the criminal proclivities of the working class as a whole. The higher incidence of crime in urban slums quickly attracted the special attention of educational reformers who sought to promote the moral reformation of those in such a station in life. The adjective moral was crucial, for without it working-class education would produce only better-educated criminals, hence the importance of Sunday schools, ragged schools and mutual improvement societies and the transformations of life they sought to achieve. This was the task of redeeming the city from all its sin, for to moral language has to be added theological: it was a sense of Christian mission that motivated so many reformers to do battle with the problems of the inner city, and for them the cause of crime was clearly theological – human sinfulness – and this belief accordingly came to inform all their writings on the subject, as also the solutions that they entertained for alleviating the situation.

Work itself was seen as a therapy that made for human rectitude or, at the very least, for keeping the working man from mischief. Thus Samuel Smiles, lamenting that "an idle brain is the devil's workshop and a lazy man the devil's toolster", characteristically argued that, "The necessity of labour may, indeed, be regarded as the main root and spring of all that we call progress in individuals and civilization in nations. An hour wasted on trifles or in indolence would, if devoted to self-improvement, make an ignorant man wise." Not all who wanted work could obtain it, however, especially in times of trade recession, but that did not deter the Victorian moralists from focusing on individual moral weakness as the cause of crime rather than on any failures within the economic system. Nor was the association of crime with the working classes limited to middle-class essayists. Engels maintained that "the incidence of crime has increased with the growth of the working-class population and there is more crime in Britain than in any country in the world", which was not perhaps surprising in so far as Britain was in the process of producing the world's first urban industrial society, where all the restraints of the familiar world of the rural economy were being put under strain, indeed were in the process of breaking down.

Varieties of crime

In the subtitle to his massive documentation of *London labour and the London poor*, published in 1851, Mayhew directs attention to three categories of person: "those that will work, those that cannot work, and those that will not work". His full description of the third category had to await his publication of a fourth volume 11 years later, which he devoted to describing the habits of the lawless, "the outcasts and enemies of society, who supported themselves by preying upon the vice or credulity of their more prosperous neighbours". Not all those described in this volume strictly speaking lived illegally, for a large section of the book is devoted to the lives of prostitutes. The life of a prostitute was not of itself illegal though many illegal acts surrounded its practice – soliciting, procuring, the keeping of brothels and the traffic in women to and from the Continent, especially when they were under age. An age of innocence was contradicted by "thousands of neglected children loitering about the low neighbourhoods of the metropolis, and prowling about the streets, begging and stealing for their daily bread". Mayhew thought this life of plunder was in part caused by the keeping of bad company, part by the loss of parents, but worse by the actions of unprincipled parents who deliberately trained their offspring to steal, so that in adolescence they graduated to becoming more serious criminals.

Mayhew's second largest category is that of thieves and swindlers, about whom he notes that "thousands of our felons are trained from infancy in the bosom of crime". Three main categories are noted: the common thief, the pickpocket and the burglar, together with those who commit highway robberies by menace, whose low exploitation of their fellows is carefully distanced from the reckless romance and bravado of the Dick Turpins of former years. In 1834 Dr Dawes, a surgeon from Longton, the southernmost of the six Pottery towns, was returning home when he was accosted by three men, provoking him to scream out "murder!", which caused one of his assailants to stuff his finger in Dawes's mouth. With considerable acumen, the surgeon snapped his jaws shut with great force so that the assailant was forced to retreat minus the end of his finger. The next day he sought treatment for his wound, was immediately arrested, and the severed finger produced in court as convincing and convicting evidence of the doctor's testimony.

Mayhew delighted in analyzing categories of criminals in detail, exposing their special skills, most frequently deployed tricks and ways of operating. To river crime, from the activities of mudlarks to smugglers and river pirates, Mayhew gave special consideration. He also identified clearly the important role of those prepared to receive stolen goods.

Workplace crimes

The workplace provided a ready arena for much fiddle and fraud, from petty pilfering by the workforce to acts of unfair trading by tricky salesmen – adulterating and tampering with the weights being the most common.

The establishment of national standards of weights and measures coupled with the arrival of the new police helped greatly to bring control to this arena.

In workplace crimes, there were difficult lines of demarcation: gleaning, for example, was an accepted traditional right of the poor, but excessive taking could lead into an indictment for theft. The garnering of fallen timber was and had long been acceptable, but not the felling of healthy trees. In redrawing that line, it has been claimed an important change in society, evermore cash orientated, was taking place in the criminalization of the taking of perks, which only served to confirm that the worker was now a waged employee rather than a valued part of the community. At the same time the widespread nature of workplace misdemeanours and fiddles challenges the notion that the criminal was somebody outside of normal society who posed an insidious threat to its good order: the offenders here were very much in the midst of normal social experience and were vulnerable to the opportunities for gain it presented in the course of ordinary day-to-day affairs.

In industry likewise, the workers traditionally had claims upon seconds and leftovers, but within reason. Certainly the stealing of a master's materials or the substituting of others of inferior quality led to criminal charges. Printers were allowed a proof copy of what they produced, but not multiple copies. In the nineteenth century, in certain parts of the country, the penalties for workplace thefts became quite high. However, there were perceived injustices built into the world of work that favoured the master rather than those he employed; for example, laws of contract bound an employee to his master for a whole year at a time, regardless of changing conditions or available employment, while the paying of wages in truck, often goods of an inferior quality bought cheaply but valued extortionately in the pay-packet, was perpetuated by a number of employers in defiance of the legislation that sought to outlaw it.

Miners were allowed coal for their own use, but were not expected to remove that which enabled them to set up as petty traders. In some areas colliers' children frequently purloined coal, which it was difficult and sometimes well nigh impossible to guard, at the behest of their parents for them to sell on, making the task of the magistrates in dealing with the children exceedingly difficult (*Staffs Advertiser*, 3 February 1855). All trades seem to have offered temptations to unprincipled opportunists, with goods in transit being particularly vulnerable to the covetous gaze of those who delivered them. Sometimes employers overlooked such behaviour or took cognizance of it in a different way. Thus it was said that the London General Omnibus Company kept its wages for conductors at 4s for a 17-hour day because it recognized that its employees added to that a certain percentage of the day's takings. Similarly, some dairy owners took into account the frequent watering down of milk when fixing the wages of those they employed. The trader's systematic adulteration of his commodity and the selling of inferior grade or short weight were deemed much more serious than petty theft. Emsley cites the judgement of James Greenwood (1869) upon such a person who was

> by far a greater villain than the half-starved wretch who snatches a leg of mutton from a butcher's hook, or some article of drapery temptingly flaunting outside the shop of a clothier, because in the one case the crime is perpetrated that a soul and woefully lean body may be saved from severance, and in the other the iniquity is to pander to the wrongdoer's covertous [sic] desire to grow fat, to wear magnificent jewellery, and to air his unwieldy carcase annually at Margate.

Checking food for adulteration, one of the requirements of the new regulatory state in defence of the health of the people, was difficult: it was hard to secure enough samples, and there were scarcely enough chemists to provide reliable analyses. Bread was often contaminated, sometimes with the introduction of inferior grains or, more seriously, of poisonous agents to make the bread white, such as copper sulphate of alum. The battle was set between those who sought voluntary reform and those who argued that the health of the nation could not wait for that and that regulation by government dictate was therefore necessary. The first Adulteration of Food Act was accordingly passed in 1860 with the consequent commissioning of the nation's first public analysts. Appointed by local authorities, they were not, however, to act preventively, but only "on complaint made". Fines imposed were small, while redress was against the manufacturer, whom it was often difficult to trace, not the retailer. Local authorities were slow to appoint analysts until improved legislation was passed in 1872 and 1875. Even so, the level of fines remained low, and to that extent working people remained unprotected in their diet.

Body-snatching may be thought to represent a different sort of workplace crime in so far as some of the earliest people involved in the trade were medical students desperate for experience in anatomy, but without resort to corpses, for the only legal supply occurred when judges on rare occasions assigned bodies to the anatomists as an additional discretionary sentence and indignity upon those on whom the death sentence had been imposed. By the early nineteenth century the trade had passed largely into the hands of the resurrection men, working-class operators who stole from coffins for profit. If caught about their macabre business, punishment seems to have been fairly light, a few months in prison at a time when an apprehended poacher could be subject to transportation. Resurrectionists had more to fear from an incensed mob than from the law until the Anatomy Act of 1832. This made available for dissection unclaimed corpses from hospitals, prisons and workhouses on condition that they were subsequently given a Christian burial. The process was to be supervised by the first publicly financed inspector, who was appointed under the act.

Cash and crime

After 1838, debt, now distinguished from pre-meditated fraud, ceased to be an offence worthy of imprisonment unless there was reasonable suspicion that the debtor showed signs of absconding. That was a significant advance, for in the period 1830–34 between twelve and fifteen thousand debtors were given custodial sentences. It was not, however, until 1869 that debt was finally decriminalized. By contrast there was a long tradition of those who literally made money. The more specialized activities of working-class coiners, who made counterfeit coins out of base metal, were described by Mayhew; he offered his readers a complete prescription for making moulds and filling them with molten metal and finally instructed them in the effective means of electroplating the finished product. Apprehending such illicit craftsmen was noted as particularly hazardous, because they constantly worked with fire, molten metal and acid, all of which could be thrown in the face of any law officer attempting to arrest them. Similarly, Mayhew had no difficulty in illustrating the many deceptions deployed by forgers of various kinds, by those who cheated at various games and by those engaged in other frauds, swindles and confidence tricks.

Figure 9.2 Imitation banknote etched by George Cruikshank, satirizing the infliction of capital punishment on those found guilty of forgery. From A. Griffiths, *Mysteries of police and crime*, vol. 1 (1902), p. 231.

Whilst the temptation to embezzle challenged the morality of such middle-class people as cashiers, travelling representatives and secretaries of Friendly Societies, embezzlement was often the work of young clerks and shop assistants. Of these, says Mayhew, they "are wretchedly paid by their employers and have barely enough to maintain them and keep them in decent clothes. Many of them spend their money foolishly on extravagant dress, or associating with girls, attending music-saloons." While Mayhew begins to suggest mitigating circumstances, he cannot free himself from identifying such criminal behaviour with the moral failing of undisciplined spending. In all his long catalogue of the crimes of London, it is property that dominates, not crimes against the person unless property is first involved. Embezzlement and fraud have already begun to take the analysis out of the area of those crimes whose perpetrators mostly came from the working classes. Such crimes are also testimony to the added temptations associated with the growing complexity and influence of business. The world of investment, while crucial to the development of Britain as the "workshop of the world", also opened up new possibilities for deception and fraud, as also for economic casualty. At the end of 1843 the *Illustrated London News* wearily lamented, "If we progress at the same rate for half a generation longer, commercial dishonesty will become the rule, and integrity the exception. On every side of us we see perpetually – fraud, fraud, fraud."

The railway company, the bank (provincial or metropolitan), the insurance company, the large trading company, the Friendly Society – all were vulnerable to dishonest action. Cases of fraud in such prestigious banks as Barings, and Matheson and Jardine, can be mirrored with a minor event in a provincial town. The local newspaper in Longton opined that 1866 was a year "fraught with sad trouble to hundreds of families in the borough owing to the failure of Harvey's Bank, many preferring the local notes to those of the Bank of England". Months previously another Harvey family business, that of J. C. Harvey, a local ironmaster, had failed with £32,000 outstanding. This in itself provoked rumours about the soundness of the bank that were immediately countered in the local newspaper. All too soon experience was to belie the statement, when it was revealed that there had been much malpractice, inaccurate bookkeeping, too many unsecured overdrafts and the early withdrawal of family funds taking advantage of insider knowledge prior to the unfortunate collapse of the bank. On 29 June, W. K. Harvey, hitherto a much respected citizen who had but recently received the Prince of Wales as a masonic visitor to the borough, hastily left Longton to confer with his London agents, the Alliance Bank. In fact he took with him £400 in ready cash and was not to return. With £44,351 at risk he embarked at Southampton for America on 2 July. Panic ensued within the local community, followed by a run on the bank the next day and its inevitable closure. As a consequence there were 14 company bankruptcies; the gas company, the guardians and the town council all lost substantial sums. What precisely was illegal in this situation it is hard to detect, although there was more to the situation than simple cash-flow problems; local society clearly suffered more from such an event than many petty thefts although these remained the focus of police concern. As will be seen in a later chapter, parliament was slow to define the limits of acceptable behaviour in the newly emerging commercial world.

More filthy lucre

Nine years later a similar event cast its shadow over Longton life. The local newspaper announced on 10 April 1875, "a very painful sensation has been called in Longton by the disappearance of Mr Enoch Palmer, house and estate agent". This was made worse by the fact that "no-one was more generally respected or enjoyed more completely the confidence of the public than Mr Palmer". Palmer's detention in London for several months was explained initially in terms of physical accident, but later financial injury became apparent: "The cause of his disappearance is said to be serious defalcations in his accounts, which rumour has magnified into what appears a fabulous amount." Subsequently the sum was shown to be in excess of £17,000. Corrupt practice was clear, involving improper auditing, loss of ledgers and confusion between personal and society funds. Palmer himself was not brought to court, although he appeared as a witness; but the steward of the Longton and Fenton Building Society, John Beech, Palmer's accomplice, was charged with the theft of money not deposited in the bank according to society rules, and of defrauding the society of funds through the creation of fictitious mortgages over a period of more than twenty years. It is abundantly clear Palmer had been a knowing partner and almost certainly the primary agent in these devices and obfuscations. The magistrates hearing the charges before they were transferred to the assizes were all former intimates of Palmer and themselves involved in the direction of local building and friendly societies.

In the assize trial Palmer, although not in the dock, seems to have received judgment, at least by observation, alongside Beech. Lord Pollock, who tried the case, expressed his astonishment at the pattern of events: "Every year from 1852 to 1872 the prisoner at the bar, and no doubt the secretary [Palmer] also, were enabled so to cook the accounts of the society as to conceal their deficiencies and embezzlements from the auditors." He later interrupted a witness to comment that it was shocking that poor people should suffer from such neglect and malpractice, while Beech's counsel made reference to "one of the most consummate scoundrels who had born the name of Palmer", a remark all the more offensive because Palmer was also the name of the famous Staffordshire murderer. Enoch Palmer was the man who ought to have been in the dock, for if Beech, who notwithstanding his advanced years was sentenced to seven years' penal servitude, had been guilty of misappropriating hundreds, Palmer was guilty of diverting thousands. The new world of scrutiny did not seem to be working so far as these vital matters were concerned. Under cross-examination Palmer would not agree that the £11,000 restitution made by him had only been made on condition that charges would not be preferred against him, nor did he admit, committed Methodist that he was, to being found intoxicated in his offices in the middle of the afternoon or that "a lady of the town" had swindled him out of £40. He did, however, make the damning admission that "any money appropriated by him had been appropriated for purposes in connection with other societies", which might suggest that an initial attempt to deal with a temporary cash-flow problem in his various societies had led the respectable Mr Palmer deep into illicit dealings, with great hurt to the ordinary people of Longton.

This was but an early reflection of the difficulties that these and other similar societies were facing nationally. For example, George Howarth had all the credentials of respectability as a Quaker cotton spinner and land agent in Rochdale, serving as actuary to the Rochdale Savings Bank, but on his death in 1849 it was shown to have a deficit in excess of £70,000. This had accumulated because Howarth had falsified the accounts to conceal his defrauding of its humble depositors. Other local savings banks faced similar problems, those made public falling a little short of £230,000. Building societies were peculiarly vulnerable. Certain societies, especially those developed on the Starr-Bowkett principles, were highly speculative but not actually illegal until proscribed by legislation in 1894. Starr-Bowkett was a package offered to local managements that involved an element of gambling. A regular ballot was to be held for interest-free loans repayable over ten years from the proceeds of subscription and repayment income.

Offences against the person I: battered wives

The greatest energies of the law and law-enforcement officers were focused on maintaining order and defending property, often of a petty kind, and most criminal statistics relate to this. Offences against the person only account for about 10 per cent of all indictable crimes in the nineteenth century. While popular fears were of an encounter with a violent and nervous burglar or of an insane maniac, in perhaps half of the cases of violent crime it seems likely that the victims recognized their violators, and indeed in most were related to them. Significantly, a large number of what the courts called aggravated assaults (one "attended with circumstances of peculiar outrage or atrocity") were of women, and their husbands were those who misused them. Very often the violent event occurred in public amidst a crowd of onlookers so that many more than the direct participants witnessed violent crime. It has in fact been suggested that no working-class person could escape exposure to such crimes because of their frequency in working-class neighbourhoods. The crime perpetrated was seldom premeditated and rarely the action of professional criminals. Its criminality was seen to be in its ferocity, which was all too often only an extension of that level of violence in relationships generally tolerated in many working-class societies. Local newspapers are littered with accounts of such offences – assault upon the wife who discovered her husband leaving his mistress's house, the attempt to drag a drunken husband away from a public house and his violent retaliation, and various forms of wife-beating that at most seemed only to secure six months' imprisonment, and even that only when the police could be persuaded to follow the case up, for there is considerable evidence that this only occurred in a few cases. (See, for example, the *Staffs Advertiser*, 14 May and 17 September 1853, 5 August 1871.)

Occasions provocative of wife-beating were frequent enough. A lack of respect for a husband's mastery in his own house was commonly at the root of the problem. Irate husbands accordingly felt provoked when their wives declined to carry out their wishes, failed in errands or commissions, sought to defend their children against vengeful paternal disciplining. All such incidents would normally be interlaced with a torrent of verbal abuse on both sides before words gave way to blows. The difference was that a husband's use of bad language was guarded by prerogative, while his wife's was considered a further sign of insubordination. Money and drink belonged closely together, but this was nothing new: the Victorian attack upon the public house as the source of all social indiscipline and folly stood in a tradition of considerable antiquity. Nevertheless it was still perceived as a focus in society for nourishing sexual licence, indecent and depraved behaviour, sensuous and violence-begetting entertainment and reckless gambling and as the very seedbed of crime and subversion. A working-class family would be almost perpetually short of cash when the husband claimed priority over family income as the means to sustain his drinking habits. Accordingly the pawnshop was frequently the destination of family possessions. But wives too could be accused of pawning possessions to fulfil their latest fancy or addiction to fashion. Other women claimed that pawning goods was the only way they knew to keep their children from starvation. Crimes of violence were frequently committed by those under the influence of drink: many witnesses testified that the drink quite changed the characters of their partners.

Many women submitted to more brutality than they should have suffered. Some 10 per cent of court cases failed because the wives failed to appear in court to sustain charges; on other occasions a wife would appear but then withdraw the evidence against her man even though it was clear for all to see that she was a victim of abuse. Many settled out of court, for the imprisonment of a husband also wounded his family, who would almost certainly be thrown on to poor relief. Not all women were so quiescent, however; in their wrath some turned to savage response with pokers, knives and other weapons. It ill behoved outsiders to intervene in such disputes for as likely as not both husband and wife would turn upon them; but other women would frequently offer nursing or shelter to the battered wives of their neighbourhood. If the neighbours feared that the violence would produce death, or if a wife was old and infirm, or if the use of weapons had led to a visible loss of much blood, then neighbours would call the police. Working-class communities were less tolerant of violence perpetrated against women outside the family, especially if they were of respectable reputation; such women could expect solid community solidarity against any external assailants.

Nancy Tomes points out that the attitudes of sentencing magistrates varied greatly. At one extreme Edward Cox, in his *Principles of punishment*, believed that in most cases the wife deserved the beating she received: far from being the "loving wife and submissive slave brutally beaten", it was she "who has made her husband's home an earthly hell, who spends his earnings in drink, pawns his furniture, starves her children, provides for him no meals, lashes him with her tongue when sober and with her fists when drunk". Other magistrates took the wife's side contending that husbandly brutality was both unmanly and cowardly and arguing that no amount of provocation could justify an act of violence against a woman. In the second half of the century public opinion was increasingly of the second kind, which can be seen illustrated in the legislation that stiffened the sentences imposed on wife-beaters, until the Wife Beaters Act of 1882 empowered police magistrates to have offenders flogged and exposed on a public pillory. The incidence of wife-beating declined during this period, in part because of the increase in penalties, in part because of an improved standard of living and in part because of a diffusion of middle-class family values.

Offences against the person II: homicides

If the focus on crimes of violence is narrowed to cases of homicide then the sample reduces again. Only in 1865 did the incidence reach as high as 2 per 100,000 population, averaging about 1.5 and reducing to 1 per 1,000 at the end of the 1880s; it declined still further in the new century. In terms of gross numbers rarely did homicides in the period 1857–90 exceed four hundred per annum and they were down below 350 in an expanding population at the end of the century. Of these cases, a remarkable number probably involved the infanticide of illegitimate or deformed children: one survey suggested a little short of half the total number of definable homicides occurred within the family. Well into the nineteenth century, infanticide remained the most common form of homicide, even though it is widely believed that it was seriously under-reported in the second half of the eighteenth century. The other main category of victim was persons in authority. Contrasting with the cases of violence against women, 85 per cent of these cases were followed up. Newspaper reports would suggest that in very many of these cases – both husband against wife and prisoner against police – the violence was due to the drunkenness of the offender who on occasions included women (see *Staffs Advertiser*, 18 March 1876).

Sensational crime seems to have been infectious, that is to say one incident well publicized was likely to provoke others. This seems to have been the case, for example, with the Ratcliffe Highway murders in the East End of London at the end of 1811. Garrotting, highway robbery by means of attempted strangulation, seems hardly to have been recorded before the London incidents of the 1850s and 1860s, but thereafter there was an escalation of cases. Even Jack the Ripper's dramatic murders in the autumn of 1889 set off mimic crimes in the provinces.

New statutory crime

The extent to which the growing power of the state in the nineteenth century was to the advantage of particular groups in society is debatable. How far did it increase the rights of the poorest members of society? How far did it both create new middle-class crimes and create the effective means for pursuing these? How far was the state the agent of capitalists large and small to protect their interests?

Early in the century every endeavour to extend the authority of the state was seen to challenge the prevailing philosophy of *laissez-faire* and infringe the freedom of the individual, as if the most free society was that which imposed the smallest number of legal restraints upon its members. Nowhere was change more difficult than in landlord–tenant relationships with the necessary challenge to the rights of property therein involved. The earliest reforms came under the heading of public health and were facilitated by the incidence of cholera, which did not confine its attentions exclusively to working-class people. The pattern was for a given municipality to pioneer reform; this was subsequently "nationalized" by legislation which recommended such policies to the nation at large, first as permissive legislation but later as mandatory requirements, what London's pioneering medical officer of health called "sanitary legislation with teeth in it", that is legislation with sanctions that could be deployed against defaulting parties. Thus, for example, Torrens' Artisans and Labourers Dwelling Act of 1868 was the first to breach the sacred rights of property and to impose upon landlords "the obligation to keep their rented houses in reasonable repair". This was a considerable advance: five years earlier a judge had given it as his judgment that "there is no law against letting a tumbledown house". The tenant's redress was to seek to get his contract implemented or, perhaps more often, to move elsewhere.

Early factory acts accomplished little because of their failure to include any mechanism for implementation. That is why the 1833 act marked a breakthrough, because, for the first time, inspectors were appointed to ensure the implementation of the terms of the act, which sought to regulate the hours worked by children and young people. These were further refined in 1844, as were the hours worked by women, and added the requirement that dangerous machinery should be fenced. To achieve the aims an inspector needed certain bureaucratic support, as for example the certification of children's ages and the availability of a public clock to measure time. In practice the inspectors can be shown to have been more rigorous in their task when trade was healthy and more indulgent to manufacturers when trade was slack. In such times manufacturers seem to have adopted a "calculational" defiance of the law, assessing whether it would be more costly to conform to legal requirements or to pay the fine for failing to. It has to be remembered, however, that the legislation was initially confined to cotton and wool production and was only slowly extended to other industries. The other principal hindrance to fulfilling the intention of the act was the widespread deployment of systems of subcontracting by which factory proprietors were not themselves responsible for the employment of children and young people.

R. H. Greg, the cotton master, objected to the fundamental philosophy underlying such acts:

> The Inspector's regulations are founded upon the principle of the master being a tyrant and a cheat; and that the operatives must look to the Inspector rather than to him for justice and protection. Regulations framed in such a spirit, necessarily throw the master into a false position and throw power into the hands of the work people, of which, it is too much to suppose, they will not sometimes avail themselves.

In such a confession the passage from the old paternalism to the controls of the new regulatory state are clearly to be seen.

Railways posed similar questions of the law: from 1842 the Board of Trade became responsible for their safe running: the maintenance of the permanent way, the checking of signalling, the testing of braking systems. In fact the railway proved to be a most important catalyst in the development of state control of the agencies of national life. If accidents could be the results of what was now termed criminal neglect, then a new area of criminal behaviour was in process of definition.

Conclusion

This chapter has sought to provide some appreciation of the great diversity of criminal behaviour in the nineteenth century. The prime concern of those who sought to impose the law was not the protection of life and limb but the protection of property very often of an inconsequential order. It was in the realm of petty theft that the magisterial mind chose to set up the crucial boundary between acceptable and criminal behaviour, fiercely sentencing those who dared to cross that boundary or were unfortunate enough to be caught in the earlier part of the period. In the context of a developing capitalist industrial society some traditional practices were questioned, and the norms of legitimate conduct redefined, leading to the suggestion that an evermore cash-orientated society was in the process of criminalizing certain customs, for example the taking of perks within particular trades that hitherto had been deemed legitimate. A major discussion, both then and among historians, has turned on the issue of whether a self-perpetuating criminal class existed. A better case can be made for arguing that those in their teens and twenties constituted a crime-prone generation. As the century progressed and the sphere of government increased there was more sentencing of those whose behaviour conflicted with the demands of the new regulatory state. New crimes also arose out of the temptations to abuse for personal profit the increasing complexities of commerce and manufacturing. Both these developments witnessed an increase in the number of middle-class offenders, who therefore suffered not only the penalty of the courts but some measure of social ostracism.

Crimes against the person only accounted for 10 per cent of indictable crime: within this category the main groups at risk were women, from wife-beating husbands; persons in authority, from the criminals they sought to control; and illegitimate and deformed children, from the parents who potentially had to support them. Sensational crime provided good copy for newspaper editors but it remained a very small part of the whole. The general pattern of criminal incident was a steady expansion of crime between the period of the Napoleonic Wars and 1842, a lesser peak in 1848, and a continuing decline in indictments for both theft and violence during the rest of the century.

Chapter 10
The policing of society

The pressures of the growth of a mass society

In some senses old English society with its small-scale, finite communities can be said to have been self-policing, so that the supposed bumbling inefficiencies of Shakespeare's Dogberry, Verges, Elbow and Dull, which later generations made fun of, did not in fact jeopardize the security of society. They were, however, all too easily made to be the stereotypes of the old order by the reformers of the 1820s, anxious to secure a better disciplined and more highly trained force to fulfil their purposes in the new uncertain world of town and machine that was coming into being. Whereas informal disciplines had worked well enough in the static world of finite rural communities, the scale and rootlessness of the new towns made different demands and needed a more formal response. A clergyman giving evidence to the Select Committee on Criminal and Destitute Juveniles in 1852 commented on the detrimental effect of the growth of one-class districts in large conurbations, for it brought to an end "that species of silent but very efficient control over their neighbours" exercised by persons of a superior class: "In small towns there must be a sort of natural police operating upon the conduct of each individual who lives under the public eye; but in a large town he lives if he chooses in absolute obscurity."

In the earlier period, by contrast, the public was apprehensive of efficiency as smacking of the centralizing authoritarianism of continental autocrats, which contrasted with their own strong pride in the local, the parochial and what they believed to be the long traditions of British freedom. Indeed the very idea of a uniformed policeman patrolling the streets to secure order and prevent crime was anathema to the civilian conscience of the late eighteenth century. To many, therefore, there were considerable merits in the law being administered by part-time, occasional officers under the authority of lay magistrates.

But already things were beginning to change, especially in urban areas where the old machinery was seen to be inadequate, and in some parishes relatively efficient watches were established by the end of the eighteenth century. As was discussed in Part I, the reputation secured in London by the two Fieldings, Henry the novelist and his half-brother, Sir John, the capital's chief magistrate, was well deserved. From the middle of the eighteenth century they had campaigned for a more coherent and organized police force. Not all their plans were implemented; but a start was made, including a scheme whereby provincial magistrates transmitted to London details of incidents in their areas together with the names of known criminals, which were published in a government-subsidized journal, the *Hue and Cry*, an early if small recognition of the acceptance that, notwithstanding the tensions and the competitiveness that existed between London and the provinces, crime had to be viewed as a national problem.

London and the provinces; public and private provision

That was a significant divide: "What appeared of value from the centre of London to suppress the city's unique crime problem", observes Emsley, "had little value outside." London, the nation's largest city, necessarily led the way in police reform. The Middlesex Justice Act of 1792 established seven district police offices for London, straying across the Thames to plant one on the Kent and Surrey side of the river. Attached to each of these were to be three stipendiary magistrates and six constables. This provision was supplemented in 1798 by the creation of the Thames Police Office at Wapping, again with three stipendiaries who eventually were to supervise a force of one hundred constables in policing the river. So London already had a sizeable police force before Peel's 1829 act. Emsley presents figures for 1812 which show that not far short of three hundred men were engaged in keeping the peace if patrols, watchmen, superintendents and river police are all included.

Various private agencies were also operating in the field. There were, for example, the thief-takers, a recognized trade in the eighteenth century, who lived by collecting rewards. Rural England had long been well supplied with gamekeepers. There were also those local organizations that developed at the turn of the century, which are variously known as either felons associations or prosecution societies or associations for the protection of property; they began to appear in fair number, perhaps as many as four thousand in total, in the second half of the eighteenth century.

Their purpose is clearly encapsulated in the concern of the Hanley Felons Association, "to pursue and prosecute any person or persons who shall commit or attempt to commit, any felony or robbery, against or upon our person or property". There was a sliding scale of rewards for successful prosecution, graded from capital offences to petty crimes. The existence of such bodies reveals the usual expectation that a solution to a given problem should be local action not government intervention. The latter was suspect as being that which came from outside, from a body which had not, as yet, won a reputation for effectiveness. More significantly, such early non-statutory initiatives were, without exception, associations of the propertied joining together to protect their corporate existence against the property-less. Thus a typical felons association would be made up of shopkeepers, manufacturers, householders and small masters, and the object of their attention would be employees, vagrants, servants and the like, all in fact who threatened their financial stability.

Similar interests were developed by the various improvement commissioners set up by private acts of parliament, which allowed them to raise rates for the benefit of their own localities. Thus the act creating the improvement commissioners in Newcastle under Lyme indicates that they were "empowered and requested as they think expedient to provide and set up watch houses, watch boxes, and to employ watchmen and night patrols" who were charged with preventing fires, murders, burglaries, robberies and disorders and were to arrest night-walkers, felons, vagrants and disturbers of the peace and lodge them in the borough prison. For this purpose they were equipped with staves, lanterns and rattles. As with the felons associations, the search for improvement also represented the action of the propertied deploying their energies to defend themselves against the propertyless. Because of this, only those parts of a town that represented its commissioners' interests were protected and improved. Much of the response at this time was provoked by specific incident or apprehension: Newcastle under Lyme set up its own police force in 1834 because of a continuing high incidence of crime, which local ratepayers believed to be the work of a determined but undiscovered gang of "banditti" descending on the town from their neighbours, the rapidly urbanizing pottery towns. Funding came partly from the improvement rate, partly from the highways rate and partly from the poor rates. The last two grants were conditional: the first on supervising paupers to keep the streets clean, the second on the constables acting as market watchers. Certainly early convictions involved the pursuit of those who had absconded from the workhouses, who were charged with the crime of stealing workhouse clothes, or those refusing to undertake hard labour. Other early prosecutions involved such misdemeanours as "contemplating a cock fight" and "being in a house which contained an illicit still".

On the other hand, petty interests often delayed effective policing. No less a person than Josiah Wedgwood II, of the famous pottery factory at Etruria, obstructed the formation of a police force in neighbouring Hanley, largely by reason of self-interest, for he argued that it would be wrong for manufacturers like himself who had their factories out of town to be required to pay the same rate as those living and working in the centre of Hanley where the hazard was greater. Behind the reasoning was the familiar argument that each locality should pay for its own crime or rather its own protection against criminals.

Legislative changes

There is a danger in writing the history of policing as from Westminster outwards by concentrating on successive patterns of legislation. Nevertheless the stages whereby police jurisdiction was extended needs to be recorded. In 1829, after seven years' experience of the Bow Street Day Patrol, which Peel had set up immediately after he was appointed home secretary, his Metropolitan Police Act was passed. Its purpose was to implement the recommendations of a committee of inquiry of the previous year that London should have a centralized, uniformed, preventive police force. Thus the capital was to be provided with comprehensive police cover: three thousand uniformed constables were to patrol its streets in an attempt to prevent crime and track down its perpetrators. The ideal of a waged police force, accountable before the law, totally impartial in pursuing its business, had been established. But the London model was not the only one as Carolyn Steedman has strenuously argued.

In provincial England there developed a quite different model of local forces responsible to local authorities or local magistrates. Already by 1842, the year of the Plug Plot Riots, it has been estimated there were across the country some ten thousand embodied policemen, but the threats and indeed the reality of civil disobedience of that year only served to reinforce in the official mind the need for even more efficient policing, and a large part of efficiency had to do with sufficiency of number. Early industrial communities, embracing a dynamic rather than static population that made for widespread anonymity, a ready cloak for criminal activity, were not easily disciplined by traditional mechanisms of control: some changes were required, but those changes did not have to follow the London model.

In carrying out their duties, however, the Metropolitan Police gained valuable experience, which was often courted by provincial forces seeking a new professionalism, particularly in recruiting trained manpower. The other main sources for this were the Royal Irish Constabulary and the English militia. Trained manpower, and that alone, was the level at which the Metropolitan Police influenced the new provincial forces. This is very different from the assertion that the metropolitan model of establishing a well-disciplined preventive police force was transplanted into provincial England. In the provinces the overriding concern remained the protection of property by locally organized forces under the control of local magistrates, a function which was well appreciated by lesser property owners – the artisan home-owner, the corner shopkeeper, the smallholder – as much as by gentlemen, entrepreneurs and aristocrats.

The Municipal Corporations Act of 1835 required all incorporated boroughs to set up watch committees to supervise the work of local police forces, interpreting policing in its widest sense to cover the general supervision of the borough streets including the removal of nuisances, some Poor

Law responsibilities and the supervision of weights and measures. In theory this legislation secured the policing of all the boroughs of England and Wales, but a number of emerging urban communities were slow to seek borough status, and others were dilatory in setting up local forces: by 1838, 78 out of 178 boroughs had yet to establish forces. However, in that same year W. C. Taylor confidently affirmed, "That crime has proportionately decreased is undeniable. Who now sleeps with pistols beneath his pillow or hangs a blunderbuss within reach of his bolster?" Even at the mid-century six boroughs had not yet implemented the requirement to establish forces, while many others had forces that were woefully inadequate. All these forces were to be answerable to local committees, whereas the metropolitan force was to be directly responsible to a minister of the Crown. The hope was that the introduction of such forces would reduce even to the point of extinction the use of the army to maintain public order, but this was not achieved until the 1850s and 1860s, while the Fenian difficulties in the 1870s saw renewed dependence upon the military to secure public order. One response to the limited uptake of the Municipal Corporations Act was the Town Police Clauses Act of 1847, which provided towns with an alternative to the introduction of local policing. Any local authority, a board of guardians, a vestry, a corporation could use the powers of the act to appoint a superintendent of police and an appropriate number of constables.

Four years after the Municipal Corporations Act, the Rural Constabulary Act of 1839 provided permissive legislation for the establishment of rural police forces. This arose out of the Royal Commission on the Rural Constabulary set up three years earlier. Its labours revealed that Britain was far from being unpoliced, but that there were other patterns for this than that offered by Peel's Metropolitan Police Act. In particular, highly local forces, the jurisdiction of whose officers was normally confined to a given parish, whose vestry called them into being and sanctioned the poor rate from which they were paid, continued. Some of these local constables were appointed under the Lighting and Watching Act of 1833, which generalized clauses that were to be found in many local improvement acts. Lighting was seen not so much as a social amenity as one of the most obvious measures to be undertaken to limit the actions of criminals. The act, which provided for the appointment of an inspector by the vestry to supervise locally appointed, paid watchmen, offered an economical means of providing some kind of police cover – albeit of a limited kind, for the watchmen were not empowered to protect property and could not even serve warrants – more cheaply than the implementation of the 1839 act. The detail of the organization of parish constables was refined by legislation in 1842 and 1850, the legislation of the latter year providing for the appointment of superintendents, paid out of the county rate, whose area of jurisdiction was to be a petty sessional division of a county, but without direct control or payment of parish constables within their areas. Such legislation and the way it was used reflected the fact that as yet the ambit of many people's thinking and practice was confined to the parish, the manor, the village, the small town, that is the immediate context of their lives, not yet the broad themes of national concern. For them the agency of centralization was not yet seen as a remote London but as the county, whose quarter sessions seemed to threaten the effective action of the more locally based petty sessions and the local magistrates. Beyond that, the variety of legislation under which policing could be undertaken emphasizes the pluralistic approach adopted by successive governments to urge and persuade local authorities to make proper provision for their neighbourhoods.

The scale of police provision in rural England up to 1839 is of great importance and justifies Carolyn Steedman's judgement that "the prescriptive pattern for nineteenth-century policing was rural not urban". These two models – urban and rural – embodied very different philosophies of administration, the Metropolitan Police reflecting most directly the interests of central government. Accordingly, focusing on their role tends to reflect a view of nineteenth-century administration that inexorably moves towards government intervention and the burgeoning of bureaucracy with little by way of counter-emphasis on the situations in particular localities. For its part rural policing was clearly conceived within a matrix of local communal rights, and contributed much to the continuity of the authority of the local magistracy and pre-industrial modes of local government in the industrial world. For all that, the police were in the process of becoming as important to rural counties as to urban communities. "The early nineteenth-century crisis of rural, southern society propelled an increasing number of gentlemen", argues Robert Storch, "to 'buy into' a new ideology of order created elsewhere by urban moral entrepreneurs and theorists, and proceed to redefine the threshold and relocate the 'baseline' of tolerate behaviour in the countryside. In doing so they contemplated something which their fathers or grandfathers would never have entertained – the extension of a policed society from urban to rural England."

Metropolitan Police Commissioner Charles Rowan observed of country policing: "a rural police was rather to prevent crime by detecting offenders rather than to protect it by their actual presence in every village" (*The Times*, 15 October 1850). The rural police, then, were well established as the servants of property within well-defined and regulated local communities. This framework of reference is emphasized by the other tasks assigned to the police locally: inspectors of nuisances, Poor Law relieving officers, market inspectors, inspectors of weights and measures. "All", in Carolyn Steedman's words, "made them more complete servants of property within the local financial structure of local forces."

The threatened withdrawal of the army from areas prone to riot and disorder could easily persuade magistrates of the desirability of appointing an adequate police force. Such advice from the Home Office to the

Staffordshire magistrates in 1842, advising that the military could not "be allowed to supply the place of constables", had exactly this effect: the magistrates immediately adopted the Rural Constabulary Act for the Potteries and in the following year extended their action to the whole of the county. The argument was partly or even largely financial, as became clear in correspondence with the magistrates for the West Riding of Yorkshire: General Brotherton noted that while it might be economical and convenient for such magistrates, who were mainly textile manufacturers, to have troops resident in their area to protect their property, this was a misuse of those troops and not in the end conducive to public safety. In the countryside, as also in the boroughs, a not inconsiderable part of the police force was privately financed and patently existed for the defence of property. The 1840 Police Act allowed for the appointment of "Additional Constables". Specially funded by an individual or group of individuals, they dressed like any other constable and were subject to the general discipline of the forces to which they belonged. Their responsibilities, however, were the defence of particular pieces of property, which could be a public institution such as a market or a harbour or a private factory or landed estate: Steedman, for example, cites the Duke of Grafton's financing of a constable to police his Pottersbury estate in Northamptonshire following an increase in crime in the area in 1855. She offers the estimate that in the 1860s and 1870s, up to a quarter of the police in the northern county and borough forces were made up of these privately funded additional constables, appointments which continued to be made up to the beginning of the First World War.

Edwin Chadwick, who had drafted the "Report on rural constabularies", wanted a close link with the New Poor Law, which he had already set on the statute books. In 1829 he had supported centralization, but in 1853 when addressing the Select Committee on the Police he showed himself willing to support the local supervision of local forces, thereby underlining that there is in police history no "slow but inexorable" process moving the responsibility for policing from the local to the central. Only after 1880, and even then with considerable resistance, was the need for local forces more and more to become agencies of central government pressed upon provincial police forces. In 1839, the notion of a 25 per cent subsidy for the new forces and a requirement that the Metropolitan Police be involved in training them failed to be written into the law. Local authorities were greatly concerned about costs, even for a necessary service, and were resentful of anything suggesting that they were being told what to do by higher authority. As with the implementation of the Municipal Corporations Act, progress in implementing the Rural Constabulary Act was slow: by the mid-century only about one half of county units had police forces, while some of these provided less than comprehensive cover.

The whole system was regularized by Sir George Grey's County and Borough Police Act of 1856, which placed on all local authorities the obligation to appoint adequate police forces. By this date, although the police forces in most of the largest towns were sizeable enough to operate efficiently, those in medium-size towns and more especially the smallest boroughs gave grave cause for concern. Grey's act was the legislative response to the findings of the Select Committee on the Police set up by Palmerston in 1853. Into that investigation were fed a number of hopes and ambitions, for example, a desire for greater uniformity across the country and the notion that the police might form an auxiliary defence force, a kind of home guard, for mid-Victorian England. At the same time there was a widespread consciousness that soldiers returning from the Crimean War could lead to more incipient violence in English society. Beyond this lay a much more general fear of local insurrection and the need to develop an elaborate apparatus of control, both formal and informal, to deal with that possibility. Furthermore, the ending of the transportation system led to the judgement that, "If the country must for the future, learn to live with its criminals, it must pay the price of protection against them." However, the centralizing tendencies prominent in the remedies for such concerns as were laid out in the report encountered all the well-entrenched forces of localism that even the personality of Palmerston could not overcome. He decided to withdraw his Bill, which would have implemented these recommendations, rather than have it rejected: "The heart that Russia could not terrify, nor Austria beguile, had quailed before the 'bureaucracy' of Manchester, Birmingham, Chester, and a deputation of county wisdom" (Radzinowicz). It was left to Sir George Grey to introduce a weaker Bill.

Accordingly the 1856 act did not yield all that the inquiry wished for, nor all that Sir George Grey initially hoped for: plans to unite small forces were far from being wholly implemented; local control was maintained, even increased, though with two modifications. First, a national inspectorate of constabulary was established, which was the vehicle for extending Home Office norms of policing out to the English boroughs. The personnel of the Home Office, who have been shown to be experienced in local government, were well positioned, therefore, to offer counsel on the problems of local policing. Thus when mayors and other dignitaries wrote seeking guidance about how to handle incipient outbreaks of violence, clear and well-informed advice was given, which normally suggested expanding the local police by swearing in as many specials as was feasible, seeking the support of a neighbouring county's constabulary, and only as a last resort calling in the military.

Secondly, the Treasury agreed to pay 25 per cent of the pay and cost of uniforms of those forces deemed to be "efficient", a judgement mainly deriving from the size of a force in relation to the population it served. This payment of grant by the central government to local authorities was a major innovation in domestic administration. In part, at least, it recognized that crime was as much a national as a local problem. Four years earlier, the

Edinburgh Review had opined, "Crime concerns, not only the individual, the parish, or the county, but the nation generally", and on the basis of this diagnosis had demanded that "the effort for its extirpation should be national likewise". Grants were initially made only to efficient forces, but by 1890 when a number of small borough police forces had disappeared, all police forces, except that of the City of London, which did not need support, were in receipt of Exchequer aid; after 1874 this was no longer restricted to 25 per cent of costs. These two innovations, the creation of the inspectorate and the offering of a conditional Treasury grant, introduced by the act, justify Radzinowicz's judgement that it successfully blended together "a minimum of direct compulsion with considerable indirect pressure". Summarizing the impact of the 1856 act, Carolyn Steedman argues that

> it outlined a realistic professionalism, not only in the appointment of government inspectors to enquire into the state and efficiency of local forces on an annual basis, but also in the clauses that dealt with the physical provision for police operations – police stations, charge rooms, cells. By this new act, a career body was delineated and superannuation funds were established.

The championing of the civilian nature of the police by some advocates of the British policing tradition has perhaps been taken too far, even to the ignoring of the very considerable impact of the military ideal on police development, especially at the mid-century. In fact Emsley notes how the 1856 act marks an increasingly clear perception of the police as a form of domestic soldiery. Before 1856 only 7 out of 23 chief constables in English counties had a military background, whereas from 1856 to 1880 the proportion rises to 22 out of 24. "Many magistrates perceived their county constabularies as the first line of defence against an internal enemy, which, in cases of popular disorder, led to them being deployed in a military fashion."

The new police at work

The new police of the 1840s and 1850s, it has been argued, were hardly new, because of the many precedents for their creation and because of the continuation of traditional policing methods long after 1856. In personnel too there was continuity in many places from the old to the new. In the historiography of the nineteenth-century police, there have been two main approaches: the first, sometimes called the Whig approach, has tended to lionize the reformers of the early nineteenth century, who are seen as bringing order out of chaos and seeking to implement a police strategy that finds its fulfilment in the idealized police forces of their own time. Historians of the Left, by contrast, conceive of the creation of the new police as essentially an episode in class history reflecting the desire of ruling elites to destroy working-class culture and impose an alien discipline on the poor in order to produce a malleable proletariat shaped to play its part in the development of Britain's great adventure in industrial capitalism. This same capitalism gave birth to a consumer society with considerable middle-class affluence, which simply meant that many bourgeois households had more possessions vulnerable to theft and burglary. Thus in David Jones's words, we have "two models of police history, the one involving consensus, the other conflict". If the Whig historians, influenced by the rhetoric of the early reformers themselves, emphasized change rather than continuity in policing, and this they certainly did, then Marxist historians have perhaps been too influenced by working-class fears of the new police, causing them to attribute to the latter a more sinister role than can be justified.

The new police, charged with the maintenance of public order and the control of society in the widest sense, embarked upon an unceasing surveillance of all aspects of working-class life, although this narrowed down particularly to the detection and, as their capacity allowed, the prevention of crime. The introduction of this "bureaucracy of official morality" into the urban communities of northern England was, in Robert Storch's words, "a significant extension into hitherto geographically peripheral areas of both the moral and political authority of the state". Seeking support for his argument that "it was in fact in its policeman guise rather than its paternalistic guise that the Victorian state was first to demonstrate its power and its purposes", Gatrell calls as witness the feminist Josephine Butler, who in 1879 pronounced, with very obvious regret, that "police government combines the evil of extreme centralisation with the activity, in every corner of the nation, of a vast and numerous agency of surveillance". So the new police busied themselves regulating working-class leisure activities not so much because such practices might offend middle-class sensibilities as because, uncontrolled, they might lead to a challenge to the peace. It was thus in Storch's judgement inevitable that "the new police would inevitably personify both alien values and an increasingly alien law, in the inner core of the modern industrial city". Working-class opinion was quite obviously hostile: for the new police were to them at once spies and a species of military, "the minion and paid servant of the Government" as the *Poor Man's Guardian* described the policeman (11 October 1830). The other side of this coin was the police's built-in reluctance in the earlier part of the century to pursue middle-class offenders of the law, for which activity the average police constable with only a modicum of training was poorly endowed and worked without well-founded hope of effective backup from his superiors. Only slowly was the idea of the policeman as an agent of government and of the bosses' class softened as patiently the reputation of non-partisanship was nurtured and developed.

Not surprisingly there was much popular hostility to the introduction of this "plague of blue locusts", for working-class fears were many. Were these men in blue the standing army, so long opposed, under a new guise? did their usefulness justify their cost? were the new police the lackeys of authority against all political questioning? were they created to enforce the New Poor Law, to break strikes and more generally to work for capital against the interests of labour? Storch gives clear answer: "The police came as unwelcome spectators into the very nexus of urban neighbourhood life." Given those fears and suspicions, the widespread incidence of anti-police riots is not surprising. Their concerns varied: unrealistically they sometimes sought to secure the withdrawal of the new forces, more realistically at other times the aims were more limited to preserving popular recreations and customs, avoiding police intervention against strike action and making timely protests against police excesses in discharging their duties. Sometimes the objection seems to have been to the introduction of the police *per se*, elsewhere riot seems to have relied upon some local catalyst to release pent-up feelings.

While much of the worst violence both by and to the police took place at a time of heightened political concern, when Chartism seemed to threaten the security of society, Storch convincingly shows that the introduction of a police force in quieter times, as in the West Riding in 1857, still provoked a bitter and at times violent response; open warfare during the period of introduction, as in Lancashire in the 1840s, gave way to a sustained period of "armed truce". As far as the police were concerned their arms were, except in the most exceptional circumstances, limited to their truncheons. These they carried concealed until 1863, being instructed to use them sparingly as part of a strategy of deploying minimum force. As late as the 1880s the people of Flora Thompson's Candleford Green still regarded the police as "a potential enemy, set to spy on them by the authorities".

Richter has argued that the securing of public order often had independent causes: "whatever order did prevail was due as much to crowd restraint as to police effectiveness". Jones, however, still persists in affirming, from his study of police diaries and criminal statistics, the importance of the police: "respectable citizens now rested more comfortably in close proximity to those three great 'moral teachers': the gaol, the workhouse and the police station". In 1871 there were 10,350 London and 15,860 provincial policemen, and 16,900 London and 27,360 provincial policemen in 1901.

Uniformed and un-uniformed police

It was not enough for the new police to do their job; they had to be seen to do their job well, hence the stress laid upon their visible presence and the importance of the uniforms they wore. However, when prevention extended to detection it became equally important to work under cover;

thus the importance of plain-clothes policemen. Debates about the effectiveness of the police presence were unending: all too frequently when a crime had been committed no officer of the law was to be found in the vicinity. Serious journals like *The Times* urgently questioned, "Where are the Police?", the headline it deployed in 1875 after a raid upon a warehouse in High Holborn that must have taken several hours to effect without apparently arousing suspicion among the law keepers.

There was no real answer to the debate because nobody was prepared to carry out the proposal of a Bedfordshire magistrate who wanted the police to be wholly withdrawn from one half of his county so that the criminality there could, in a controlled experiment, be compared with that in a like area that was regularly policed. Without that evidence it has been suggested that the visible presence of a policeman did deter petty criminals and control the level of violence on the streets, confining crime in nineteenth-century England to a basic threshold of occurrence.

For their part the new police sought to demonstrate their value to society and the ratepayers who provided their remuneration by compiling numerous statistics of arrest, including many offences that annoyed their middle- and upper-class paymasters: various forms of street crime, begging, being drunk and disorderly, illegal street trading and soliciting. They also recorded the number of licensed premises in the community and monitored the number of vagrants passing through its jurisdiction, for vagrancy, which Steedman calls "a mobile anomaly in the structure of social control", was widely perceived to be the source of many other crimes, the problem being that while vulnerable property was static, the criminal, with improved communications, had become highly mobile.

In rural areas there was less argument for the wearing of uniforms, for there could never be a great police presence in such locations. Even in urban areas it was the plain-clothes men who apprehended most criminals. Some, however, thought that plain-clothes agents were rather sneaky, concern being expressed that England should not adopt continental spy tactics against her own people. The decade 1829–39 had seen plain-clothes detectives working alongside the Metropolitan Police under the authority of local magistrates. In 1842, the Metropolitan Police were compelled, if reluctantly, to appoint their own plain-clothes detectives. Only slowly did they increase in number, partly because of the suspicions already mentioned, but also because plain-clothes men were thought to be more vulnerable to corruption.

Professionalizing the police

Major problems for early police forces were low pay, even when supplemented by some benefits in kind, and a lack of training. As long as such conditions prevailed, the quality of those recruited remained low, and the margin between lawbreakers and law keepers ill guarded: it was said early in the century that the police hardly offered a career, only an alternative to unemployment. Carolyn Steedman expresses a similar idea when she speaks of working-class recruits to the police who never became policemen, in the sense that they never became the epitome of respectability, patience and neutrality that latter-day creators of stereotypes wish on the mid-nineteenth century. She has produced a remarkable array of statistics to show how rare a phenomenon the career policeman was for much of the century: turnover in police forces continued to be very high until the last decades of the century. "If the men stay for two years, there is some hope of them staying longer", reflected a chief constable in 1874, "but the vast proportion of men change within the year, or the first few months."

In Staffordshire in most years between 1856 and 1876 more than two-thirds of the force left before completing two years' service; little more than one-tenth continued, with prospects of promotion, until they had earned their pensions. By contrast, the officer class of the police showed remarkable stability; in Staffordshire 80 per cent of those appointed between 1852 and 1863 either died in service or secured their pensions. Half of the high early leakage among constables was caused by dismissals, the most common causes of which were drunkenness and living with large debts, which was specifically forbidden in some rule books: the paradigm of temperate respectability for the nineteenth-century policeman was clearly more honoured in the breach than in the rule. Given such a high turnover of manpower, there were clearly limitations upon what the police could achieve: in such a context, the worst fears of historians of the Left may appear to be exaggerated.

When local forces were established, the prevailing fear seems to have been of nepotism and undue local influence, hence the appointment of early superintendents from among those who were strangers to the area: in the event simple drunkenness and embezzlement of police funds seem to have been more immediate hazards, or so it proved in Newcastle under Lyme. Thus the first Superintendent of Police, Isaac Cottrill, was an outsider who had a similar post in Pendleton in Lancashire. By virtually garrisoning the town against any overflow from the Plug Plot Riots that ravaged the neighbouring Potteries towns in 1842, by enrolling some eight hundred specials and by displaying two pieces of cannon outside the police station, he won the special approbation of Newcastle's leading citizens. Within seven years, however, he was dismissed for two incidents involving drunkenness and absence from duty: even the special payment of £50 that was nevertheless given to him on his dismissal, in respect of "the extraordinary exertions used by him in the preservation of the peace of the borough at the time of the riots in the Potteries in 1842", was subsequently withdrawn when it came to light that he had been making more personal provision for his pension by diverting fire-service funds to his personal use over the past 12 years.

Cottrill's successor, J. T. Blood of Uttoxeter, was by contrast renowned for being difficult to extract from the police station. To such an accusation he offered the defence that his work there was necessary since he alone had to do all the paperwork as his three constables were all illiterate; more office help was agreed so that the superintendent could be seen more frequently in the town, replete with frock-coat and silk hat rather than police uniform. The borough force did not initially benefit from the subsidies offered under the Grey act, partly because of a poor ratio of police to population and partly because of the borough force's failure to co-operate with the contingent county force, which represented the borough force as interested only in driving the criminal out of the borough on to county territory. Not until 1873 did the borough spend enough on its police force to qualify consistently for government subsidy. This is not untypical of many borough forces, which were often too small to be effective; for its part the Home Office constantly reiterated the merits of "a police force essentially civil, unarmed and acting without any assistance from a military force" (Hansard). Otherwise, in times of crisis the local force would, to meet the immediate need, swear in as special constables as many as possible of its sober and upright citizens. As a matter of strict law all such citizens could be compelled to serve, unless belonging to an exempt class.

The general movement was clear enough. In 1857, 120 forces were judged inefficient; by 1875 that number had fallen to 38 and by 1890 to zero. Whereas in 1857 there were just under 19,000 policeman in the country more than a third of whom served in the capital, by 1901 that figure had risen to over 44,000; just under 17,000 of these were in London. These increases represent in part a response to the increasing population, in part an attempt to secure a better ratio of police to public. For example, in 1857 the ratio in the provinces was one policeman to every 1,365 persons; it had reduced to 1:949 by the end of the century. The London ratios for the same dates were 1:446 and 1:396. Numbers also produced results: thus Gatrell argues that from the 1850s to the eve of the First World War, "the war against criminal disorder was palpably being won by the State, and contemporaries knew it". Success had its own contribution to make to self-respect and thus to professionalization.

In the nineteenth century the hierarchy within the police force clearly mirrored that in society at large, with officers drawn from middle-class backgrounds but the much larger number of constables recruited from the ranks of the deferential rural working classes. These working-class men, in Carolyn Steedman's words, were "used as a tool of social policy by local governments". Low pay, a lack of training and poor discipline had, however, left the police of the earlier part of the century in low public esteem. In its first issue in February 1866 the *Police Service Advertiser*, which played a very positive part in developing the idea of the ordinary policeman as a professional, lamented, "probably no public servant is so ill-used by his employer as the policeman".

From the 1870s onwards many a chief constable sought to raise the professional esteem of his force by trying to get them to focus all their energies on policing and to drop their subsidiary local-government functions *vis-à-vis* the Poor Law, market-watching, weights and measures, etc., for much of which they acted as officers of the local magistracy. This was seen as distracting the police from their proper duties. In this the chief constables were successful to the extent that the Home Office in the 1870s issued several circulars to local authorities underwriting these desires for more focus in police work. In the process the bond between police and magistracy was loosened, and this was reinforced when the central government came to bear an increasing proportion of the cost of local forces. At the same time new legislation, such as the Explosives Act and the Adulteration of Food Act, both of 1875, brought new responsibilities to local forces, but these they implemented on their own authority without resort to magistrates. Increasingly public perception was encouraged to think of the police as an autonomous service seeking to implement its own professional standards.

The appointment of three inspectors of constabulary as part of the 1856 act began to improve the status of the police. Over the years they outlined to central government, and anybody else willing to listen, the need for a professional body, but they still emphasized in their annual reports the virtues of local-government policing. The most celebrated of those first appointed, Major-General Sir William Cartwright, a humane gentleman soldier distinguished in his concern for the welfare of the police, used the report to campaign for uniform scales of pay and the recognizing and rewarding of merit among those recruited as constables. Cartwright believed that the position of sergeant was critical to the development of good policing, both as a rank with which to reward loyal service and as a means to provide an additional level of superintendence throughout the district. As important as levels of pay and prospects of promotion was the need for proper pensions, which became obligatory from the 1890s. By the end of the century joining the police was becoming, albeit slowly, a way to secure economic security and social respectability for some working men.

Conclusion

This chapter has traced the development of a nationwide police service but in doing this has insisted that there is no single model of development. The Metropolitan Police Force was exceptional and hardly offered a model to provincial England. Rather the government was content to develop a plurality of legal instruments, allowing localities to develop the style of policing deemed most appropriate to their areas, noting that the defence of property was high on most agendas. Certainly successive administrations were anxious to wean local authorities away from a dependency on the army, which they hoped would be used only in extreme emergencies. In rural areas the pattern of policing often reflected pre-industrial traditions of administration with the authority of the rural magistracy carefully underlined. In the industrial north and midlands this "plague of blue locusts" was greatly feared as representing a new intrusion into working-class communities of an alien and unwanted force suspected of being intent on curbing ancient freedoms. In fact the response of many urban authorities to much legislation was slow and grudging until some local crisis brought local consciousness of a security need to coalesce with the interests of central government to police the nation. Even the offer of subsidies found many small boroughs hesitant to undertake the costs of a force large enough to meet the canons of efficiency. But it was not enough to ensure that each locality had a police presence: it had also to be ensured that it was of sufficient strength and quality to do its work effectively. Early in the century that was often not the case. The scale of remuneration was such that service in the police was hardly membership of a profession; rather it provided a temporary alternative to unemployment. It was late in the century before ordinary policemen could be induced to offer a considerable number of years in police service. For this to happen they had to be persuaded by the prospects of pensions, promotion and other improvements in conditions of service secured through the advocacy of the members of the national inspectorate. Only then did the paradigm of impartiality, scrupulous honesty and temperate respectability, the longed-for image that was coveted for Britain's police, begin to reflect any reality on the ground.

Chapter 11

Patterns of punishment

The punitive state

Punishment in the nineteenth century underwent profound changes. At the beginning of the century, capital punishment and transportation both featured predominantly, as threat as much as reality. By 1875 transportation had gone, and the number of capital offences had declined to a minimum. A second change noted by Emsley is a movement from a situation in which all the vital decisions were in the hands of the officers of the courts to one in which the forms of punishment were more and more determined by them in partnership with the experts within the prison service. This change happened partly because of a need to think more positively about the function of custodial sentences once the days of transportation were seen to be numbered. Whereas at the beginning of the period Sir James Stephen spoke of prisons as embracing "mainly a system of licensed revenge", it now became necessary to think positively about the relationship between punishment and reformation.

The "Bloody Code" of the early nineteenth century stipulated capital punishment for more than two hundred offences before the intervention of reformers such as Romilly and Mackintosh. The desire to celebrate their achievements probably led earlier historians to exaggerate the harshness of this code, and some caution is called for. One reason for the large number of offences was the over-precise definition of offences; for example, as an offence, defacing Westminster Bridge was different from defacing Fulham Bridge. Such narrow definitions meant that the number of offences was not likely to add to the number of prosecutions, let alone convictions. This could aid the accused: in 1833 John Haughton of Stoke-on-Trent was charged with maliciously setting fire to a Mr Owen's stable, but because the defence was able to show that the building was last used as a cowshed the accused was acquitted.

Secondly it is important to look not so much at the statutory penalties as at the way the courts acted under such legislation. Many testimonies bear evidence to the courts' reluctance to convict when a penalty seemed disproportionate to the crime committed. In this respect there seems to have been on occasions a strange alliance between working-class protests and the hatreds of a land-based magistracy for the new middle-class entrepreneurs, the despised millocrats. It has been argued that capital offences were not effective as deterrents to criminal action but that they did deter people from making prosecutions or the magistrates or jury from bringing in a guilty verdict.

In the early nineteenth century there was in fact a growing trend to commute even capital convictions to some lesser penalty. For example, the ready availability of transportation led to a number of capital offences being reduced to transportation for a given number of years. In 1821, the Lent assizes for Staffordshire passed death sentences on 28 people, but only 5 were actually executed. And between 1825 and 1834 only 5 per cent of those convicted were actually executed, these principally being those convicted of murder and sexual offences. From 1866 executions largely took place in private, the last public execution being at Newgate on 26 May 1868. Before the development of the concept of public prosecutions, a prosecution had to be initiated by either the victim or those who supported the victim. They had to decide not only on whether to prosecute but also on the severity of the crime for which to prosecute. Prosecuting for a crime of less gravity would give a better chance of a conviction, since the burden on the evidence would be less, as too the pressure on the jury to reject a guilty verdict. In many cases, however, the only possible way to proceed was *de facto* to pardon the offender by not taking the case to court.

An increasingly important part of the equation was the growth of public opinion, fed by a growing literature on the nature of crime and its appropriate punishment. Parliamentary reports played a major part, as did the periodicals and the social problem novels. For example, Charles Reade's "*It is never too late to mend*" (1856) transmutes significant blue-book and other evidence for Victorian fiction readers, fulfilling an important role of public education in the process. Reade's plot in this instance provided him with the opportunity to deal with transportation, conditions in the antipodean colonies and the abuses of the pre-reform style of prison management. Between 1822 and the accession of Victoria, legal reformers secured a rationalizing of offences away from a rather random scatter of particular criminal acts into a well-defined series of criminal categories; only the most violent were retained as capital offences. The list of 1837 was not extensive but by 1861 it was reduced to only four categories, which remained capital offences until 1957.

Early-nineteenth-century views of punishment

Bentham's *Introduction to the principles of morals and legislation*, although completed in 1780, was not published until 1789, while the collaborative work that he wrote with the Frenchman Dumont was published in French in 1811. The underlying assumption in Bentham's thinking was that all punishment is an evil, which, under the theory of utility, should be admitted only when it promises to exclude some even greater evil. Thus the utilitarian view of punishment is in three parts. First, it must deter wholly or confine the criminal to some lesser crime. Secondly, it must correct. Thirdly, it must be as cheap as possible and in no case exceed the cost of that which it seeks to control. Applying such principles to the death penalty, the following deductions were made. It clearly controlled the criminal and by the same token acted as a deterrent. In many cases, such as murder for example, the penalty was appropriately analogous to the offence committed and in that respect made its appeal to public opinion. Its great drawback was its inflexibility: it could not be mollified and it allowed neither for reformation nor for the mitigation of mistakes. The natural deduction was to retain it only for the most serious offences, that is "murders accompanied with circumstances of aggravation", a very radical view for the beginning of the nineteenth century. Thomas Fowell Buxton, when urging the mitigation of capital punishment for forgers and contending for imprisonment with hard labour and solitary confinement if necessary, argued that if the state was unable effectively to supply the appropriate secondary punishment then the felon ought not to suffer the more because of the incapacities of the state.

In the early nineteenth century all non-capital punishment was regarded as secondary punishment. This, in its turn, was divided into the two broad categories of custodial and non-custodial penalties. Non-custodial sentences were wider then than now: mutilation of the body had largely ceased by the early nineteenth century, but the pillory and the stocks remained available, the former for more serious, the latter for less serious offences. The problem with the pillory was that it virtually handed the punishment of the prisoner to the mob: it was all but abolished in the United Kingdom in 1815, though it was retained for perjury until 1837. The stocks continued in use for rather longer, until at least the middle of the century in rural areas.

The conscience about capital punishment soon led to objections to corporal punishment. After 1817 women were no longer whipped in public and after 1820 not in private either. The comparison here would be with the widespread legitimate use of corporal punishment in the home, extending to servants as well as to children, with the same practice common in educational institutions. In 1861 corporal punishment was abolished for males over the age of 16 except for a short list of special offences, which in 1865 were increased in response to a contemporary wave of garrotting. Clearly many members of the judiciary continued to believe in the deterrent value of flogging. In 1875 for example a number of judges argued that flogging was a wholly appropriate punishment for wife-beating husbands. It was not finally abolished for adults until 1948, though the Howard League had mounted a formidable campaign for its abandonment from the last quarter of the nineteenth century. On the other hand, throughout the period corporal punishment was a regular part of prison discipline. As bodily afflictions increasingly fell out of favour so non-custodial sentencing came to focus more on fining, in itself a testimony to the growth of a money culture increasingly permeating throughout society. At the beginning of the period fining was difficult, for it presupposed a certain level of prosperity and the ability of the courts to extract those funds: to whip the poor was so much easier.

Humanitarian reformers

Early prisons, sometimes run as enterprises for profit by those responsible for their administration, were most often places of detention for those awaiting trial rather than places of long-term incarceration. Accordingly their punitive functions were not fully worked out. The Gaol Fees Abolition Act of 1815 signalled the beginning of the end of the prison as a place of commercial profit, until recent changes in the administration of the prison service came to reverse this pattern. Such legislation depended not only on the energies of a group of reformers but also on the development of a body of public opinion that they were able to exploit.

John Howard, the most famous of early prison reformers, was a gentleman grocer from Bedford with a country estate at Cardington just outside the borough. He was a Congregationalist of evangelical persuasion, though when in London he was a hearer at Samuel Stennett's Baptist chapel. He had personal experience of prison regimes: caught by a French privateer on his way to Portugal in 1756, he was committed to a French prison, an experience which prompted him to become an international prison reformer. His knowledge of the conditions of British prisons came first from his appointment as high sheriff of Bedfordshire. The experience he gained from this office he called upon when asked to give evidence to the select committee of the House of Commons. This was of little avail, for the reformist legislation of 1774, lacking any principle of implementation, proved ineffective.

Howard virtually appointed himself a private inspector of prisons, campaigning for the removal of gross abuses, which he illustrated in apparently scientific detail in his *State of prisons in England and Wales* (published in 1777). The following year saw him giving evidence to a Commons committee against the pernicious conditions that existed on the hulks. During the decade 1775–85 he visited six continental towns in the interests of prison reform, travelling as far east as Turkey and Russia, again recording the details of abuse as a mechanism of reform.

A fellow evangelical of a slightly later generation was the Quaker Elizabeth Fry, who made her first visit to Newgate in 1813, taking up serious prison

A PLAN for a COUNTY GAOL.

Figure 11.1 From John Howard, *The state of the prisons* (1777).

work four years later when, with the return of Britain's soldiers from Europe, British prisons became desperately overcrowded. In contrast to the Benthamite concern for administrative tidiness, she embodied warm humanitarian concern, motivated by strong evangelical convictions. "Committed", in the words of one of her biographers, "to reforming the prisoner by work rather than punishing them by labour", she campaigned for prisoners' education, for Bible reading in prison and for the development of programmes of rational recreation. She collaborated with her brother-in-law Thomas Fowell Buxton, who was particularly concerned about the conditions under which remand prisoners were held, as also those held for debt.

Elizabeth Fry bemoaned the lack of proper segregation of prisoners, the lack of useful work for them, and the overcrowding and insanitary conditions they all too often encountered. The visiting committee she established for Newgate, which was made up almost exclusively of Quaker women, sought to provide proper clothing for the prisoners and to instruct them in "order, sobriety, and industry" and established a school for prisoners' children. The object of Elizabeth Fry's ministrations was an ordered prison administered under the concerns of a Christian conscience, as compared with the unsupervised chaos of many gaols of the pre-reform period. She drew up rules for the governing of prison life, sought the provision of regular work for all and campaigned for the exclusion of unhelpful pastimes. Her concern was to adapt the monitorial system to the needs of the prison, ensuring that religious instruction was made available to all. The new discipline was self-imposed and agreed to by the women themselves, who also consented to live under the superintendence of a matron paid for by the Quaker women. Such methods, together with the more subtle instrument of her own personality, were deployed in the interests of humanizing Newgate. Elizabeth Fry also proved a formidable witness before the several inquiries of 1818, 1831 and 1835.

Some argued that the evangelical humanitarians were too soft upon those who had defaulted on their social contract. Edwin Chadwick condescendingly argued, "Because of the Howards and Frys, the prisons had been so reformed by narrow sentiment and blind zeal as actually to attract vagrants and others who preferred their comfort to labour." By contrast Elizabeth Fry argued that aspects of the new discipline smacked of the imposition of deliberate cruelty, which she believed had been growing since the 1830s. She especially protested against the use of solitary confinement as a punishment, as also against the combination of dietary restriction with hard labour, a combination of penalties the effects of which were spelt out in compelling detail in Charles Reade's *"It is never too late to mend"*: the young Josephs is described as a helpless lad of fifteen "overtasked and famished for a month past and fitter now for a hospital than hard labour of any sort". Ten pages later he is found dead in his cell having committed suicide.

Transportation

Although transportation had been in use since the seventeenth century, it was most intensively deployed from 1788 to 1867; during this period some 150,000 people were transported, principally to Australia. At the peak of its use in the early 1830s, some 5,000 men, women and juveniles were transported each year. A sentence to transportation almost always entailed an initial period of waiting in the "hulks", insanitary ex-warships laid up in a number of British estuaries. The original intention was that they would offer temporary prison accommodation for a crisis period of 2 years, but they were in fact used for 80. Conditions on board were deplorable: the accommodation was damp and overcrowded, and the prisoners spent much of their time in irons. The Webbs observe: "Of all the places of confinement that British History records, the hulks were the most brutalising, the most demoralising and the most horrible." Those who stayed in the hulks for any significant length of time were susceptible to a special kind of disease, christened "hulk fever" by John Howard. As many as 25 per cent of those committed to the hulks never got beyond them but died on board: in such circumstances early transportation was seen as a reward for good behaviour. An exposé of conditions in the hulks in *The Times* in 1845 led to the gradual reduction of their use: only two survived after 1852. Thereafter, temporary incarceration in a penitentiary was the fate of convicts awaiting transportation.

Beyond the hulks lay the hazard of a difficult four or more months' journey with some prisoners dying *en route* between Britain and Australia. The worst disaster happened in August 1842 when the convict ship *Waterloo* broke up off the Cape Coast with the loss of 250 of the 330 persons on board. At first contractors were paid according to the numbers taken on board. Conditions improved when remuneration was related to the numbers safely landed in Australia. Once in Australia, the convicts were assigned either to private individuals or to various governmental institutions, largely according to the usefulness of their trade: carpenters and mechanics for example were in considerable demand by private individuals. This rather than the nature of the crime for which they were sentenced determined assignment, though some convicts, those who had proved difficult to handle during their incarceration and on the journey out and were described as "depraved characters", were retained for public works. After 1835, private assignment tended to be reserved to those on longer than seven-year sentences, for the training costs of those on shorter terms did not leave a sufficient period of benefit to the settler. In the case of juvenile convicts, genuine attempts were normally made to apprentice them to a trade.

Neither settlers nor overseers of public works programmes were themselves allowed to administer corporal punishment, but the local magistrates frequently authorized this. In New South Wales between 1833 and 1837 almost a quarter of convicts were flogged at some time, forty lashes being about the norm; at Point Puer, a special juvenile establishment, 56 per cent of the convicts were caned in 1835 and 70 per cent in 1837. Though the efficacy of flogging was much debated it was cheap and easy to apply. Moreover it was administered far away beyond the gaze of reformers at home. Convicts returned by their masters as unsuitable were automatically assigned to road gangs before being made available for re-assignment, while more serious offences led to incarceration in a penal settlement. After 1842 assignment was replaced by the probation system, whereby all prisoners were assigned to probation gangs for at least two years before being allowed a probation pass.

As in all open prisons, which were *de facto* what the Australian settlements were, discipline was effected not only by the deterrents of punishment but also by the incentives of potential privileges. The most important instrument was the ticket-of-leave system, whereby those who had a record of good conduct could apply for early release from "imprisonment" so that they could seek paid employment, on condition that they registered the location of their residence with the police authorities. Such licences were always conditional on continued good behaviour and could be instantly revoked if this condition was contravened.

The idea behind transportation in the nineteenth century was that making the labour of the able-bodied available to the new colonies was more important than punishing them revengefully for the vices they had displayed in the mother country. Sentencing could appear vicious, especially since many of those sentenced were very young: Thomas Bailey, an 11-year-old from Lane End (Staffordshire) was sentenced to seven years' transportation for stealing a halfpenny – but against his name was recorded, notwithstanding his tender years, "a notorious rogue". Hannah Hambleton, aged only ten, received seven years' transportation for stealing a handkerchief, a net collar and some ribbon from a shop in Hanley. The most youthful case was that of John Inskip, aged only nine, who was sentenced to seven years' transportation for stealing 2s 2d. But the most notorious juvenile to be transported from the Potteries was Nathan Benton, who at the age of ten was facing his 24th prosecution for stealing a watch, having first come before the courts at the age of four! No pawnbroker would accept it so out of spite Benton had destroyed it with a brick. Mercy in his case was conceived to be a separation from "those who had neglected his education both in precept and example", and for the good of "his soul as well as his body" he was transported for seven years.

The deterrent effect of transportation must have lessened when it became desirable rather than undesirable. One 16-year-old purloiner of boots in Stone may well have committed this offence deliberately, for he told the court "he could get no employment in this country and he would be thankful to be removed out of it". In similar vein, John Hartshorne's father confessed to not being able to control his 13-year-old son, beseeching the court to transport him, which it duly did on an indictment for stealing clothes and food. The stealing of food, presumably out of some kind of desperation, was not uncommon. David Leedham, aged 12, was sentenced to seven years' transportation for the theft of bacon valued at 2d, as was Joseph Bryan for stealing two pounds of pork. John Eardley, aged 17, and James Bailey, aged 20, were more severely handled: both were sentenced to death, later commuted to transportation, for the theft of a loaf of bread. Clearly poverty or hunger were not perceived as extenuating circumstances. By contrast crimes against the person could receive comparatively modest sentences Alexander Lowe of Burslem, who inflicted ten wounds upon Samuel Billings with a carpenter's awl and stabbed Richard Kettle three times, causing him to lose much blood, was found guilty of "committing an assault and battery, under circumstances of most brutal and savage atrocity" but was only imprisoned for two years.

As a general rule, receiving, after it was made a felony in 1827, was treated as a more serious crime than stealing, so that Isaac Wood and Elizabeth Woodford were sentenced to transportation for 14 years for receiving stolen clothes, while sentence on the thieves themselves was only 7 years. Perhaps the most colourful case was that of Catherine Dudley of Stoke Lane near Newcastle under Lyme, otherwise known as Irish Kit, who seems to have received stolen property on a regular basis from a number of criminals. These she concealed at her establishment, which also housed a domesticated bear and a pack of hounds. At the end of 1833, one of her accomplices eventually broke her confidence and led Broadhurst Harding, the constable of Lane End, to her residence, where he discovered a false ceiling that concealed a secret storage place for a hoard of stolen goods. The judge described Dudley as "one of the greatest nuisances that could exist in female form" and sentenced her to 14 years' transportation, allowing Harding his expenses and a reward of £10.

Breaking and entering in order to steal obviously incurred severer penalties than simple larceny, as John Fox discovered in 1821 when he acted in this way to steal £5: the initial death sentence, however, was converted to transportation for life, "to leave this country never to return". Over the next decade there seems to have been considerable consistency in treating breaking and entering cases, namely the imposition of the death penalty subsequently commuted to transportation for life. Coining was also seriously regarded as a threat to the commercial stability of the nation: Hugh Shufflebotham, who in 1849 was caught at his home in possession of both the moulds and chemicals necessary for his trade, was sentenced to 15 years' transportation, the judge warning him that in earlier times he would have "expiated his offence upon the gallows".

Contemporaries reviewing the fortunes of certain families were inclined to the view that crime ran in families. The *Staffs Advertiser* first reported on the Clare family in 1819, when Prudence Clare was convicted of stealing a 28-yard length of printed cotton; her mother Mary was convicted of receiving it. The daughter was sentenced to 7 years' transportation and her mother 14. The mother in fact died in Stafford gaol that same year, before transportation, and the daughter's sentence was commuted to imprisonment in this country, though in 1826 she was again sentenced to transportation shortly after her release. Her eldest brother was hanged for murder at Newcastle upon Tyne, another brother, Joseph, was transported after escaping from custody on his way from the Shire Hall in Stafford to the county gaol, while a third brother suffered a long period of imprisonment at home. Prudence's sister Mary was sentenced to transportation for her third conviction of stealing from a shop on market day, while another sister suffered imprisonment at home: "The history of this woman's family certainly favours the opinion that crime is hereditary", noted the newspaper. Scholars have been more inclined to stress the importance of a "criminal generation": evidence from north Staffordshire for the first half of the nineteenth century would certainly support that notion as the vast majority (72 per cent) of those sentenced to transportation were between the ages of 11 and 25.

Mary Clare was described as "a notorious bad character" and "a member of the Pottery Gang", fear of whom appears through the court records for 1828. George Greatbach, an 11-year-old, stole 15s and goods and was identified with his brother as "belonging to a gang, commonly called *The Pottery Gang*, and a more lawless band perhaps could not be found". He was sentenced to seven years' training in the hulks. This was evidently unsuccessful for Greatbach reappears nine years later for breaking and entering, for which he was given a capital sentence commuted to transportation for life. George Boulton, aged 20, and Thomas Brown, aged 13, were similarly identified as members of the Pottery Gang and each sentenced to ten years' transportation for stealing a silver watch from James Lindop in Burslem. Since they had both been before the courts on previous occasions Mr Twemlow, the chairman of the magistrates, argued "that there was no hope left of the prisoners being reformed, or of the property of their neighbours being safe while they remained in this country". Their sentences were clearly identified by the court as a deterrent to other members of the gang, while the mothers of the convicted were reported as visibly affected by the sentences.

Prostitutes were well known to relieve their clients of more than their due fee. Michael Dowd, an itinerant dealer in shawls, had access to the residence of Priscilla Heath in Burslem, "in which the purest morals do not seem to have prevailed". Heath seems to have relieved him of three shawls, which she passed on to Hannah Coupland, who made away with them and on whose possession they were found by the local constable. The two women were found guilty of theft and sentenced to transportation, while Dowd, who brought the prosecution, was reprimanded by the court for his immorality which created the opportunity for the theft to be accomplished. Immoderate drinking could also make a victim vulnerable to criminal action: in March 1849 William Brassington appears to have celebrated the sale of a couple of pigs in Tunstall with a young man named Joseph Davies, who proceeded to rob Brassington of over £3. Brassington confessed that "he became fresh but not so much as not to know what he was about". Davies was sentenced to ten years' transportation for highway robbery.

The most coherent group to be transported from Staffordshire were the Plug Plot rioters of 1842. Rudé calls them "the largest batch of prisoners to be arrested, imprisoned and transported for participation in any single event in the course of the Chartist disorders". For such "complete insurrection" 276 people were sent to trial, 116 imprisoned at home and 46 men transported, 5 for life, 12 for 21 years, 8 for 15 years, 19 for 10 years and only 2 for the common term of 7 years. Those transported all fell within the age range 17–33: no-one was transported for riot or sedition alone, the indictments always including one or more other offences. Commenting on the sentence passed on Joseph Capper for speeches made long before the riots, Charles Shaw, "An Old Potter", writes, "it was not the judge who tried him who interpreted the law. It was the overpowering sentiment of the middle and upper classes that something must be done, that some retribution must be inflicted upon every man who had been at the front in this time of agitation, however sacred his motives, and however noble his endeavours to guide this movement to true patriotic issues."

Doubts about the whole process of transportation had always existed. Some thought the punishment too soft. Sidney Smith satirized the deterrent aspect of sentencing thus:

> Because you have committed this offence, the sentence of this Court is that you shall no longer be burdened with the support of your wife and family. You shall be immediately removed from a very bad climate and a country over-burdened with people to one of the finest regions of the earth, where the demand for human labour is every hour increasing, and where it is highly probable you may ultimately gain your character and improve your future.

On the other hand stories about the appalling treatment of convicts in Australia, as presented to the Molesworth Commission as early as 1837–8 also provoked alarm, but it was to be twenty years before effective action was taken to end the system.

Reservations at home were by then effectively fortified by complaints from the Australians themselves, who objected to their colony being treated as a kind of human dustbin, especially at a time when the supply of free labour was increasingly sufficient to meet the colony's needs. Transportation to New South Wales ended in 1840, and to Tasmania in 1852, while the last convict ship left for western Australia in 1867, though for the past fifteen years or so it had ceased to be a practical option of wide utility.

Custodial sentences at home: the great debate

As early as 1779, parliament had passed, under pressure from reformers such as Howard, Eden and Blackstone, a Penitentiary Act, which was to provide for two new institutions, one for each sex, to be constructed to serve reformatory purposes. But like so much legislation of this period the act remained a dead letter: the penitentiaries were never built. The great majority of those convicted of serious offences were therefore either assigned to the hulks or transported, though some county prisons were reorganized on a reformatory basis to provide facilities for the separation of different categories of prisoner, for the prisoner's gainful employment and for the solitary confinement of the recalcitrant.

Many considered a harsh regime essential to reform. In 1791 Bentham drew up plans for his model prison, the Panopticon, a prison architecturally suited to its purpose. Instead of solid masonry it was planned to deploy iron-framed divisions and to provide a water-closet in every cell. Most importantly its cells were to be so arranged as to allow for the constant supervision of those assigned to its care. Not only that but it was also to provide for the supervision of the supervisors, since corrupt gaolers had been a large part of the problem of earlier prisons. The enterprise, to be run under Bentham's own superintendence, was to aim at profit, the inmates providing for their keep and maintenance by their own labour. In 1794 a site was secured in Millbank, but even then the finances for the construction of the Panopticon were not released: the site was later used for the first national penitentiary, the control of which was invested in the home secretary rather than in the local magistrates.

Some of Bentham's ideas were incorporated in the building of Millbank, which took four years to build, starting in 1812, at a cost little short of half a million pounds. As with the New Poor Law the disciplining of the nation was not to be achieved without considerable capital cost, nor indeed without a considerable increase in the supervisory functions of the central government. The Benthamite plan of prison architecture had much to commend it and was followed, for example, in the Lancashire prisons of the 1820s. An alternative design favoured at this period was the radial design, to which cells and workrooms were built along long corridors radiating out from an administrative centre: indeed even in Lancashire, which had initially favoured Bentham's circular design, the radial prison was becoming standard by the end of the 1840s. The small cells here provided, given the technology of the age, proved incapable of efficient and safe heating, save when overcrowding produced an undesirable overheating. In consequence such cells were more uncomfortable than even their designers intended.

In his reformist period as home secretary, Robert Peel, supported by the labours of the Society for the Improvement of Prison Discipline, secured the passing of the Gaols Act of 1823, together with helpful amending legislation the following year. This set out the long-term goals for the establishment of a coherent system of prisons in the country: abolishing all fees within the prison system, separating different categories of prisoners, drawing up basic health regulations, securing the means of enforcing hard labour, providing for religious services, and laying down the criteria for magisterial inspection, with annual reports sent to the secretary of state.

As with the administration of the police, the role of the local magistrates should not lightly be dismissed, as if they were either the agents of the central government or conversely obstructive to its reforming intentions. Rather they represented a provincial or county interest dedicated to appropriate improvements as they perceived them and believed themselves able to fund them. Originally all prisons had been licensed by them. Some greater national coherence was introduced into the system by the appointment in 1835 of the first prison inspectorate of five inspectors. As long as transportation provided for long-term sentences, the average term of confinement at home was not long: between 1836 and 1842 in the 36 largest English county prisons it was 46 days, which clearly allowed little scope for such institutions to undertake much by way of reform. But the demands on the system were changing. Arguably the changed situation needed new institutions, but many small county gaols and borough lock-ups continued to operate in situations for which they were totally unfitted.

A second national penitentiary was commissioned and constructed at Pentonville in the context of the great debate in prison circles about the best means of reform: either the silent or the solitary (sometimes termed the separate) systems. The first ensured that prisoners were not allowed to talk to one another, a regime of silence being maintained at all times. The solitary system went further by requiring the total isolation of prisoners in solitary cells; even when they attended chapel they met in separated boxes, and when moving from one part of the prison to another they had always to wear anonymizing masks. The net result of the system was to throw men in entirely upon themselves for as long as eighteen months with only a chaplain's ministrations to break the isolation, when it was hoped his gentle words might be able to shape their by now hopefully malleable minds to more social attitudes. "The opening of Pentonville in 1842", argues Michael Ignatieff, "represents a point of culmination in the tightening up of social controls underway since 1820." By 1848 a further 54 prisons had been added. Clive Emsley, however, offers a different perspective: "There is no reason to suppose anything other than that, in the popular mind, the prison was accepted as being designed not as an encouragement to them to behave, but as a place where genuine offenders were to be punished."

Although the 1835 select committee had come out in favour of the silent system, a number of inspectors, whose creation arose from the report of the same committee, had different ideas. Among their number was William Crawford, who in 1836 observed in the USA the two systems operating side by side, the separate system in Pennsylvania and the silent system in New York State. Seeing the advantages of the first he and some of his colleagues strongly advocated it. Thus when the new Pentonville penitentiary was built, it was constructed to the requirements of the solitary system.

The system was not without its difficulties, sometimes prompting violent reactions, sometimes producing psychological abnormalities in those who suffered its terrors, even provoking the most despairing to suicide. After a number of significant reports such as that following the death of a prisoner in Birmingham Prison in 1854, these and similar difficulties became generally recognized by the end of the 1850s, so that the care of prisoners was considerably modified in line with initiatives taken earlier by particular governors. Gradually rewards for good behaviour were developed alongside the dissuasions of bread and water diet, corporal punishment, hard labour and solitary confinement, to produce a more balanced regime, but for much of the century the pendulum swung too much between more liberal attitudes and severe subjugation, the latter finding new favour after the garrotting panic of the early 1860s.

Other issues hotly debated included the desirability of developing work skills instead of the pointless labour of the treadmill and the crank (making a given number of rotations against a weighted resistance), the moving of cannon-balls and the picking of oakum (pulling old rope apart to produce a material used for caulking and sealing joints on ships). In contrast to all this, Durham gaol pioneered setting prisoners to useful work producing cloth, mats, nets and rugs, all of which were sold for profit. This was a reaction as much against the evil consequences of inactivity as against the futility of existing penal tasks. The difficulty was that under the new regime setting prisoners to their tasks was often less demanding than what was demanded by many a private entrepreneur: a hatter discharged from Lancaster Castle pointedly commented, "I must now work a great deal harder than I have been doing here." Some perceived other advantages in prison life. "Men have told me repeatedly", affirmed a visitor to Dartmoor in the 1870s, "especially men from agricultural districts, that they were better fed and had better beds in prison than they ever had in their lives before."

A similar debate turned around prisoners' education: was the provision of such a service unfairly to advantage those who had abused society, offering them a facility not available to working people at large? Or was education vital to the reforming process and to the equipping of the prisoners to make a positive contribution to society? Prison diets, poor as they were, and the availability of prison medical services likewise entailed the danger of making life in prison "more eligible" than the condition of life in the communities or workhouses from which the prisoners were drawn. The consequences, in years of trade depression, were inevitable: the suspicion that crimes were committed deliberately to secure admission, especially when sentences were short.

Many governors found it difficult to implement prison discipline fully: when they tried to reduce dietary provision, mortality among prison inmates became unacceptably high. Elsewhere, overcrowding had a similar effect, especially in so far as it made the imposition of effective restraint extremely difficult. Contraband items, especially tobacco and sometimes opium, seemed to be smuggled into prison with ease. Indeed trafficking became a significant part of the subculture of many prisons, some prisoners achieving positions of dominance and others, especially any belonging to minority groups, being coerced to serve their interests. Punishments were widespread and gave to prison officers *de facto* powers to extend the judgments of the courts when prisoners offended against whatever regime was functioning in their prison, and, of course, attempts to enforce something like the silent system necessarily produced many offenders for punishment. In many undermanned prisons the problem of discipline was further compounded by the continued presence of lunatics even after the establishment of county asylums, partly because of administrative ineptitude, partly because juries were sometimes reluctant to identify insanity as a cause of irregular behaviour.

The effective administration of prisons and the securing of sufficient prison capacity continued to trouble politicians as the successful apprehension of criminals increased, as capital offences were reduced and as transportation ceased to supply an easy solution to the detention of the convicted. Prison administrators were in danger of being totally overwhelmed by numbers: by the 1830s committals in Lancashire had already come to exceed ten thousand per annum, but in 1858 they were in excess of forty thousand. In the later part of the century, when more white-collar offenders and the political prisoners arising out of the Fenian disturbances were in prison, there were more articulate people in custody anxious to use their literary skills to expose and to challenge the pointlessness of much prison routine and of the brutalities arising out of the unchecked, or inadequately checked, powers of prison officers.

Non-custodial sentences

From the world of transportation, probationary release was adopted for certain categories of prisoner at home. The application to the domestic situation of something like the ticket-of-leave system became a virtual necessity when it became apparent that some convicts awaiting transportation to Australia, where some commutation of sentence could be expected, would still be in prison in English gaols when transportation came to an end. By the Penal Servitude Act of 1853 such release on licence of prisoners of good behaviour was allowed at home, although there were difficulties because the nation lacked a court system sophisticated enough to administer a large number of criminals living freely in society but on licence. In 1864 their supervision was made the responsibility of the police. The restoration into society of such persons, as also of ex-convicts, caused all sorts of difficulties, which underlines the fact that a prison sentence was not the only punishment. It was argued that this was particularly true of those who came from a middle-class background: "To a large number of criminals", argued an ex-convict of middle-class background in 1877, "it is merely so many years being shut up in prison, restricted from doing their own will, and being compelled to labour, to a certain extent, whether they like it or not. To the man in a good position, it is moral death accompanied with ruin and disgrace to his family and relatives."

Returning the criminal to the world of work represented a challenge to philanthropists. For example, Thomas Wright (1789–1875) of Manchester, a Congregational layman employed as a foreman iron-founder earning £3 5s a week, encountered at work a discharged convict who was threatened with dismissal until Wright deposited £20 as security against his good behaviour. Alerted to the problem of the ex-convict, he began visiting prisons from 1838 onwards, but a 13-hour working day from five in the morning meant this had to be done either in the evenings or on Sunday afternoons. For many discharged prisoners he secured employment on his own guarantee. When his work was made public through the reports of prison chaplains and inspectors, he was offered the post of Her Majesty's Travelling Inspector of Prisons at a salary of £800 per year, but he declined the offer because he believed his influence depended on his voluntary status. He did accept, however, a public testimonial of £3,248 (including a small royal bounty), which provided an annuity to enable him to concentrate on his prison visiting; for some years this included attending on every prisoner sentenced to death. In a not dissimilar way, police court missionaries, most of whom were provided by the Church of England Temperance Society after the Probation of First Offenders Act of 1887, became the first supervisors of those under probation, who were often found employment on special projects set up by the society.

Juveniles were now seen as less responsible for their actions than they had been, with the consequence that prison sentences were seen to be inappropriate: the Reformatory Schools Act of 1854 and the Industrial Schools Act of 1857, the fruits of reformers like Mary Carpenter and Matthew Davenport Hill, were the results, providing a useful alternative to prison for some juvenile delinquents. But such institutions did not seem to provide the whole answer. Severe warnings, parental fines and binding young offenders over to keep the peace came to supplement not only custodial sentences, but also the services of non-penal institutions such as industrial schools and Barnardo's refuges. In this a start was made on looking for methods of punishment that diverted people from the ministrations of general prisons.

With the growth of regulatory offences and commercial, white-collar crime, fining came to take on new significance, the prison becoming not the immediate punishment but the sanction deployed against those who did not pay their fines on time. The process leading to "a decentring of the prison in criminal policy", as one author describes it, began as early as the 1880s, was well under way by the turn of the century and was confirmed by early-twentieth-century legislation.

Conclusion

The utilitarian view of punishment set the century a very reasonable agenda with its three concerns about punishment: that properly punishment should deter, wholly or in part; that it should correct and certainly not add to depravity; and that it should be economical and not in any case exceed in cost the value of that which it sought to protect. When interpreting the changes of the century it is essential to distinguish between statutory penalties, that is the penalties imposed by the courts, granted the frequent unwillingness of juries to bring in guilty verdicts, and the punishment actually carried out. This is particularly important when looking at capital offences at the beginning of the century, for juries were already moderating the law in practice by refusing to convict when in their judgement the punishments were too severe for the crimes committed. At the same time the existing non-custodial sentences – the pillory, the stocks, flogging and whipping – were also being challenged, while fining was of limited scope for those of meagre income. The great panacea was transportation, the vision of the Australian colonies as one vast open prison, with, it has been estimated, 150,000 convicts transported before the practice came to an end around 1852. While prison reformers like John Howard and Elizabeth Fry had sought to stamp out the worst abuses in English prisons, many local prisons continued to function in a far from reformed manner. The great debate was over what system was to be adopted for the new national penitentiaries: whether this should be the silent system, which allowed no conversation between prisoners, or the solitary system, which imposed total isolation on those detained. Both systems presented difficulties that had to be resolved once transportation ceased to be an option. Thereafter prison ceased to be a place for remand prisoners or those given short sentences; so alongside deterrence and retribution, attention had to be given to correction and reform, without the penal institution becoming "more eligible" than life outside. More attention had to be given to non-custodial sentences that involved taking the Australian ticket-of-leave system and transforming it into the modern probation service. Attempts were made to take groups such as juveniles and lunatics out of the prison system altogether, while, with the growth of regulatory offences, fining came to take on a new significance.

Part III

The making of the modern criminal, 1875–1960

Chapter 12

Patterns of crime

General trends

The final century covered by this book is the era of numbers. From 1857 onwards, crime was counted. A patchwork of official statistics had been available since the beginning of the century, but with the reorganization of the returns after the 1856 County and Borough Police Act, there became available a systematic annual summary that recorded indictable and summary offences and also offences known to the police. Although the figures were still surrounded by a variety of more fragmentary or impressionable evidence, ranging from an ever-increasing volume of newspaper reports to episodic scares about particular phenomena such as garrotting, hooliganism and drugs, it was by the published reports that society increasingly understood the incidence of what was considered to be crime. Every prisoner was allocated a number as a symbol of the loss of individuality, which was central to the process of punishment. Every policeman, who was himself numbered, was conscious that through his labour he was contributing not just to a diffuse goal of maintaining order but to a table of crimes and convictions, which would be avidly read at the local as well as the national level. The state's capacity to collect and analyze the figures was a measure of its power and rationality in the face of the disruptive and irrational behaviour of a minority of its inhabitants. Modern scholarship has taught us to treat all criminal statistics as a form of suspicious behaviour: the only certainty is that they tell us more about the subjective practice of those who defined the law than about the objective actions of those who broke it. None the less, they constitute the point of departure for any understanding of how relations between the enforcers and transgressors evolved in the concluding period of this history.

The general movement in the figures conforms to a broad if uneven and very indistinct U-curve. During the second half of the nineteenth century, the trends were generally downwards. Trials for indictable offences per head of population fell by 43 per cent between the early 1860s and the end of the century and then began to rise very slowly. Most crimes were committed by men against property. Larceny and related offences accounted for about nine in ten trials for indictable offences, thus their incidence mirrored the overall figures. Only the much smaller number of burglaries failed to register a significant fall before 1900. Not until the mid-1950s did the upward lines on the graphs begin to resemble the similar but far less reliable trajectories of the early nineteenth century. In terms of known figures in the modern period, Macmillan's announcement in 1957 that "most of our people have never had it so good" may have been as true of the thieves as of the affluent electors whose votes he was seeking. A sharp rise in crime during the Second World War was briefly checked during the period of post-war austerity before recommencing with renewed vigour. The number of indictable offences known to the police, of which 85 per cent were still larcenies or receiving, increased by two-thirds in the second half of the 1950s and doubled in the following decade.

The post-war growth was of increasing concern to contemporary society, but it needs to be put into perspective. At the end of the period covered by this book, just under three-quarters of a million indictable offences were known to the police. In 1994, the figure for the roughly comparable category of "more serious offences" was 5.3 million, which was paraded as the second consecutive fall in the graph, which had reached a peak of nearly 5.6 million in 1992. The final section of this book begins with the growing sense that the state and its agencies were winning the battle against crime and ends with the first intimations that the problem was running out of control. The developments in the years since 1960 make the past within living memory a very distant place. For every one indictable offence committed in the bleak years of the Great Depression, twenty are now recorded.

In the official view, property became safer as the Industrial Revolution was consolidated, and so also were people. Crimes against the person accounted for about 4 per cent of indictable offences in the middle of the nineteenth century and, with the exception of sexual offences, fell per capita as fast as those against property during the remainder of Queen Victoria's reign. By the Edwardian era, the common assault rate was more than two-thirds lower than in the first of the modern returns. Although the figures are difficult to use, it seems likely that cases of violence within the home, particularly by husbands against wives, declined in the later nineteenth century. There was some increase in the levels between the wars, but as late as 1945, less than five thousand offences of violence against the person were known to the police. By 1960 the figure had risen to nearly sixteen thousand and would pass two hundred thousand in the early 1990s. Violence among neighbours and especially within the family was particularly susceptible to variable reporting by the victims and to inconsistent intervention by the police and the courts. Murder, on the other hand, with the possible exception of infanticide, was perhaps as near to an absolute criminal fact as could be established. In this case, the decline was steeper and longer than for any other category of offence, and the rise slower and later. The English homicide rate, which stood at 1.5 trials per 100,000 population in 1871, fell to 0.6 in 1911 and was halved again by 1931. The figure was still 0.3 in 1951, and crept up by only a single decimal point in the following decade. It was a paradox of the death penalty that the melodrama of trial and sentence, reprieve or execution, riveted public attention on the one area of crime that was the least cause for concern. Conversely, the abolition of capital punishment in 1965 took place as the rate doubled, reaching a level in the early 1970s not seen since the 1890s.

The official narrative of progress and then varying degrees of regression needs to be treated with some respect. Those who paid the rates and taxes that supported the police and the courts read the figures that suggested that their money was well spent during the later decades of Queen Victoria's reign, and thereafter increasingly ineffective and under threat. In terms of the published data it appears that person and property were probably safer at the end of the nineteenth century than they had been half a century earlier and certainly than they would be a century later. The closely related issues of scale and causation are much more open to debate. How the lawmakers and enforcers explained why the law was broken deeply influenced how the law was constituted; this in turn affected the precise levels of reported transgression in any category at any particular time. A central feature of the modern period in all areas of detection and punishment was the idea of classification. Knowledge and the action which depended on it required first that the problem should be broken down into its constituent elements. While the categories that were developed could imprison understanding even more powerfully than the larger and vaguer generalizations, they do equip the historian with some tools for digging beneath the surface of the published tables. If we look more closely at variations in the criminal population by age, by gender and by class, we can begin to glimpse the dynamics of change in the period.

The young

Crime was, above all, the business of the young. At the beginning of the modern period, children between the ages of 7 and 12 were still coming before the courts and receiving prison sentences. The introduction of reformatories and later juvenile courts removed the very young from the penal system, but those in their mid and late teens, together with men in their early twenties, remained the focus of activity and concern on the part of both the law-enforcement agencies and public opinion in general. There is some evidence that later in the nineteenth century the average age of those committing more serious crimes was rising. The prison population grew older in this period, although this in part reflected the success of attempts to find alternative means of punishing younger offenders. However, the courts were dealing with an increasing volume of prosecutions of juveniles for lesser offences, and the compilation of more precise age-related statistics from the mid-1890s onwards revealed large disparities between sections of the population. In the late 1920s, the highest incidence of males found guilty of indictable offences was in the 14–16 age group, at 628 per 100,000. This proportion was 50 per cent higher than that of the 21–30 group and four times larger than that of the over 30s. And whereas the level of convictions rose only slightly for all men over 20 throughout the subsequent crisis of unemployment, it almost doubled for those in their mid-teens. By the 1950s, two-thirds of convictions for indictable offences were of men under 30, and half were of juveniles under 21.

There is no reason to suppose that encounters between the young and the prevailing forces of law and order were in any way unique to the later nineteenth and early twentieth centuries. For this area of criminal behaviour, more than any other, the dramatic changes were in perception, labelling and the legal process. So great was the increase in complaint and activity that the most important association between crime and the young tends to be overlooked. In Victorian Kent, 43 per cent of all homicide victims were under the age of 12. Just over half of these were cases of infanticide, while the remainder lost their lives as they struggled to grow up. By contrast, in 1994 only one in eight homicide cases involved a child under 16 and there were only two cases of infanticide in the whole of England and Wales. In the later Victorian era, sexual abuse took place on an immeasurable scale, in the countryside as well as in the overcrowded slums; day in and day out there was casual violence from parents, older children and employers. The gradual reduction of child labour and the increasing external intervention in the behaviour of families, especially following the foundation of the National Society for the Prevention of Cruelty to Children in 1889 and the Children Act of 1908, meant that early-twentieth-century children probably had a better chance of growing to adulthood without serious emotional or physical scars than those of any preceding generation.

If, over time, children had less to fear from adults, the reverse was not felt to be true. The publication in 1853 of Mary Carpenter's *Juvenile delinquents – their condition and treatment* marked the culmination of two decades of growing concern about lawbreaking by the very young. Whereas once child-offenders were seen as interchangeable with adults, now they were viewed as doubly the victims of the grown-up world. These "ownerless dogs" had been abandoned by their parents and then misunderstood and mistreated by a penal system that traditionally accorded them full responsibility for their actions and moral development. State recognition of reformatory and industrial schools in 1854 and 1857 had set in motion the development of a separate legal process for children, but did little to calm public apprehension. At the end of the nineteenth century a further series of scares and reports culminated in the discovery of the hooligan, and then of the explanatory category of adolescence. In part this was a repackaging of old concerns. The rowdy apprentice had long attracted censure, and the hooligans were lineal descendants of the roughs and street arabs who had preoccupied observers throughout the nineteenth century. In part it was a reflection of the growing tendency to encroach on the responsibility of parents to discipline their offspring. Once mothers and especially fathers were felt to be too lenient for the public good or too savage for the good of the erring child then the work of the police and the courts was bound to increase. Around the turn of the century humanitarian and disciplinary concerns coalesced in a new emphasis on puberty as a period of both licence and vulnerability. Older concepts of sin and temptation, poverty and play were translated into psychological and biological terms that denied young males, and to a lesser extent young females, full responsibility for their actions yet presented them as a particular threat to society. The adolescent was brought on to the stage of crime, older than the child, who as far as possible was removed from the drama, younger than the mature male, whose criminality would decline as he grew older.

This invention involved finding a new explanation for the petty thefts of food, clothing and sometimes toys that had long been committed in the name of want, mischief or greed. It also accelerated the increasing attempts to involve the courts in disciplining activities that once had lain outside the legal process altogether. The young were being brought before magistrates in growing numbers for playing rowdy games, shouting and whistling, throwing snowballs, sliding on wet grass or ice. The bicycle craze of the 1890s involved the young in traffic offences, and it was above all in the street that the dividing line between legality and illegality was drawn and contested. Any adolescent male, and in particular any group of them, were an immediate object of suspicion. Either they should be brought to the attention of the school attendance officer or they should be in the workplace and subject to the authority of employers. On the street they were evading either education or work, or were engaging in forms of learning or money-making that were of long-term benefit neither to them nor to society at large. The difficulty of finding healthy recruits to fight in the Boer War intensified concern about the moral and physical degeneration of those upon whom the future defence of Britain's greatness depended. In an increasingly hostile international environment it was more important than ever that the transition to manhood was accomplished in a purposeful and above all disciplined fashion.

With education compulsory until 12 from 1880, 13 from 1902 and 14 from 1918, attention was concentrated on the myriad of casual occupations through which most working-class children passed on their way to an adult occupation or lack of one. Most of these took them out of doors, as van boys, delivery boys or street traders in every kind of marketable item, by whatever means it had been obtained. It became the task of the police and the courts to distinguish proper from improper occupation, and gainful presence in open places from loitering, drinking, gambling, vandalism and dangerous play. Legislation on child labour, which previously had concentrated on structured employment, was extended to street trading, which after 1919 was prohibited under model by-laws to boys under 15 and girls under 16. The apparent crime wave among the young at the turn of the century was a consequence of a rise in behavioural rather than property offences. Although violence at football matches was already a cause for concern, the incidence of physical assault in public was in decline. The object of fear now was not the specific damage done to individuals and their property, rather the more diffuse but critical harm done to the young themselves and as a consequence to the nation whose future depended on them.

Ironically, the dependence of the crime statistics on variations of perception made it almost impossible to understand the dynamics of change. Hermann Mannheim's classic study *Social aspects of crime in England between the wars* devoted two long chapters to "juvenile delinquency", but could reach no very firm conclusions about why young people broke the law in increasing numbers. He found a third of a sample of Borstal boys had lost a parent, that almost all had received only a basic education and that most had very limited career ambitions; but he recognized that none of these factors amounted to a rigorous explanation. The post-1950 growth in the rates brought into focus the quality of parental discipline, supposedly undermined by the disruption of war. But as the products of the peacetime baby boom reached the age of criminal responsibility and the rate accelerated still further, this factor became redundant. The offspring of the most stable family structures in recorded history were still damaging or purloining property and disturbing the peace in their neighbourhoods and in holiday resorts. Attention once more shifted to the combination of relative prosperity and complete irresponsibility in the late adolescent, which merely took the argument back to where it had been a century earlier, when patterns of youthful consumption were first connected to the fear of crime.

The only consistent feature of the young people who came before the courts was the indigence of their home backgrounds. Whether it was poverty itself or a sudden rise of consumption in the midst of deprivation, there was no doubt that the offenders were drawn from the lower strata of society. An insight into the fragile boundaries between one side of the law and the other in the world of poor children is provided by the recollections of the East End criminal Arthur Harding, born in 1886. Brought up partly by his deserted mother, who had taken to drink, and partly in a Barnardo's home, he ended his schooling with no prospect of gaining entry into a secure trade. So he became, in his own words, "a street Arab, hanging about street corners at night and making a nuisance of myself to the police". Gradually he was drawn into a ritual of conflict with the law. His arrest and then acquittal for obstruction raised both his standing among his fellow loiterers and his visibility to their uniformed enemies. Casual jobs selling newspapers and carrying luggage at Liverpool Street station multiplied opportunities for casual theft, and eventually he was convicted of removing a bale of rags from a wagon. Other members of his family, other children in the neighbourhood came through their late teens and early twenties with their respectability more or less intact. Harding, by contrast, proceeded from street corners to become one of the first of the "Borstal boys". Here he learnt how to be a professional criminal, as also did the leading East End gangster of the next generation, Billy Hill, who gave proper thanks in his *Boss of Britain's underworld* (1955) to this most valuable phase of his education.

Women

The relationship of women to crime, like that of young people, was fundamentally conditioned by perceptions of their identity. But whereas, in the midst of the panic about adolescence, criminality was seen as almost the natural condition of those approaching adulthood, it was held to be the denial of everything that femininity represented. As the cult of domesticity became entrenched during Victoria's reign, the angel of the hearth was charged with special responsibility for the moral wellbeing of her family, and thus of society in general. Her influence was both passive and pervasive. Where her menfolk strove in the public arena, she ruled the home through her gentle, exemplary conduct. Nevertheless she made up four times as large a proportion of the prison population as her successor in the present day. She got drunk in the streets, she sold her body and stole the money of those who bought it, she sold other people's possessions, she forged money when she could not steal it, she committed acts of violence on members of her family and other women in the neighbourhood and, at the beginning of the modern period she constituted 40 per cent of all those charged with murder. A society that prided itself on its celebration of the virtue of women was regarded by European criminologists of the second half of the nineteenth century as possessing the highest proportion of female delinquency.

The conflict between the ideal construct of the domestic manuals and the reality of the penal system arose out of a particular intersection between class and gender. Whereas the vision of nurturing innocence was held to be descriptive of the middle-class woman, it was seen as largely prescriptive in the case of her less prosperous sisters. Respectable women came to court only as victims. Their purses were purloined in the streets, their possessions were stolen by their servants, occasionally they were subject to rape or sexual assault. Poor women, by contrast, appeared as defendants as well as complainants and where they did seek redress for some form of violent attack found it much more difficult to press home their charges within a court system inhabited exclusively by middle-class men. If their behaviour in any way transgressed the domestic and sexual conventions, the legal process was all too ready to attribute to them complicity in their own downfall.

In formal terms, there was complete equality. The offence of rape, now so frequently represented as the defining criminal act against women, had by the nineteenth century been divested of its association with property. It was conceived purely in terms of the physical and emotional suffering of the victim, and where a charge was proved it was treated very seriously. Until 1840, the crime was subject to the death penalty and thereafter attracted long sentences. In practice, if a poor woman was to sustain a case, particularly against an employer, she had first to prove she possessed the virtue she claimed to have lost. A respectable woman, especially if the attacker was her social inferior, would not find herself on the defensive. In her case, it was much more likely that the initial complaint would be proceeded with and less likely that it would be downgraded to assault or dismissed altogether. Even so, the public rehearsal of sexual experience, however involuntary, was humiliating, and for their different reasons both respectable and non-respectable victims of rape had such strong reasons for avoiding the courts that the precise incidence of the crime was impossible to establish. All that can be said is that the published figures were low and remained so. For instance, in Victorian Manchester, the shock city of the era, arrests for serious sexual crimes, including rape, sodomy and bestiality, never exceeded 15 in a year. In Victorian Kent, only five cases of rape a year were proceeded with. Between the wars, the number of rapes known to the police in England and Wales as a whole was around a hundred a year. There was a steady rise after 1945 to about three hundred and fifty a year by the mid-1950s, but even so they represented a tiny proportion of all known crimes. In 1955, rape accounted for just 1.4 per cent of indictable offences against the person, and eight in ten thousand of all indictable offences. Whatever multiplier needs to be applied to these figures to reach the true level, there is little reason to contradict Roy Porter's speculative conclusion, based largely on literary evidence, that fear of rape, at least in open spaces, was not widely experienced by women and did not need to be.

The belief among middle-class observers that by committing crime women unsexed themselves was in some respects borne out by the profile of female criminality in the published tables for the later decades of the nineteenth century. About a fifth of summary convictions for drink and violence were of women, and of those coming before the magistrates just as large a proportion of female defendants as men were charged with assault, and more with drunkenness. The same was true of the indictable offence of simple larceny, although larceny from a person was more of a female speciality as it was closely associated with prostitution. Given the flexibility of prosecuting practice, it is difficult to isolate prostitution from theft, violence or drunkenness. If the women were not themselves inebriated, they frequently made it their business to ply their clients with drink before robbing them with varying degrees of gentleness, leaving the police, who in York constituted their second biggest category of customers, with a range of possible charges. What may be said is that in spite of the moral panics of the period, prostitution constituted only 9 per cent of summary convictions of women in 1870, and thereafter all offences involving physical misconduct declined in significance together. Between the wars there was a steady fall in the number of women coming before the courts, largely accounted for by a further reduction in crimes of drink, sex and violence, and by the fact that few of them were driving motor cars, which were introducing a different combination of injury through aggression or drink or both. By 1930, only eleven hundred prostitutes a year were convicted in England and Wales, a tenth of the pre-war figure. This figure tripled by 1939, but even so remained a minor element of female criminality.

During the last three decades covered by this book, the amount of crime committed by women fluctuated at around a seventh of the male rate, with a slight rise during the Second World War as the men were conscripted. By the end of the period, the pattern of offending was much more distinctive than it had been in the later nineteenth century. Women brought before the courts were now five times less likely than male defendants to have engaged in violence against either persons or property. Nine out of ten convictions were for theft or fraud. Their profile of crime had in a sense become more feminine, but it had also become less domestic. While the two thousand recorded crimes of violence mostly occurred in the home, the bulk of their encounters with the law took place in shops or in their places of work. As they encountered a wider range of temptation in larger and better-stocked retail outlets, shoplifting began to become a concern, especially after the introduction of supermarkets and their open shelves. And as women became more widely present in the workplace, so the opportunities for fraud became more numerous. Although prosecuted less often than their menfolk, the chances of falling foul of the law were scarcely negligible. In 1959, statistics began to be collected which permitted the calculation of cumulative conviction risks. These suggested that one woman in twelve was likely to offend during her lifetime, compared with nearly one in three men.

White-collar crime

Most crime hidden from contemporaries and historians alike in this period was not undertaken by the young, nor was it directed against women as such, although as they began to deposit savings and buy shares they came to be numbered among its victims. The phrase "white-collar crime" was coined in the 1940s to describe offences committed by the respectable classes in their occupations. As so often, this was a case of criminology attaching labels to what had long been perceived as a discrete and disturbing problem. Criminality in commerce had a history stretching back to the South Sea Bubble and beyond, but around the middle of the nineteenth century it acquired a new and much more pervasive character. The cause was the second phase of the Industrial Revolution, driven by the railway boom. The need to generate unprecedented sums of capital at very great speed stimulated the emergence of the modern stock exchange and the accompanying structure of company law and limited liability. Legislation between 1855 and 1862 created an arena for promoters, speculators, investors and managers in which those with little competence and less morals could multiply and flourish. Where once coining was seen as the greatest threat to the integrity of the economy, now embezzlement on a vast scale and fraud in ever more ingenious forms threatened the health and reputation of what was becoming the world's leading economy.

Most of the malefactors so far discussed in this chapter were traditional figures in new clothes. It may be argued, however, that men such as the company promoter Albert Grant, whose fraudulent promotion of schemes such as the Emma Silver Mining Company of Utah and the Lisbon Tramways Company financed a career as an MP before his downfall in 1877, were the period's one original contribution to criminal history. They were a product of an intersecting series of developments. The most obvious of these was the sheer buoyancy of the mature industrial economy. The availability of large profits encouraged the dishonest to persist with their schemes in the hope that future gains would conceal past losses, and enticed the gullible to part with their savings for projects whose viability they were all too content to take on trust. The growing sophistication of the commercial infrastructure meant that more and more money was being handled by those who did not own it or who were not directly responsible for putting it to work. Through increasingly complex paper transactions, money was being used to make money, out of the control of those who had invested it, and outside the discipline of the simple profit and loss accounts of the small partnerships that had financed the first phase of the Industrial Revolution. The financial services sucked in a myriad of men for whom breaking the rules was a tactical rather than a moral choice. The standard definition of white-collar crime, that it was committed by "men of respectability", puts the cart before the horse. There were of course reputable officials who fell victim to temptation, such as the 70-year-old secretary of the Canterbury Savings Bank, who was found in 1865 to have quietly embezzled £9,300 over the previous twenty-five years, but for many fraud was not the ill-judged betrayal of respectability but the calculated path towards it. At the upper end of the spectrum were men like Sadlier and the great railway promoter George Hudson, who built careers in politics and high society out of their illicitly acquired instant wealth. At the lower end were the thousands of ill-paid clerks who misappropriated a few pounds in a desperate attempt to cling on to the lowest rung of the ladder that would lead them out of the working class. It was self-help by the most direct route available.

In the volatile economy, where bankruptcy continually threatened honest and dishonest alike, the risk of exposure seemed well worth taking. For most of the period, the law was outpaced by its enemies. Much of the difficulty stemmed from the novelty of the activity. Either established offences, such as embezzlement, were conducted and concealed by original devices, or entirely new crimes had to be distinguished amid the morass of practices that were merely over-ambitious or mismanaged. Share-rigging, for instance, needed to be defined before it could be punished, as did issuing false prospectuses and failing to keep proper accounts. Committed as it was to the self-acting virtue of *laissez-faire*, the state was slow to admit to the possibility of systemic faults in the new structure of company law. Such improvements as took place during the later part of the nineteenth century were largely a consequence of a growing expertise in management techniques reinforced by the professionalization of accounting. This had the effect of reducing major bank fraud significantly in the final quarter of the century, but it had little impact on the share market. The first major legal reform came in 1900, when more rigorous controls over the contents of prospectuses and balance sheets were established, and new regulations introduced over the issuing and ownership of shares by company directors. The legislation improved the quality of information available to investors but still left those in charge of their money with far more latitude than was enjoyed in any other European state. None of the changes had much impact, for instance, on the career of William Preston, a university-educated solicitor's son who received sentences for forgery in 1894, 1902 and 1910: he was still busy issuing bogus shares in 1930. Not until 1948 did Britain's regulatory system come into line with the other advanced economies, and only then did Scotland Yard set up its Fraud Squad to deal with commercial crime.

The tardy and ineffective response of the legal system partly explains the double standard in polite society's response to financial malpractice. On the one hand, the problem of crime was conceived of in terms of the activities of a semi-barbaric criminal class which infested the slums of the urban centres and preyed on the property of respectable outsiders. On the other hand, the deeds of the early railway crooks and of the swindler and journalist Horatio Bottomley, whose career, like those of several before him, encompassed both parliament and prison, attracted immense public interest. The City of London, which lay at the heart of Britain's international economic power, was generally regarded, especially in the period of its greatest growth in the second half of the nineteenth century, as a nest of improper practices ranging from the incompetent to the totally dishonest. But however immoral and threatening to the country's reputation and prosperity, such activities occupied a compartment separate from the humdrum larcenies and assaults that preoccupied penal reformers. As Canon Horsley observed in his study *How criminals are made and prevented* (1913), the connections were never made: "in none of the books on crime and its causes which I possess is there any mention of a low standard of commercial morality as a great cause of offences against property". White-collar crime did not fill the statistical returns because much of it was either dealt with by civil rather than criminal prosecutions or concealed altogether in order not to damage confidence in the firms which had suffered the loss. The figures rose steadily throughout Victoria's reign, but in the early twentieth century only about a thousand criminal cases a year involved embezzlement and another three thousand various forms of fraud and bankruptcy offences. And it did not feature in the tables because the real cause of concern was not the scale of villainy but the volume of suffering. In cases of burglary or violence, there was a roughly one-to-one ratio between criminal and victim, but where sums equivalent in today's values to tens of millions of pounds were misappropriated, one individual could destroy the savings of many thousands of small investors. If the incidence of burglary highlighted the criminality of all the labouring poor, the occurrence of fraud emphasized the vulnerability of all the propertied classes. Capitalism required a different scale of measurement to estimate its malfunction.

Poverty

As long as crime was conceived of as a matter of figures, there was little to be gained from counting its respectable component. Sindall's attempt to prove that there were more middle-class criminals than working-class in the late-Victorian period, and that they stole more money, rests on a shaky statistical base and misses much of the point. It may be true, but we cannot know it and the past society would not comprehend it. The problem for the agencies of law and order was the nature of the relation between deprivation and crime. As the vast majority of those who came before the courts were from poor backgrounds, the question was whether moral failure caused or was caused by their poverty, and whether the misappropriation of other people's goods was undertaken out of need or greed. These questions are so walled in by contemporary perceptions and definitions as to resist historical analysis, but it is possible to generate some limited insights from the available evidence.

The nineteenth century provides apparent support for the argument that dearth caused crime. Until about 1850 the figures for crime, scanty as they were, moved in inverse relationship to the trade cycle, and as the long Victorian boom set in, so the rate of convictions began to fall. Within any given year through to the end of the period, the incidence of property crime was higher when the weather was colder and the need greatest for small items of clothing, food and fuel, which comprised the bulk of stolen property. Conversely, drink-related violence peaked in the long hot summer evenings. Over the period as a whole, however, the fluctuations suggest that deprivation was losing its explanatory power. During the second half of the nineteenth century, the rates were much less consistently vulnerable to downturns in the economy than once they had been, and while the levels did indeed begin to rise in the midst of the Great Depression they were, in the early 1930s, far less volatile than the numbers of unemployed. As a contemporary observer of the recession-hit northeast noted, "one of the most remarkable features of the post-war depression has been the absence of serious crime among unemployed workers". The increasingly sharp climb in the graph in the 1950s coincided with the virtual abolition of unemployment and sent commentators off in search of prosperity rather than poverty as the underlying factor. Now it was not the absence of goods but their plenitude that was destroying respect for property. Either material gratification was so easily available as to undermine the self-discipline once required to earn it, or there was simply so much to steal in shops and homes as to overwhelm with temptation members of an increasingly individualistic society.

It is not just the poverty of the statistics that qualifies this simple transition in causation. At the outset, the model confuses the direction of fluctuation with its total scale. During all the great crises of the industrializing economy, from the post-Napoleonic War depression to the Wall Street crash more than a century later, the most striking feature of the recorded crime rates is their inertia. Whatever their impact on public disorder, which will be discussed in a later chapter, the short-term sufferings of the propertyless did not provoke a wholesale collapse of respect for the rights of the propertied. This was partly because of the consistent youthfulness of the offending population. In both the Victorian and interwar periods, there is evidence that the loss of job prospects and pressure on the family economy together did further increase the criminality of teenagers. But adults who became unemployed were usually too embedded in structures of respectable behaviour to respond to their difficulties by turning to crime on a large scale. This was especially true of those who frequently were the greatest victims of recession, the late-middle-aged, who took longest to find their way back into the economy, and might never do so. A law-abiding 50-year-old was not likely to turn to burglary to avoid the workhouse or eke out his dole.

The inertia also reflected the sheer ubiquity of poverty among the labouring population, from whose ranks most of the prison population was recruited throughout the period. The question of the relation between unemployment and crime could not properly be asked before the 1920s, because until the coming of unemployment insurance there was no precise means of distinguishing those with work from those without. Periodic underemployment and idleness were the lot of even the most skilled artisans; few working-class family economies were insulated from the life-cycle of troughs and temporary recoveries identified by Rowntree in 1901. In this context, the incidence of secular depressions were of relative insignificance. What mattered was the persistence of deprivation and its continuing association with crime. The underlying continuity of behaviour can best be demonstrated by the content of the property crimes that made up the bulk of the statistics. As had been the case during all the centuries covered by this book, the objects that were stolen were mostly trivial items of food and clothing or household possessions with little resale value. The exact nature of the goods inevitably varied as patterns of distribution and consumption evolved, but as late as 1955 one larceny in a hundred was so petty as to be literally worthless. In the midst of the burgeoning consumer society, almost a third of such offences involved property valued at less than a pound, and two-thirds less than five pounds. The poverty of ambition or skill of most of those brought before the courts reflected their general indigence. If it was need, the thief had to be genuinely desperate; if it was greed, then some other term has to be invented to describe the behaviour of those who were embezzling huge sums from companies and banks.

The factors of youth and poverty also undermine the main explanatory category of the first phase of modern penal theory, that of a sharply delineated criminal class. The widespread belief that the principal challenge to law and order was posed by a subculture within the working class served to deflect attention from larger and more intransigent questions of economic and social justice. If the problem was not the poor in general but merely those brought up to habits of vice by their already degenerate parents, then punitive or remedial activity could be confined to policing, remoralizing or eventually demolishing the slums in which they lived. That crime was largely the province of professional criminals was in the first instance contradicted by the varied ages of those who came before the courts. The sharp rise to a peak around the ages of 13 and 14 and the accelerating fall with the onset of manhood, meant that lawbreaking was a phase, in some cases perhaps a rite of passage, for a great many who subsequently settled down to a law-abiding existence throughout the remainder of their adult lives. The working-class communities were full of men, and to a lesser extent women, with a past but no future in the criminal records.

There was, of course, an association between bad housing and crime, and slum clearance may have helped to reduce the rates, although by the time the programme was gaining momentum in the 1930s the graphs were beginning to rise once more. Equally there were career criminals, possessed of their own conventions, rules of conduct and thieves' cant. The culture of the underworld, which had fascinated polite society for centuries, was revisited for the mid-nineteenth-century middle class by Henry Mayhew. Thereafter, there was a temptation to act the part for each new generation of journalists and publishers, but men like Arthur Harding and Billy Hill, although tempted into respectability later in life, had undoubtedly seen crime as an occupation, had worked in the company of other professionals and, as with any skilled artisan, had prided themselves on the combination of tradition and innovation in their calling. And as in the world of labour, there was a development towards more sophisticated organization; the Messina brothers, for instance, diversified from vice to property ownership between the wars. Such gang-leaders were a real threat, but not much of an explanation. Most of what came to be termed after 1880 as recidivists were not full-time bank robbers but pathetic serial drunks and incontinent petty thieves. The most precise calculations made at the end of the period, using five or more indictable offences as a yardstick, could identify a little under ten thousand serious offenders in England and Wales.

The persistent criminal for the most part stole the same things as the occasional amateur, and both came from much the same background as those who resisted temptation or discovery. Among young men in particular, as among young women who drifted into and out of prostitution, the wall dividing the criminal from the non-criminal was far less solid than most observers liked to believe. This much has become clear from the careful work undertaken by historians in recent years, but in conclusion to this chapter it should be noted that such findings have merely opened up a new set of research questions. While the notion of an enclosed criminal class may no longer be sustainable, nor is a model of working-class society that sees going on the streets or mugging a passer-by as being as inconsequential an act as borrowing a cup of sugar or cadging a cigarette. We know from other studies of working-class cultures that the barriers of respectability ran right down through the homes and streets of the urban poor. The poverty-driven but entirely legal act of visiting the pawnbroker, for instance, was permeated by evasion, subterfuge and loss of face. In Walter Greenwood's *Love on the dole*, prostitution and theft are treated with radical sympathy and understanding, but the drama of the novel, and subsequent play and film, revolves around the breach in domestic and neighbourhood conventions that such actions implied. Just where these lines were drawn in the case of crime, how far they varied according to the period, the nature of the offence, the type of community, the degree of poverty, the age and sex of the offender, and what the consequences were of crossing them – all require much further study. Some light on these important issues of popular perception and practice can, however, be cast by looking more closely at purely behavioural offences and at the systems of policing and punishment, which will be the concerns of the final three chapters.

Chapter 13
Bad behaviour

Victimless crime

For the greater part of the modern period, most policemen spent most of their time trying to make people behave themselves. Until the invention of the motor car, their target was mainly the labouring poor, but as the roads gradually filled with careless, speeding or drunken drivers, so increasing numbers of the respectable classes came to their attention. The growth of what is loosely termed victimless crime was a characteristic of the age. The forces of the law had always had a concern with order, but not until the middle decades of the nineteenth century did the ambition extend to controlling all public spaces, particularly in towns and cities. In earlier times, disorder attracted concerted attention only when it directly threatened the possessions or wellbeing of the propertied. Now order was seen as an end in itself. The educated classes had a right not to encounter immoral behaviour as they went about their business but a responsibility to rescue the less educated from the consequences of their excesses. The concept of victim was enlarged from the particular and the immediate to the general and the potential. Drunkenness, vagrancy, prostitution and gambling and, later homosexuality, drug-taking and bad driving were stigmatized for the danger they posed to civilization at large or for the harm they might do to families, innocent bystanders or the perpetrators themselves.

This is a history of the growth of bureaucratic morality, which resulted in a large increase in the work of the courts and in the range of people who came before them and caused the expulsion of a variety of practices from the public to the private sphere. There was a long-term growth in the authority of the state over personal conduct and in the range of agencies and specialized groups that enforced it. Behind these more general developments, however, lay a series of complex negotiations and adjustments. In practice, the state intervened unevenly and often uncertainly, with varied and not always predictable results. The courts and the police were not always working to the same agenda or in accordance with the demands of a succession of political campaigners and social purity groups in various manifestations. Throughout the modern period the police, especially those on the beat, were less concerned about public morality than most reformers and more about traditional issues of public order. There was a continuing debate about what the law could do and what it had achieved. As the man on the beat always knew but his masters often forgot, effective intervention was conditioned as much by what the neighbourhood as the state perceived to be legitimate. The subjects of the increasing intervention sometimes met the objectives of the legislation for reasons other than the law itself and sometimes so frustrated them as to force a law's eventual repeal. The trajectories of each category of behaviour were so varied that they resist simple generalization, but each illuminated important aspects of the evolving relationship between the police and the policed in this period.

Drink

At the outset of the modern period drunkenness was seen as the defining problem. The excessive consumption of alcohol exemplified the responsibility of the poor for their failings and dramatized the threat they posed to the rest of society. Intervention was required to break the culture of moral deprivation that enveloped each succeeding generation and to undermine the structure of criminal activity, much of which was thought to be directly or indirectly inspired by drink. There was, however, little prospect of outright prohibition, except in the very small number of industrial settlements. On the one hand, it would destroy for ever what chance the new police had of gaining acceptance in the working-class communities. On the other, the politico-brewing complex was too powerful, and the dependency of the state on excise duty too great. At the beginning of the final quarter of the nineteenth century, as recorded alcohol consumption reached its all-time peak, 43 per cent of national revenue was derived from the sale of drink. Thereafter the proportion declined as consumers found more diverse ways of spending their money and the state introduced more varied means of extracting it. None the less, as late as 1939, one pound in every eight of taxation was derived from this source.

Rather than banning alcohol, the state settled for attacking the way it was drunk. Until 1872 mere inebriation was not an offence. However, the Licensing Act imposed penalties for being drunk or disorderly, rather than both together, and for being in charge of a vehicle or a firearm while under the influence. At the same time, the police were encouraged to be much more rigorous in their application of the law. No longer were wheelbarrows kept at stations to convey the incapable back to their homes. Once, only persistent offenders were taken to court; now there were fewer warnings and more prosecutions. Just as the figures for total consumption were complicated by the shift from home to commercial brewing, so those for drunkenness were conditioned by changes in the behaviour of the law enforcers as well as of the lawbreakers. Whatever qualifications need to be made, the published statistics offered little comfort to the teetotal movement after three decades of agitation. The number of summary convictions relating to the excessive consumption of alcohol was three times higher in the mid-1870s than it had been two decades earlier. This growth occurred at a time when the incidence of other offences was beginning to fall, and by 1870 a quarter of the work of the magistrates involved drink in some form. The police spent an increasing proportion of their time dealing with drunks in the street and supervising the conduct of public houses, whose opening hours had been restricted on Sundays in 1839 and at night in 1864. So much contact with drink and its victims increased both work and temptation. Most of the dismissals of police in this period were for sharing in the practices they were supposed to be controlling. Occasionally members of respectable society so completely or persistently disgraced themselves as to make it impossible for the police to ignore them, but the principal target of the increased activity were those who had to go out to find drink and comfortable surroundings in which to consume it and who had neither horse nor servant to help them get back again. As long as the streets were quiet, how much was drunk inside the home, and with what consequences, was of no concern to the law.

The gradual fall in per capita convictions after 1875, punctuated by increases following good years in the economy, suggested that the campaign against public drunkenness was beginning to have some effect. It is likely, however, that the police were pushing at a door which was opening of its own accord. Once the licensed premises had been the principal sources of warmth, light, sociability, jobs, news and amusement; now the more mature urban centres were developing a wider and more specialized range of facilities. New forms of mass entertainment and organized sport emerged, finding and being paid for work became less closely associated with consuming alcohol, and the holiday industry began to tap a working-class market. Although Thomas Cook's first railway excursion was for a temperance outing, few of these new diversions were entirely dry. Nevertheless, getting plastered was more often the occasional by-product of spending money on a good time than its central objective. There were journeys to make through the streets other than to the nearest pub, and the rolling, rowdy drunk became more noticeable to his neighbours as well as to the police. At the same time, and for connected reasons, crimes of violence were declining. Gradually the open urban spaces were getting quieter.

The First World War accelerated the decline (although it increased the use of cocaine). Those drinkers who were not in the trenches faced higher prices, yet more dilution of their pints and, from 1915, day-time closing hours. It can be argued that here, as in other aspects of the consumption of food and drink, the war saved lives, especially in respect of the alcohol-induced neglect or smothering of young children. Peace was celebrated in the time-honoured fashion, but convictions for drunkenness climbed back to 80,000 a year, half the pre-war level. Whereas once unemployment and alcohol consumption had been inversely related, both fell in the 1920s, after the short post-war crisis was over. The onset of the Great Depression intensified the decline, and although the economic recovery later in the 1930s produced a rise in all categories of convictions, the rate for drunkenness in 1939 was still only a quarter of the Edwardian figure.

Beneath the aggregate patterns, subtle changes were taking place, presaging the emergence of modern patterns of alcohol abuse. While the towns were generally more drunken than the countryside, gradually the pre-eminence of the north of England and inner London was being challenged by the affluent, suburban Home Counties. As women began to leave the home in increasing numbers to earn money and spend it, concern was growing about their drinking habits, although the proportion of women convicted was less than 20 per cent of the total. With more drinkers using cars to get to the pub, convictions for drunken driving were beginning to show up in the returns, the numbers rising from two thousand in 1933 to three thousand in 1937. By the mid-1950s, summary convictions for drunkenness were 50 per cent higher than before the Second World War and still rising; however, because of the explosion in motoring offences, their significance in the work of magistrates' courts was steadily falling. For every drunkard brought before the bench, seven drivers were prosecuted. The problem of undisciplined behaviour in the streets and highways was taking on a new form.

Vagrancy

In the later decades of the nineteenth century, vagrancy was seen as almost as great an evil as drunkenness, and in some ways a more complex one. The Vagrancy Act of 1824 had, in common with other reforms of the decade, reduced some of the more draconian punishments associated with the offence, but extended its scope. The police had powers to arrest a wide variety of undesirables found loitering in the streets, ranging from beggars and tramps to fortune-tellers, unlicensed pedlars, Poor Law offenders, riotous prostitutes, sellers of obscene literature and persons suspected of intending to commit more serious crimes. By and large, it was not work the police enjoyed. They could use the legislation to take out their feelings on the most helpless or troublesome of their customers, but they resented the time spent arresting and charging those who would be back committing the same offence once a pointless period of imprisonment was completed. They found themselves caught between unpredictable surges of sympathy for down-and-outs on the part of the public or magistrates, and irrational outbreaks of hostility on the part of MPs and senior officers which resulted in periodic purges on the streets. The relation between the official returns and actual practice was further complicated by the intervention of charities that attempted to find non-statutory solutions to the problems, but such figures as are available suggest that each year up to 1914 between five and twelve thousand tramps were prosecuted for sleeping rough; about twice as many beggars were prosecuted. The arrests of those demanding money were more volatile than those of tramps, partly because begging was more responsive to economic depression and partly because attitudes were more variable towards those who actively pestered passers-by.

In practice, the distinction between drunks and vagrants was often arbitrary, and the two groups performed a similar function in clogging up the legal system with men and sometimes women who were more of a danger to themselves than to the public at large. At the beginning of the twentieth century, 30 per cent of all males in English prisons were "without fixed abode and with no regular means of subsistence"; about half of them were birds of passage charged specifically under the Vagrancy Act. After the First World War, the profiles of the two categories of offence were very similar. As for drunkenness, prosecutions for begging and sleeping out recovered after a wartime slump but never regained Edwardian levels. And as with property crimes, the most striking feature of the vagrancy offences was how relatively unresponsive they were to the Depression. Either the unemployed stayed at home, or they were accommodated in casual wards in what was left of the Poor Law system. Orwell noted in *The road to Wigan Pier* that, "in the industrial towns the old communal way of life has not yet broken up, tradition is still strong and almost everyone has a family – potentially, therefore, a house. In a town of 50,000 or 100,000 inhabitants there is no casual and as it were unaccounted population; nobody sleeping in the streets for instance." A reform of the Vagrancy Act in 1935 confined the law to those persistently refusing the offer of a bed or directly causing a nuisance. Mere sleeping-out ceased to be a crime. Prosecutions for begging remained well below the early-twentieth-century figures. At the end of the period, barely a thousand tramps and beggars a year were being brought before the courts. As campaigns in the 1960s were to demonstrate, homelessness and destitution had not been abolished, but for the most part they were for the welfare system not the police to deal with.

Prostitution

In the absence of specific legislation, the third main social problem of the period, prostitution, was initially dealt with as an instance of one of the other two. It was far from uncommon for the "unfortunate" to be drunk, and if sober then she was open to the charge of loitering in the street. Despite the rising tide of concern about sexual misconduct, the police approached the problem as a matter of public order rather than of private morality. Brothels were usually raided only when activities inside the house or in the street outside annoyed the neighbours, or when some additional offence was suspected, such as the robbery of clients or the serious mistreatment of the women who worked there. Discreet transactions between the well-born and the highly paid were not likely to attract the attention of the police, whatever the view of the Church and a growing band of moral investigators. It might be the case, as was widely believed, that the incidence of prostitution was rising as the towns and cities expanded and that the future of family life was thereby imperilled, but both the police and parliament were reluctant to move directly against it. All sex outside marriage was wrong, but it was illegal only if it disturbed the peace.

The number of reports and investigations multiplied around the middle of the century, but their conclusions were so conditioned by prior assumptions as to tell us a great deal more about the observers than about the observed. However, recent work by historians, concentrating on those who were brought before the courts, has done much to dispel the myths that surrounded the problem. In many respects, the findings endorse the practice of the police of placing streetwalkers under the headings of drink and vagrancy. As with most men convicted for such offences, their essential characteristic was not their immorality but their poverty. They were on the streets because their homes were too squalid to support any sort of business activity, and they drank because their lives were too harsh to offer any other kind of reliable comfort. Although the numbers are impossible to quantify, some may have been attracted to the profession by the prospect of easy living, and a few may have enjoyed a level of financial independence and personal autonomy denied to their sisters in any level of society. But rather than concentrate on the contrast between fine clothes and low morals that so scandalized respectable commentators, it is more appropriate to place the prostitutes in the context of the strategies of the poor in general. Throughout the period covered by Part III, those without an adequate, regular source of income instinctively turned to the nearest available form of private enterprise. The most active capitalists in the late-Victorian economy and beyond were those who were its greatest victims. Under-employed men and ill-supported women roamed through the interstices of the economy, making and bartering whatever they could and, in the absence of any other product or skill, selling their bodies when purchasers could be found. Prostitution was an applied form of penny capitalism. Always there was a prospect or at least a dream of comparative wealth, almost always there was the reality of hunger and insecurity, reinforced in the case of the streetwalkers by disease and physical mistreatment. Those who responded to the urban missionaries who went among them were looking not for forgiveness but a square meal. The attraction of the moral reclamation programmes was the pathway offered to a more secure form of income.

For these reasons, there is evidence of considerable mobility in and out of the ranks of prostitution. Some reappeared in the courts time after time, but others went back to occupations such as dressmaking from which they had been temporarily detached by a depression in the trade. The line within working-class society was not so much between the decent and the indecent, but between those who could afford to keep their financial affairs private and those compelled to adopt a range of shameful devices openly, of which prostitution was one, pawning possessions another, and entering the workhouse probably the worst. By the same measure, streetwalkers were accepted in communities where everyone's affairs were forced into the open, tolerated where some attempts were still being made to preserve privacy and ostracized where working-class families were prosperous enough to keep themselves to themselves. The loss of status was confirmed by the kind of men who purchased their services. Rich young libertines and philandering middle-class husbands were a real but comparatively insignificant presence in the market. Most clients were poor men paying very small sums to even poorer women. Serious money was usually available only when some farm labourer came hopefully into town with his harvest pay in his pocket. Plied with drink and relieved of his clothes, he was liable to lose more than his virtue. Inexperience and ill-judgement were more important defects than immorality and more likely to land the client in court as a plaintiff.

Magistrates were not always sympathetic to such gullible hayseeds and indeed for the first two-thirds of the nineteenth century were little interested in the business of buying sex. The first category of client to excite specific legal intervention was members of the armed forces. The Contagious Diseases Acts of 1864, 1866 and 1869 were in part a reaction to the shortcomings of the army in the Crimea a decade earlier. The fear that fighting men might not be fit enough to defend the British Empire was to be a recurrent theme of social and legal reform for the next half century. Where later the concern was of more general forms of physical or moral weakness, here the focus was on venereal disease. The acts empowered special plain-clothes police officers in garrison towns to arrest any suspected prostitute, compel her to undergo an internal examination and, if she were found to be diseased, imprison her in a locked ward until she was pronounced cured. The significance of the acts lies less in their impact on the targeted clients, who, if nothing else, soon learned to patronize the brothels on the day after medical inspections, and more in the opposition they engendered. In 1886 the acts were repealed as a result of a powerful campaign led by Josephine Butler, which combined a deep moral conservatism with a radical assertion of women's rights. On the one hand, the prostitutes were presented as passive victims of male lust, and the monogamous marriage was celebrated as the only location for sexual intercourse. On the other, the legislation was attacked as an extreme version of the double standards that characterized the treatment of women in Victorian society. The prostitutes were being penalized for their own misfortune, while the men who seduced and infected them and who might also be infecting their innocent wives were left unpunished.

Extending the sanctions to the clients as well as to the prostitutes was never seriously contemplated. Throughout the period, the law was applied to every aspect of the problem except the right of men and women to engage in sex for money. Greater protection was given to women and especially to young girls who were thought to be vulnerable to physical or moral coercion. The raising of the age of consent from 12 to 13 in 1875 and to 16 in 1885 was associated with a campaign about white slaves, and further legislation in 1898, 1912 and 1922 sought to deal with the manipulation of prostitutes by procurers, pimps and brothel keepers. The principal effect of police activity was to shift the location of off-street prostitution from brothels to apartments and the focus of censure from the women to those who lived off their labours. The central issue remained the public incitement to immorality. As poverty diminished and women began to experience a wider range of economic opportunities, the volume of prostitution and the incidence of prosecution fell, the latter reaching its lowest point in the middle of the inter-war period. Thereafter, convictions for street offences began to rise, slowly at first but with increasing speed from the late 1940s. The interaction between growing police vigilance and mounting public alarm culminated in the Street Offences Act of 1959, which systematized and extended penalties for outdoor soliciting. The clients were still free, and the prostitutes were still more exposed to concealed commercial exploitation.

Gambling

The final member of the quartet of offences against public order and morality shared many characteristics of the other three. Gambling first became an object of inquiry and censure at the same time as drink and prostitution and thereafter became a significant part of the workload of the new police forces, especially in the urban areas. The Betting Houses Act of 1853 had attempted to prohibit ready-money gambling with bookmakers, and further legislation in 1874 and especially in 1906 sought to deal with the growing volume of street betting. Hostility to the practice derived from a familiar combination of moral criticism of unearned, irrational gratification and social concern about the consequences of diverting money away from the family economy and attention away from the workplace.

The element of class discrimination was more blatant than in any other form of misbehaviour. As Charles Muir noted in 1936,

> the general effect of the betting laws is that a man who has a telephone and credit or can personally attend racecourses may bet with impunity, whereas a man who has not those facilities but

engages in exactly similar transactions for cash in a street or "resort" is guilty of a criminal offence. This is a clear case of one law for the rich and another for the poor and is difficult to justify.

It was far from unknown for a magistrate to convict a series of street book-makers and then retire to place his own long-distance bets. The illegal practices were inextricably bound up with public houses, where bookies rested out of sight while their runners lurked in back alleys collecting bets. The trade in general represented perhaps the most extensive and successful incidence of penny capitalism. Thanks to the law, there were no premises costs to incur and no income tax to pay. It was open to anyone with energy and a head for figures to enter the business, and although many went broke the wealth of figures like Sam Grundy in *Love on the dole* was far from fictional.

There were, nevertheless, critical differences between wagering on the future and more immediate forms of gratification. The most important of these was that the campaigns against drink, vagrancy and prostitution were to a greater or lesser extent moving with the general flow of social and economic change. The growing prosperity and security of working-class families and their homes, the increasing variety and sophistication of urban recreations and the gradual introduction of non-punitive forms of welfare all tended to work with, rather than against, the efforts of police, magistrates and legislators. Although there remained wide areas of tension and conflict, there was some consonance between evolving concepts of respectable behaviour held by the law enforcers and by the working-class communities in which they operated. The reverse was the case with gambling. From the middle of the nineteenth century onwards, the tide of history was running strongly against prohibition, while the state was more and more committed to achieving it. The most important developments were in the field of communication. The rapid growth of the sporting press, together with the application of the electric telegraph, shrank time and space in betting on horse-races. Once the papers began to print starting prices in 1884, factory workers and slum dwellers in the industrial north could rub shoulders with the racegoers at Ascot or Newmarket for the cost of a few pence. It was one of the ironies of the age that the massive investment in elementary education bore fruit just in time to exploit this urgent but unimproving application of literacy. For many of the working class, reading the list of runners and calculating the odds was likely to be the most complex use they would ever make of the skills they had learned in the classroom.

The Street Betting Act of 1906, which replaced a tangled mass of statutes and by-laws, was a response to a general concern about national efficiency and a particular alarm about the remorseless increase in gambling. At this stage senior policemen, fresh from their statistical victories over other categories of crime and misconduct, were eager to apply their new powers. The constables on the beat, however, were always less sanguine about a task that evoked so much hostility and so widespread and ingenious resistance. Bookmakers became so well organized that their scouts would wait with bicycles near police stations and follow those sent out to pursue them. Within two decades, the scepticism of the rank and file had spread throughout the forces. The investment of much time and effort was producing no measurable reduction in the practice and was instead having a discernible effect on the morale and reputation of the police themselves. Failing so obviously to enforce the law undermined their authority, which was damaged still further by frequent cases of corruption. Enforcing moral standards had always threatened the morality of the police, and whereas drunkenness on duty and consorting with prostitutes had declined since the raw early days of the police forces, using and being bribed by bookmakers had not. At the same time the magistrates began to be less zealous, resorting more often to fines than to imprisonment.

The basic problem was the breadth of the public's acceptance of betting. The practice was not confined to a stigmatized and diminishing subculture but spread right through the labouring population, male and female, old and young, at work and at play and up into the white-collar class. Successful bookmakers were respected for their defiance of what was generally considered as an unjust law and thanked for the provision of jobs as runners and look-outs for those down on their occupational fortunes. There was a vein of indigenous censure associated with nonconformity and self-improving socialism, and there was bitter hostility in families wrecked by what now would be recognized as compulsive gambling. But usually the betting was of small sums invested in doubles and trebles designed to yield only fleeting wealth. It was an entertaining, mostly harmless and perfectly rational means of providing small intermissions in the monotony of life. With the rise of dog-racing and in particular the football pools, which by the 1930s were attracting ten million customers a year, all hope of eradicating gambling from the working class disappeared. The only way forward was to transfer the ambition from prohibition to control. That at least would break the worrying but probably overstated link between gambling and organized crime and enable the police to enlarge the sphere of consent within which they operated. After the Second World War, a royal commission confirmed that the law was in disrepute and that the harm caused by gambling was far less than once had been feared. The subsequent Betting and Gaming Act of 1960 finally legalized off-course betting by the mass of the population. Like the Street Offences Act of the previous year, it was designed to clear the open spaces, removing a still somewhat disreputable but seemingly inevitable activity from the public gaze.

Homosexuality

Although their treatment was given a new form in the late-nineteenth century, drunkards, whores, vagrants and gamesters had not been strangers to the legal system before then. In a sense, the first of the three behavioural issues that have come to obsess twentieth-century moralists also had a long history. Buggery was a capital offence from 1533 to 1861 and thereafter attracted a sentence of ten years to life. Special attention had always been paid to it in the armed forces. However, the crime applied equally to acts between men and women and between men and beasts and was seen, like rape or assault, as a momentary aberration rather than a way of life. The category of the homosexual, denoting a discrete group of sexual deviants whose very existence was an affront to public decency, was an invention of the closing decades of Victoria's reign. It entered the legal process via the Labouchere Amendment to the Criminal Law Amendment Act of 1885, which made acts of gross indecency between two men a misdemeanour punishable by up to two years hard labour. The introduction of the lesser offence and sentence made possible a much wider range of prosecution, ensnaring Oscar Wilde ten years later after the failure of his libel action against Lord Queensberry. Unlike the other behavioural legislation of the era, it applied to acts in private as well as in public. Importuning in the street was dealt with separately by a Vagrancy Act of 1898 and another Criminal Law Amendment Act in 1912.

With homosexuality, more than any other form of nominally illegal behaviour, it is extremely difficult to take a measure of the relation between practice and prosecution. Oscar Wilde's two court cases in 1895 were a defining moment. He was struck down at the very height of his fame amid unprecedented press hysteria. His insistence on the right of the artist to set his own moral standards and the exposure of his use of the late-nineteenth-century equivalent of rent-boys entrenched the image of the homosexual as an alien and corrupting figure. The court, staffed by men with compromising memories of their public-school days, declared its outrage at such practices. It was said that six hundred men crossed to France the night Wilde was found guilty, ten times the usual number, and thereafter sexual relations between men were shrouded in fear and secrecy. Those between women were concealed by incomprehension and incredulity. Even when the existence of lesbianism was finally brought to the attention of law-makers in the 1920s, it was felt that to stigmatize the activity would serve only to publicize a deviancy of which most women must be blissfully ignorant. Because their sexuality was held to be essentially passive, there was much less danger that their actions would corrupt the innocent.

In 1912, Havelock Ellis observed that England possessed the most draconian laws against homosexuality, but in contrast to countries such as Germany used them more sparingly. Between the wars, offences of indecency between males known to the police doubled to about three hundred a year, but the figure bore no relation to the impact of the legislation, which from time to time continued to bring the rich and famous into the dock, particularly if they had been consorting with their social inferiors. In the first decade after 1945, the work of the police increased sevenfold, a reflection of increasing official concern at a practice that at the height of the Cold War had become linked to national security. Following a series of spy scandals, particularly that of Guy Burgess, who was unduly fond of both men and the bottle, positive vetting was introduced into the civil service. Homosexual tendencies, however they were recognized, became grounds for exclusion from sensitive work and, in extreme cases, for dismissal. But as with gambling and prostitution, the work of the courts served only to emphasize the impossibility of some final victory. In 1954 an interdepartmental committee was set up under Lord Wolfenden to consider both prostitution and homosexuality. Its report, published three years later, found that, while the practices remained morally wrong, it was sensible to confine police activity to public order and to cases of direct coercion and corruption. That which the law could not prevent was better left to other agencies of education and censure. As hostility to homosexuality ran much deeper than hostility to illicit heterosexual behaviour, it took longer for the state to pluck up its courage to intervene, but in 1967 the Labour Government permitted the passage of a Private Member's Bill which legalized acts between consenting males in private, providing they had reached the age of majority. Public indecency remained a crime and was prosecuted with increased vigour.

Drugs

The consumption of drugs initially had much in common with drink. It was an everyday, unremarkable practice, engaged in by men and women from all walks of life. Opium was available from any corner shop in a host of forms. It was made up into pills, lozenges, plasters, liniments, enemas, sweets, vinegar, wine and tinctures. It could be bought in a variety of patent medicines claiming to cure or at least relieve the symptoms of a wide range of ailments. Children were sent out to buy it for their parents and, in the form of preparations such as Godfrey's Cordial, it was given to fractious or hungry babies to quieten their crying. Like alcohol, its use straddled the recreational and the therapeutic fields. Laudanum (the alcoholic tincture of opium) would be found in any medicine chest, to be taken to relieve both physical and mental stress. For the labouring population it was a cheap alternative to official medicine and a welcome antidote to the pains of physical toil. A pennyworth of opium would in many cases do as much good as the doctor with his fees and more expensive prescriptions. For the educated classes, both male and female, the drug was employed as an unstigmatized relaxant. Its famous users included not only the romantic poets but such pillars of Victorian respectability as Florence Nightingale and William Gladstone.

One of the claimed applications of opium was as an antidote to the delirium tremens. In the middle of the nineteenth century, there was no recognized condition of excessive dependency, and no record of users threatening public order or disturbing the peace. They were unlikely to congregate together in a threatening manner, but tended to consume their purchases at home where the lawmakers wished them to be. When under the influence they did not assault each other, or the police, or their wives. Yet whereas the sale of drink was subject only to a permissive system of licensing the sale of drugs was gradually excluded from the free market altogether. The influential Society for the Study of Inebriety, founded by Dr Norman Kerr in 1884, saw alcohol and drugs as differing forms of the same problem of intemperance, but only the latter was coming under strict supervision. The initial cause of the divergent paths of criminalization was the structure of manufacture and distribution. From the eighteenth century onwards, the drink industry was at the leading edge of developments in mass production and sale. From the great brewers wielding their influence in parliament to the myriad of licensees who sold their products, alcohol represented capitalism at its most energetic and aggressive. Drugs, by contrast, occupied a territory contested by commerce and medicine. On the one side, the patent-medicine vendors embodied the more imaginative and less scrupulous aspect of Victorian enterprise. On the other, doctors and pharmacists were coming to see the control of drugs as integral to their professional development.

Legislative interference began with the Poisons and Pharmacy Act of 1868. This restricted the sale of dangerous substances and required that less harmful drugs, including opium, should be labelled as poisons. As the act excluded patent preparations, which like alcohol were a source of government revenue, its impact on levels of consumption was negligible. Its importance lay rather in the assertion of responsibility. The pharmacists, who had gained legal recognition in 1852, staked a claim to authority over drugs. Without their intervention, the market could not be trusted to supply a safe product, and the customer could not be relied upon to consume it sensibly. Public-health statistics were deployed to raise fears about the adulteration of drugs, their use in suicides and the incidence of accidental overdosing, particularly of very young children. A broader concern for the conduct of working-class families was given a scientific twist by an emerging medical profession anxious to reduce the sphere of self-doctoring. For the time being, however, the police and the courts had little role to play. The path to drugs raids and banner headlines lay through the discovery of the addict. In the final quarter of the nineteenth century, the debate shifted from the substances to the users. Attention was focused on the consumption of morphine, an alkaloid of opium, taken initially under medical instruction by means of the newly introduced hypodermic needle. A growing body of research into the obsessive consumption of both alcohol and narcotics was given added urgency in the case of a substance that doctors had promoted and were indeed themselves using on a disturbing scale. At this stage, addiction was conceived of as a physical reaction giving rise to a moral breakdown. It was to be countered by controlling supply where possible and exposing sufferers to systematic exhortation and re-education. The 1890 Lunacy Act included drug addiction as grounds for official guardianship. Once opium and its derivatives were a means of medical intervention; now they were coming to be seen as a justification for it. At the end of the century, cocaine began a similar transition from promising anaesthetic to dependency-inducing menace.

What finally drove the issue from medical anxiety to public panic was the association of drugs with the corruption of young women. Before and immediately after the First World War, a series of well-publicized tragedies highlighted the supposed vulnerability of unsupervised girls to unscrupulous and usually foreign traffickers. A host of fears about national integrity, so severely shaken by international conflict, and the purity of women, newly threatened by their growing role outside the home, coalesced in the tableau of the drugs den, in which innocent females were divested of their moral and physical health by malevolent suppliers, often of Chinese extraction. The police, who had found it difficult to intervene under the 1868 act despite its extension in 1908, were given more effective powers by the Dangerous Drugs Acts of 1920 and 1923, which consolidated regulations first introduced during the war to protect the fitness of fighting men. The sale of opium, morphine and cocaine was controlled by doctor's prescription, and the import, export and manufacture of the raw drugs were forbidden except under licence. A burst of police activity in London, Liverpool and Cardiff resulted in three hundred cases a year, but once the main supply networks had been broken up the figure fell to below a hundred, half of which involved opium and the remainder morphine and cocaine. In 1926, the medical profession was advised by the Rolleston Report that addiction should be dissociated from vice and treated as a purely physiological condition by a variety of therapeutic interventions, including carefully monitored prescribing. The subsequent low level of prosecutions reflected both the efficacy of the police and the continuing availability of drugs from doctors, as well as what may have been a real fall in consumption during the remainder of the interwar period. In the 1950s public concern was renewed; cannabis, which had been used for medical and recreational purposes for a century, was the new threat, and teenagers replaced young women as the vulnerable population. This time the passage of further legislation in 1965 marked not a reduction in use but the beginning of its steady escalation.

Motoring

Within this period, the amount of public concern about drugs generated little additional work for the legal system. The reverse was the case with the final category of behavioural crime, the range of offences associated with the motor car. In 1900, six years after the first vehicle appeared on the roads, transgressions of the law constituted just four cases in a thousand found guilty in magistrates' courts. By 1930, with a little over two million vehicles on the road, they accounted for 43 per cent of all non-indictable offences and had passed 60 per cent by the time war broke out. Whereas a hundred murders and fourteen hundred felonious or malicious woundings took place each year in the early 1930s, six and a half thousand people were killed on the roads – 50 per cent more than in 1991, despite an eleven-fold increase in registrations – and two hundred thousand were injured. The majority of sufferers were "non-combatants" – cyclists and pedestrians inadequately protected from careless, incompetent and reckless drivers by either road design or the law. In spite of vigorous resistance by the Automobile Association to all legal controls, the internal combustion engine had come to dominate every other category of misbehaviour dealt with by the police and the courts, whether or not a victim was involved. Across the centuries covered by this book, no form of activity had so profound an affect on relations between the law and the public in so short a period.

The most striking change was in the identity of the offender. In general terms, the history of crime and punishment had mainly been one of the propertied directly or indirectly prosecuting and punishing the property-less. To a large extent this had remained the case with the body of legislation that grew up to regulate horse-drawn and then pedal-driven traffic in the Victorian streets. Although an otherwise blameless citizen was occasionally convicted of drunken riding or driving a vehicle "recklessly, negligently or furiously", most of the activity was directed against drivers of commercial vehicles, such as carts or cabs. But as the possession of private cars remained the preserve of the middle and upper classes until after the Second World War, so it was from their ranks that most of the increasing number of defendants was drawn. The speed limit was raised from 4 to 12 miles per hour in 1898 and to 20 in 1904, where it remained until it was abolished in 1930; it was reimposed in 1935 at 30 miles per hour in built-up areas. This meant that as ownership spread into the middle classes during the first three decades of the century, the limit was consistently below the attainable cruising speeds of even the least sophisticated vehicles, making driving almost illegal by definition, rather like drug-taking in contemporary society.

For the first time the police found themselves dealing on a large scale with their social superiors, and magistrates with their social equals. The police in particular found it a disagreeable experience. They were diverted from protecting property to preventing accidents. Boring, cold, noxious hours were spent on busy junctions, until the introduction of traffic lights in the 1930s began to relieve them of this work. They had more traumatic encounters with injury and suffering caused by drivers than ever they did on Saturday nights after the pubs emptied. And when they arrested a transgressor they were met with a mixture of condescension, incredulity, abuse and bribery. Their efforts to set speed traps were frustrated by the Automobile Association, which employed scouts to warn motorists, and those they did arrest were not always treated by the magistrates with the rigour that had been reserved for the traditional, lower-born defendant. In the very early years, rural justices, outraged at the disturbance of the countryside, collaborated with the police in enforcing the law strictly, but as they and their friends became car owners themselves their vigour waned, much to the frustration of pedestrian and cyclist pressure groups. All kinds of excuses were accepted in mitigation, and the penalties caused little pain. In 1938, only eight hundred out of 438,000 convictions resulted in custodial sentences. Offences that had caused death or serious injury rarely attracted more than a small fine.

The only real gain for the police was in relations with the working-class population, who as pedestrians were especially vulnerable to careless or drunken driving. For the first time the literal man in the street could see the uniformed constable making a systematic attempt to protect him and to apply the law across the social divide. In return, he found himself going to the police to give information or to seek redress on a scale that would have been inconceivable a generation earlier. The rise of the motor car dramatized a development that had not been so visible in the fields of drugs and homosexuality, if only because the prosecutions for them had been so much less frequent. When once the increase in behavioural policing had been a means of criminalizing the poor in the name of middle-class respectability, now the process was beginning to operate in reverse. And while the spread of car ownership after the Second World War brought more of the less prosperous into the courts, the later increase in drug-taking further expanded the liability of the privileged, or at least of their children. The courts had scarcely become havens of social equality, but they could no longer be viewed simply as agencies of class control.

Chapter 14

Professional law

Professionalization

Between the County and Borough Police Act of 1856 and the Police Act of 1964, England and Wales gained what was routinely described as the best police force in the world. It was celebrated for its particular combination of political neutrality and civilian restraint. Policemen did not carry guns, they did not favour party interests. They were at once distinct from the communities they served and subject to their control. The reforms that had been set in motion by Peel in 1829 bore fruit in a disciplined force that, at least until the closing years of the interwar period, contained theft and made the streets safer to walk along. The police were an integral element of a drive towards professionalization that embraced not only the men on the beat but the lawyers who conducted the trials and the prison staff who administered the punishment. In this sense the middle decades of the nineteenth century represented a major watershed in the history of crime. Before the reforms, the systems were both amateur and inefficient, in the aftermath, they were remunerated and competent. In the *ancien régime* the line between private and public procedures was essentially blurred; in the modern world there was a clear and necessary distinction between those who enforced the law and the people who paid for their services and reaped the benefit of their labours.

However, as Barbara Weinberger and others have pointed out, care has to be exercised when applying the model of professionalism to the police. In such critical areas as organization, recruitment, training, working methods, ethical standards and general effectiveness, it is not easy to associate the police with either the formal definition or the particular corporate bodies which emerged in the Victorian period. And the wider the gap between the police and the classic professions, the shorter seems the distance between the new forces and the much derided patchwork of parish constables and watchmen they replaced. Just as the crime figures that apparently demonstrated the success of the police can be shown to be at least in part a construction, so the journey from Dogberry to Dixon of Dock Green can be seen more as fiction than fact. There is no simple resolution of this debate, which can be located within the development of the service itself, nowhere more bitterly argued than in the unfinished struggle of chief constables to escape detailed control by lay members of watch committees. But it is

Figure 14.1 Two policemen at Eccleshall, 1907 (copyright
Staffordshire Museum Service).

possible to gain a measure of the nature and scale of change by focusing
attention on two related issues. First, if it is facile to merge the histories of
policemen and lawyers, it is necessary throughout this period to place the
men in uniform in the context of a broader legal system, which included as
active participants not just the other paid functionaries but also members of
the public, both propertied and propertyless, who retained a pivotal role in
the maintenance of law and order. Secondly, if the increasingly elaborate
body of Home Office internal regulations and disciplinary procedures did

mark a real element of differentiation between the new and old constables, it is necessary to pay close attention to the element of discretion that informed law enforcement. Stiff and unbending as he may have seemed as he paced his measured beat in his new uniform, the police constable had to exercise judgement in all that he did. By the same measure, those on whose behalf he was employed had to decide whether and in what way to co-operate with him. How these choices were negotiated influenced both the changing meaning of policing and the criminal statistics that were used to measure its progress.

Careers

The single most important reform of the late nineteenth century concerned not the work of the policeman but how it ended. The case for the disparity between the amateur and professional officer is most clearly displayed in the introduction of a proper pension system by the Police Act of 1890. Since 1839 there had been a variety of superannuation arrangements, but these were too inconsistent and underfunded to represent a predictable benefit. Now there was to be a properly financed scheme, one that guaranteed a pension after 25 years of service or after 15 if the retirement was on medical grounds. This reform had three crucial consequences. In the first place, the replacement of a series of *ad hoc* local arrangements by a single national structure was the most potent statement of the existence of a single police force. Within the reformed structure there were in fact three different kinds of police organization: the Metropolitan Force, answerable to the home secretary; the borough forces, controlled by watch committees made up of councillors; and the county forces, subject to a committee of magistrates until 1888 and thereafter to a mixed body of justices and county councillors. Across this tripartite structure were spread as many as 188 separate forces, reduced by a third in 1946, of widely differing size, culture and responsibilities. During the period, there was a piecemeal growth in the authority of the Home Office, beginning with the powers it acquired in 1856 to inspect forces and withhold grants to those deemed inefficient, and accelerating in times of national crisis, when the interests of the state could more easily override local sensitivities. But, although it was advocated from time to time, the case for a single national force was always resisted, partly in the name of recently invented county and borough traditions and partly in response to a continuing mistrust of central government. The new pension, by contrast, introduced at a stroke a uniformity to conditions of service, guaranteed by the state, which profoundly influenced if not external perceptions then certainly the attitudes of those who had committed their financial wellbeing to the forces. All ex-policemen were now alike, however distinctive their previous employers thought themselves to be.

Secondly, the pensions were the foundation of policing as a career. The early forces had mostly recruited either from the existing bodies of parish constables or from the pool of unskilled or semi-skilled labour. The initial starting salary of around 19s a week was unlikely to tempt many respectable artisans to exchange their independence and status for a uniform and public obloquy, but it represented an attractive prospect for farm workers anxious to escape the confined prospects of the countryside and casual urban workers struggling to keep their jobs for more than a day or two at a time. Few of the new recruits regarded police work as a vocation, still less as a lifelong job. For most it was a temporary refuge from the storms that continually buffeted the lower reaches of the economy, or a shaky stepping-stone on a journey from the country to the town or from the unskilled sector to the skilled. Having survived physical and educational tests more rigorous than for any other manual position except the parallel uniformed occupation of the Post Office, they were then faced with a potent combination of fierce discipline, communal hostility and wide temptation that soon detached from the service all but the most dedicated. Half of Peel's first force were sacked within two years, four-fifths for drunkenness, with a further third leaving of their own accord, and the pattern was repeated as the new borough and county forces were established. There was a gradual improvement as the century wore on, but until the 1890 act, few recruits could be certain of lasting long enough to earn a pension whose existence and value was far from guaranteed. Now, with superannuation set at the attractive level of two-thirds of wages, there was a real incentive to view policing as the central event of a working life. Apart from the other uniformed manual occupations, no trade, however dignified and however prosperous at good times of the year, could offer this level of security from entry to death. Nor was sick-pay generally available until the National Insurance Acts of 1911. There was a marked drop in voluntary resignations immediately after 1890, and the rate of turnover overall, which had begun to fall in the 1870s, continued to decline until it reached five per cent in 1914, where it remained as the interwar rise in unemployment further enhanced the value of a permanent job. Conversely, when the welfare state and the era of full employment arrived, the occupational benefits of police work became less distinctive and the restrictions of uniformed labour began to seem more irksome.

Finally, the pensions consolidated the system of internal discipline. It was crucial to the projected identity of the new forces that the behaviour of their officers embodied a code of conduct that was superior to almost every other occupation in the community they policed. In the private sector, only the railway companies attempted to achieve similar levels of sobriety, timekeeping and obedience. During the early years simply sacking large numbers of recruits did little to achieve this end. With a good chance of finding an equivalent rate of pay elsewhere, and scant prospect of ever gaining a pension, the new officers had little incentive or opportunity to internalize the behavioural norms that their chief constables required of them. Gradually the forces began to develop more sophisticated systems of personnel management. The idea of incremental progression emerged both here and in the other uniformed occupations. The ranks of constable and sergeant were subdivided into separate grades, and an increasingly complex series of regulations controlled movement between them. In place of the drama of sudden death there was established a long game of snakes and ladders, with accumulated virtue leading to good conduct stripes and an extra few shillings a week, and petty infringements to their loss. A proper pension scheme represented the coping stone of this system. An officer with some years of service under his belt had far more to lose by dismissal and was encouraged to concentrate his attention on maintaining his performance until the 25 years were finally completed. The introduction of a modern career structure strengthened the authority of chief constables but at the same time gave the rank and file policemen some sense, however illusory, that they could manage their own progression.

Training

Although the early occupational structure was based on a military model, and most of the nineteenth-century forces were run by former army or naval officers, the guaranteed income for life and the accompanying pattern of incentives and penalties represented a real innovation in the world of manual labour. By the end of the century the distinctiveness of police work went much deeper than the uniform. The longer the career, the more the opportunity of developing a genuine occupational culture, and the closer the service came to the professional model of vocational commitment and ethical performance. It is not, however, possible to generalize from the systems of personnel management to the work of the police as a whole. In the first instance, the constable on the beat remained a working man, with none of the status, privilege or income of the lawyer or doctor. Those recruits who had fled the constrictions of agricultural labour found where and with whom they lived once more subject to surveillance by their employers. Prospects of real promotion beyond the minor incremental advances were slight, and not until the interwar period were chief constables of the provincial forces routinely drawn from serving officers. Attempts to unionize from 1872 onwards provoked an increasingly bitter series of conflicts that culminated in the police strikes of 1918 and 1919. The first represented a temporary victory of the men over a government struggling to come to terms with the ending of the war, the second a catastrophic defeat leading to mass sackings and the installation of an in-house organization, the Police Federation, which was prohibited from ever again withdrawing labour.

More broadly, the business of policing showed nothing like the same degree of progress. At the outset, the police forces and the Post Office were the only manual institutions to impose a formal literacy test on recruits. Constables were required to record their work daily, and those whose command of English was not up to the task were either given additional education or dismissed. In his painstaking copperplate and stilted, formulaic prose, the nineteenth-century policeman probably made more use of the written word than any other product of the elementary schools of the period. There was not, however, a substantive body of abstract professional knowledge to study and be examined on. Induction to the force consisted only of military drill. Once they had learned to march, constables, like all other working men, were expected to pick up their skills on the job. It took half a century for the idea of systematic teaching to take hold. In 1902, a small training unit for detectives was established in Scotland Yard, which led to the opening of the first police training school in London five years later. Between the wars, the larger constabularies began to follow suit, but the smaller forces, with only a handful of new recruits a year, were reluctant to invest in what seemed at best a marginal activity. Not until after 1945 did all entrants to the service have to undergo a period of residential training before setting out to complete their education on the beat. By this time, formal learning was a constituent part of the promotion process. From the 1860s onwards, various forces had introduced tests on educational subjects and police duties for advancement to sergeant and beyond. These qualified the candidates for consideration, the final decision resting on an assessment of character and record. In 1919, qualifying examinations became compulsory throughout the service, but not until 1958 was a serious effort made to ensure conformity of standards between the forces. By this time, preparation for advance to the higher ranks was provided by the National Police College, which was established in 1947.

Technology

The slow and hesitant acceptance of the relevance of paper-based learning was mirrored in the application of technology to policing. It was evident from the beginning that the Industrial Revolution represented a double-edged weapon in the fight against crime. In an economy with an ever increasing volume of cash in circulation, it was far from clear which side stood to gain most from innovation. Coining, an obsessive fear of earlier centuries, at first became more difficult as the Royal Mint developed new techniques, then easier as electroplating introduced new possibilities of home production. An unending struggle began between safe-manufacturers and safe-breakers, with every improvement provoking a new method of circumvention. There were widespread fears that the penny post, which had been introduced in 1840 in an effort to spread the habit of written communication to the lower orders, had merely facilitated the conduct of long-distance criminal conspiracies, and for this reason the Home Office refused to abandon its reserve powers of letter-opening, in spite of a public outcry in 1844. Yet for every forger, safe-breaker and international criminal, there were tens of thousands of petty larcenists and burglars. Across the decades, the bulk of crime was committed by those with the most limited intellectual and physical resources, and by the same measure policing was conducted with the most primitive machinery. Only with the advent of the motor car did technological innovation seriously intrude into the daily routines of the constable on the beat. At first it was an uneven conflict between speeding drivers and policemen who could travel no faster than a horse or a bicycle would take them. Some forces experimented with cars before 1914, but not until the 1920s was serious use made of motorized patrols. Attempts were made to link these by wireless, at first using Morse code, and in 1934 the Metropolitan Force set up an information room to service a grand total of 50 wireless cars.

During the latter part of the nineteenth century, progress was confined to a limited use of new methods of communicating and recording information. From the late 1860s police stations were linked to each other by telegraph although there was still considerable reluctance to embrace the telephone at the end of the century. The basis of a national criminal record system was laid down in 1869 with the creation of the Register of Habitual Criminals, but its effectiveness was severely hampered by the absence of a reliable method of identifying and describing lawbreakers. The camera had been employed almost from the invention of photography, but in the end it was as fallible as the human eye that interpreted the pictures. A series of miscarriages of justice culminated in the scandal of Adolf Beck, who was sentenced to seven years' penal servitude in 1896 after being mistaken at a number of identity parades for a habitual fraudster named John Smith, who was also, as turned out to be relevant, a Jew. The error was eventually exposed when attention was drawn to the fact that Beck had not been circumcised, but this technique of identification scarcely had a wider application. As was often the case in this period, the main advance was made in the colonies. India exemplified the problem of alien policemen identifying unfamiliar faces writ large. As early as 1858, William Herschel had developed a system of fingerprinting to deal with corruption in Bengal, and eventually the possibilities of this method were taken up in Britain by Francis Galton, who published the first scientific study in 1892. In the 1890s, the Metropolitan Police experimented with both fingerprinting and, less successfully, the French system of anthropometry, which based identification on the measurement of body parts. Finally, in 1901, the Inspector-General of Police in Bengal, Sir Edward Henry, was appointed assistant commissioner of the Metropolitan Force and brought his methods across with him, setting up a specialist fingerprint section and remodelling the Habitual Criminal Bureau into the Criminal Record Office, based on what was held to be a foolproof method of identification.

The more direct application of modern science was slower still. The array of techniques with which Conan Doyle equipped Sherlock Holmes remained outside professional policing for another half century. In the early decades of the twentieth century, assistance was increasingly sought from private chemists and pathologists, but not until the arrival in Britain in 1934 of the former Government Chemist of Ceylon, C. T. Symons, were steps taken to set up a properly equipped in-house service. Police laboratories were established at Hendon for the Metropolitan Force and in seven regional centres, but as late as the Second World War, entire counties were being policed without any scientific resources at all. At this stage, some of the smaller forces still lacked a specialized detective section. The modern detective was created in fact and in fiction in the early years of the Metropolitan Force, yet he remained for a long time a minor element in the struggle against crime. Between 1842 and 1868, the number of full-time plain-clothes policemen grew from 8 to just 15, although in the capital, as in the provincial forces, officers could be taken out of uniform to respond to particular problems.

In this respect much was made of the contrast between London and every other European capital city of the time. English civilization was defined by the absence of spies and secret policemen out of uniform. To the extent that other countries depended on hidden surveillance, so they appeared to lag behind the cherished freedoms of the liberal state. Ironically, what finally provoked a major reorganization and expansion of the detectives was the discovery of widespread corruption in this embodiment of national liberty. An increase in plain-clothes men in the early 1870s outstripped the quality of their control, and in 1877 three of the four chief inspectors were convicted and jailed for turf frauds. It had to be admitted that lessons could be learnt from abroad, and, following a study of the Paris Sûreté, the Criminal Investigation Department (CID), was set up under the direction of a young barrister, Howard Vincent. Within six years he had a force of eight hundred men at his disposal, with its own command structure, rates of pay and *esprit de corps*. His example was followed with varying degrees of enthusiasm by the provincial forces, especially those in urban areas, and by the end of the century the idea of detectives had become accepted, even if their presence across the country was far from consistent. The plain-clothes men began to make systematic use of informers, a practice that earlier in the nineteenth century had become associated with peculation and repression. This aided the fight against crime, but exposed the officers to new forms of corruption, which their increasing corporate strength served to protect rather than expose. By the early 1920s, according to David Ascoli, the metropolitan CID "had become a thoroughly venal private army". The creation of something like a national standard of plain-clothes policing had to await the work of the Home Office Committee on Detectives, which between 1933 and 1938 established proper co-ordination between the separate forces and laid down the basis for the systematic use of scientific methods.

Knowledge

For much of the period, the central process of policing was walking the beat. The main difference between the new borough and county forces and old parish constables was merely that the basic activity of maintaining a visible and watchful presence in the neighbourhoods of the propertied was subject to more systematic organization. The beats were measured out – longer in the daytime than at night and in the countryside than in the towns; the rate of progress was set – two-and-a-half miles an hour in London and slightly faster in the counties, where there was a greater distance to cover; even the side of the pavement along which the constable was to patrol was specified – inside at night, to check doors and windows, outside during the day. In 1869, the "fixed-point" system was introduced, which required a constable to arrive at particular stages in his beat at certain times, enabling his sergeant to find him when he needed to and check that he had not taken an unauthorized deviation or rest. This remained the only means of co-ordinating the work of the division until the provision from the late 1920s onwards of police boxes, linked to the station by telephone. Until the introduction of team policing in the 1950s, which properly exploited the potential of the radio-controlled police car, the constable was on his feet and by himself for most of his working life. In the early years of the reformed forces, toiling labourers were wont to protest at the good fortune of those paid regular wages merely to walk about, but from the perspective of the newly recruited policeman the work was arduous, unrelenting and boring except when it was actively dangerous.

The steady, pre-ordained tread of the man in uniform was what the ratepayers required and for most of the period was as much as the chief constables could supply. The essence of policing was passive knowledge. With the exception of the small and initially mistrusted detective sections, it was not expected of the constables that they should go actively looking for crime or for evidence about criminals. They were there first of all to register the presence of the law, secondly to deter outbreaks of disorder and thirdly to absorb and if possible commit to memory such information as they observed while they walked or they heard as they conversed with law-abiding citizens. The knowledge they acquired, which defined such identity as they possessed as specialized workers, was of people rather than of events, of personal characteristics rather than of psychological generalizations. The only significant technology that could aid them in this work was associated with storing such information over time. The early use of photography, the creation in most police stations of registers of local inhabitants who had committed or might commit crimes and the attempts to set up a national register of known criminals were natural extensions of the basic work of the constables. Without such techniques, the departure from the beat of an experienced man reduced that area of a force's operating knowledge to zero. In this context it may be argued that the real break with the past came not with the creation of the new forces and the arrival of designated detectives but with the introduction half a century later of fingerprinting, which was the first method of policing not to depend on what could be seen and heard and the first technique that could be applied only by genuine specialists.

The public

The reliance on personal observation was at the root of a major paradox in the work of the forces. On the one hand, the police were required to behave like physical automatons, far more so than the soldiers on whom they were partially modelled, who spent a much greater part of their time lounging around in their base. On the other, they were continually engaged in categorizing human behaviour in ways that demanded constant individual judgement. While the Home Office compiled ever more elaborate tables of cold, abstract statistics, the constables upon whose work it depended filled their mental archives with living, named, differentiated personalities. In the absence of more sophisticated theories or evidence, such judgement was informed by stereotypes of likely criminals. These fell into three categories: first, those who had already come before the courts; secondly, those who were in the wrong place at the wrong time, such as roughly dressed men in polite neighbourhoods, factory workers out of doors during working hours, people carrying bundles after dark; thirdly, those who were on the wrong side of the law by definition, who included vagrants, especially from outside the area, unemployed youths, persistent drunks, known prostitutes and all the inhabitants from notorious houses or streets.

The archive of criminals predated the crimes. The task of the policeman was to fit a known suspect to the offence once it had been committed. This in turn required the active co-operation of the victim and the witnesses, which introduced a second paradox into the work of the forces. Whereas the essence of the reforms was the differentiation of the professional policeman from the private citizen, the reforms' success was largely dependent on co-operation between them. The bland generalization, articulated by the first commissioner of the Metropolitan Police and by chief constables and home secretaries across the decades, that good policing depended on the confidence of the public, had a much sharper meaning in the day-to-day struggle against theft and violence. The new police had relieved the ratepayers of the task of arresting offenders and supervising their journeys through the legal system, but they still lacked the power to initiate prosecutions for most of the non-behavioural offences with which they dealt. Increasing the security of persons and property required the victims to report the crimes, to assist in nominating the suspects and to appear in court to confirm the identifications. The chances of clearing up a crime were greatly enhanced if those who saw it could match a face or a name to one on the formal or informal police register. Conversely, where there was no witness and no progress could be made by stop-and-search or rounding-up the usual suspects, there was little prospect of a successful outcome. In this activity, civilians were just as dependent on personal knowledge structured by stereotypes as the police. If, for instance, a shopkeeper did not catch a thief red-handed, he was likely to nominate either a suspicious-looking stranger or a local person who previously had stolen from him. The process of labelling deviancy, which is often seen as a central characteristic of modern policing, was in reality a broader social process, with an active dialogue taking place between professionals and citizens based on what was often a shared set of assumptions.

There is evidence that from the beginning this mutually supportive relationship extended well beyond the ranks of the propertied classes. Local studies have established that working-class victims reported crimes, nominated suspects and appeared in court as plaintiffs or witnesses, especially when solicitors or magistrates could arrange for their expenses to be met. At the same time there are ample examples, especially from the early decades of the new forces, of widespread hostility to the men in uniform among the lower orders, which was embodied in a range of sanctions up to and including individual and collective assault. This remains an area in need of further research, but it is possible to clarify some aspects of the apparent contradiction. In the first instance, a distinction needs to be drawn between the categories of police activity. For instance, the fluctuations in hostility that have been charted in the third quarter of the nineteenth century frequently stemmed from changes in official policy to drunkenness and to other customary forms of rowdy activity. In the early decades of the twentieth century, the most serious conflict between community and police standards was provoked by the ultimately vain attempt to suppress off-course gambling. Just as tactics in these areas varied according to the type of force and the personalities of those in charge of it, so the pattern of non-co-operation or outright conflict showed inconsistencies across the country. Throughout these hostilities, the same men who fought with the police on Saturday nights or placed bets down dark alleys were perfectly ready to summon the aid of the law when their houses or their workshops were broken into or when they felt themselves cheated by landlords or employers.

Even in their most rigorous phases, the police had to exercise discretion about whether to lock up a drunk or a bookmaker or a motorist and about how diligently to pursue a thief. As Stefan Petrow observed, "Discretion enabled these police to strike an operational balance between the demands of the law, their superiors, and moral reformers, and the often different attitudes of the residents in the local areas they policed, and their own views and backgrounds." This element of choice was replicated among the propertyless. There was neither a total rejection of policing nor a once-for-all acceptance of the role of professional law keeping. During the later part of the nineteenth century, poor people sought the help of the police when they thought it appropriate and sorted out their problems within the neighbourhood if they did not. They shared with the middle class a general sense that theft was wrong and brought in the local constable if it was worth the trouble and there was likely to be a result. Wife-beating was moderated by local surveillance and censure unless it caused serious injury or involved another man's wife. They tolerated some forms of violence, dealt with others themselves and went to the law if it was particularly excessive or if the victim was especially vulnerable. They sought redress when the perpetrator was outside the community, either as a stranger or as an economic superior. As commercial and legal transactions became more complex, they used the police and the courts to compensate for their lack of skill and authority in the market place. The escalation in the role of pawnbrokers, whose numbers reached an all-time high in the years before the First World War, generated a growing volume of legal business as the desperate managers of overstretched family economies sought affidavits to replace lost tickets or took out summonses on the grounds that they had been overcharged. By the Edwardian period, a million claims for debts were being processed by magistrates' courts each year, usually for trifling sums by small traders in danger of joining the ranks of the destitute unless they obtained redress.

A series of judicial reforms, notably the Matrimonial Causes Act of 1878, the Maintenance of Wives Act of 1886 and the Summary Jurisdiction (Married Women) Act of 1895, embroiled magistrates' courts in the conduct of working-class families. A wife could seek protection and enforce financial support on the grounds of assault, desertion or cruelty and, with the 1902 Licensing Act, of her husband's habitual drunkenness. Wives went to the courts because the informal neighbourhood sanctions, whether verbal or physical, could not compensate for their powerlessness within the home. Just as much of the domestic conflict in the end stemmed from the lack of money, so most of the advice and action they sought from the magistrates concerned their need to obtain adequate financial support from their husbands. So far from rejecting the paraphernalia of the law, they seemed to have overestimated its potential, inundating magistrates with requests for information and intervention that were beyond their ability to meet. By the final quarter of the nineteenth century, some attempts were being made to co-ordinate the work of the police and courts with the missionary endeavours of the churches and the philanthropic societies, and as professional health visitors and social workers began to emerge after 1900 it became possible to deflect some of the advisory functions of the legal system to professional helpers. At the same time, however, the welfare responsibilities of the courts continued to grow, especially after the Children Act of 1908, creating a complex network of state intervention which was variously welcomed and resented according to the perspective of the victim.

The magistracy

A critical role in the relationship between the law and the poor was played by the magistrates. While their administrative functions were increasingly assumed by centrally appointed bureaucrats, their legal responsibilities steadily increased. A succession of statutes, most notably the Criminal Justice Act of 1855 and the Summary Jurisdiction Act of 1879, transferred offences from the quarter to the petty sessions, which dispensed justice without the aid of judges and juries. In one sense, the reforms reversed the trend towards professionalization. Although increasing use was made of stipendiary magistrates, the traditional representatives of the old ruling order, reinforced by members of the newly prosperous anxious to parade their status and integrity, gained a new lease of life. In some of the smaller boroughs, there were for several decades more justices of the peace than policemen, and in the counties the amateur tradition lived on largely undisturbed. It remained an upper-middle- and middle-class male preserve until the property qualification was abolished in 1906 and women were admitted to the bench in 1918. Whether paid or not, none of the magistrates received any kind of formal instruction, although they made increasing use of clerks who had and who thereby gained substantial and largely unsupervised authority in the courts. Courses became available after 1945, but only in 1966 did training become compulsory for new JPs, which meant, according to Esther Moir's standard study, that "at last the Bench is coming into line with other spheres of government in accepting the need to be professional".

As individuals and as a collectivity, they possessed immense discretion as to how they dispensed justice. Their relationship with the emerging police forces was complex. They saw their duty as protecting and enhancing the role of the initially unpopular officers. A clear distinction between the parish constables and their better-organized successors was that the latter more often appeared in court and had a greater expectation that their evidence would have privileged status. But the magistrates also acknowledged a broader responsibility to maintain confidence in the local legal system as a whole, of which the police were not always a sober, sensitive or honest part. Whether out of personal idiosyncrasy or mature judgement, they were on occasions capable of taking the side of the poor against their oppressors, in uniform or out of it. Their identity as local dignitaries and the very distant authority of the Home Office encouraged them to see themselves not just as agents but embodiments of the justice of the judicial process.

Class conflict

There was, in this sense, a strong element of continuity between the eighteenth and late nineteenth century. In both cases, much of the intervention on the side of the poor had a symbolic function. Temporary concessions were made in order to maintain confidence in a system whose essential purpose was to preserve order in the interests of propertied people. For all the use made of the law by the dispossessed, it remained the case that the bulk of the work of the courts concerned the prosecution of labouring men and women by their social superiors and their agents. As was noted in the previous chapter, not until the arrival of the motor car did the middle class begin to appear in large numbers as defendants. In late-nineteenth-century Manchester four-fifths of the cases in magistrates courts concerned behavioural offences in which the orderly sought to discipline the unwashed. Poor men and women coming before the courts still received harsh sentences for trivial offences against the property or peace of the better off.

Three general points can be made about the issue of class bias. In the first place, the poor did not need criminologists to tell them of its existence. The modernization of policing was viewed through a long-standing double perspective by which the law was seen as at once the birthright of all free-born Englishmen and the servant of the ruling order. Those without economic and political power approached the judicial system with a hazy instrumentality, exploiting it where they could, evading it if possible where they could not.

Secondly, over time the bias became increasingly nuanced. By the end of the nineteenth century, it was no longer the law against the lower orders, but rather the increasingly broad category of the respectable against those stigmatized as yet to be civilized. However misleading an analysis of the actual characteristics of criminal behaviour, the concept of a criminal class that informed both theoretical approaches to policing and the behaviour of the constable on the beat was at least a statement of confidence in the bulk of the working class who lived outside what were seen as degenerate and corrupting slum districts. The middle-aged, native-born, gainfully occupied, relatively prosperous, adequately housed and reasonably sober working man enjoyed a relationship with the forces of law and order quite different from that of the young, unemployed member of a notorious family or community. He was largely untroubled by patrolling constables, who now tended to be recruited from his sector of society, and he increasingly appreciated the reduction of theft and rowdy behaviour. On the other hand, to be Irish or, at the end of the period, Black, to be under 20 and without a secure job, to engage in almost any kind of economic activity on the streets, whether operating market stalls, taking bets or selling your body, was to invite constant attention from the police and barely concealed discrimination by the courts.

The third point to be made about bias is the extent to which the state managed to dissociate itself from the participation by the police in forms of class warfare. When it came to public order, the increasingly elaborate distinction between criminal and non-criminal types tended to collapse. The outbreaks of violence at general elections, which persisted for much of Victoria's reign, could not be attributed solely to the dregs of society, and the disputes between masters and men, which were taking a more organized form as the century drew to its close, involved precisely those sectors of the working class that had been accepted within the pale of civilization. The repeal of the Master and Servant Act in 1867 relieved the police of the responsibility to intervene in conflicts between employers and individual employees, but the growth of trade unions and working-class political organizations generated a new set of problems. The basic approach of the Home Office was as far as possible to disengage itself from any actions taken against strikers and protesters, particularly where those actions went wrong. This was true even in London, where the police had a statutory responsibility. The two major disturbances in the capital during the second half of the century, the Hyde Park riot of 1866 and the unemployed workers' riot of 1886, left the politicians in place but accelerated the demise of one commissioner of the Metropolitan Police and terminated the career of another. Elsewhere, forces were officially left to their own devices, their relations with marchers and strikers varying according to the personality of the chief constable and the profile of class relations in the area.

By the final quarter of the nineteenth century, however, confidence in the stability of the state was beginning to seep away, and more initiatives were taken by the centre. For the most part, governments were able to exploit their well-established licence to evade parliamentary scrutiny of security measures. Secret policing, which had been quietly discontinued with the collapse of Chartism, was equally quietly reintroduced in the 1880s, first in the form of the Special Irish Branch of the Metropolitan Police, set up by Howard Vincent in 1884 in response to a mainland bombing campaign by the Fenians. This dropped its specific association with Ireland the following year and, without any statutory sanction or even public announcement, became the basis of modern police undercover work. Postal espionage, which had also fallen into abeyance after the stabilization of class conflict in the middle of the century, unobtrusively recommenced at the same time. The capacity of local forces to cope with strike action was called into question in 1892 when two miners were shot dead at Ackton Hall Colliery after an overstretched chief constable had called in the army. The unprecedented strike wave of 1910–12 finally emboldened the Liberal Government to assume more interventionist powers, sending troops around the country to assist beleaguered forces, and issuing instructions on the maintenance of police reserves. Alongside the growing role of the Special Branch in the struggle against anarchists, Irish republicans and suffragettes, the Secret Service Bureau, the forerunner of MI5, was set up to combat what was seen as the growing threat to national security from foreign spies and domestic malcontents. With the exception of the Aliens Act of 1905, which for the first time imposed systematic controls over the residence of political refugees, and the Official Secrets Act, which was rushed through the Commons in less than an hour in 1911, none of the state's erosion of traditional civil liberties was subject to parliamentary oversight. While chief constables were engaged in an increasingly complex relationship between the Home Office, the army, the Special Branch, Secret Service spies and their often confused and hostile watch committees, the general public was largely unaware of the extent to which the conventional boundaries between the centre and the locality, between overt and covert surveillance and between civilian and military policing had been undermined.

During the First World War a range of new powers and restrictions were assumed under the Defence of the Realm Act, and with the return of peace and the emergence of the twin threats of domestic unemployment and international communism a number of these were consolidated under the Emergency Powers Act of 1920. The Home Office now possessed formal authority to deploy police to aid other forces and to co-ordinate responses to national crises, such as widespread strike action. Less publicly, the Special Branch, under the command of Basil Thomson, another ex-colonial, instituted a vigorous programme of collecting what was frequently inflammatory information about subversive activity. A prime target throughout much of the interwar period was the National Unemployed Workers' Movement, which was engaged in organizing hunger marches and creating local networks of assistance, recreation and protest. Its association with the small Communist Party, which became more pronounced as the Labour Party drew back from direct action, exposed it to a host of undercover devices, ranging from black propaganda and phone-tapping to the installation of a Special Branch officer on the organization's central committee. Widespread casual violence between the police and groups of unemployed men culminated in a ban in 1931 on all demonstrations outside any Labour Exchange. In 1934, the National Council for Civil Liberties was established in response to the perceived misuse of state powers.

However, despite the Public Order Act of 1936, which gave chief constables increased authority to control demonstrations, it remained possible to preserve the image of the stolid, peaceable, accountable policeman, open in his relations with the public and neutral in his response to class conflict. Major breakdowns in self-discipline, such as the police riot against poor districts in Birkenhead in 1932, were dismissed as aberrations. At all times, the repression was less overt and the protests less destructive than in contemporary European states. The reputation of the forces was further enhanced by their conduct during the second great war against continental tyranny, and in 1945 the new Labour home secretary was able to describe them as an "object of universal admiration" as he introduced a new police Bill. As with the prison service, which will be examined in the next chapter, the first signs of a weakening of their reputation coincided with the acceleration in the crime rate in the late 1950s. Doubts about the continuing efficacy of the forces, which still placed more emphasis on traditional foot patrols than on modern technology, were reinforced by a series of minor corruption cases and the re-emergence of serious conflict between entire communities and the law with the Notting Hill and Nottingham race riots of 1958. In 1959 a royal commission was set up to investigate whether the police were capable of responding to changing times, and although its final report in 1962 recommended a series of improvements to their conduct and control there was no road back to the age of low crime rates and unquestioning public confidence.

Chapter 15
Ordering punishment

Order and reform

Jabez Balfour was one of the occasional symbolic victims of nineteenth-century justice. Using extensive nonconformist connections he had established the rapidly expanding Liberator Building Society, which attracted the savings of working people anxious to become home-owners. On the basis of his financial success, he entered parliament as a Liberal MP and established himself as an authority on commercial matters. In 1892 his business empire collapsed and he fled to Argentina. The contrast between his public celebrity and the private suffering caused to thousands of thrifty citizens was so blatant as to force the state to make an example of him. The cumbersome extradition machinery was put into operation, and in 1895 he was brought back to England and sentenced to 14 years' penal servitude for a series of frauds associated with the failure of the building society. After brief periods in Wormwood Scrubs and Parkhurst, he was sent to England's version of Alcatraz, the island convict prison of Portland, "a heart-breaking, soul-enslaving, brain-destroying, hell upon earth" as he later described it. There he underwent the standard nine months of solitary confinement, broken only by an hour's exercise a day, and was then allowed to associate with other convicts in the prison workshops, spending the nights in an unheated "corrugated iron kennel" measuring 7 feet by 4 feet. The routine was harsh and unbending, "unredeemed by any moment of recreation or leisure, other than the brief period allowed for reading", and embittered by the endless "petty tyranny" of the warders and the periodic, humiliating strip-searches of the prisoners.

Yet Balfour also found, even in Portland, a prison officer who treated him with "great humanity and patience" and other convicts who had preserved their personal identities, especially some Fenian dynamiters. Conditions noticeably relaxed during his sentence, and he spent his last few weeks busily completing a "much wanted" new catalogue of the prison library at Parkhurst. He had entered prison just as the most rigid phase of penal policy was coming to an end, and his *My prison life* was itself a contribution to the increasing debate about the nature and function of incarceration, even if his final recommendation that transportation should be reintroduced was unlikely to be taken up. His experiences raise two broad questions that have preoccupied historians of the development of the modern penal system. First, how destructive and inhumane was the structure of the punishment that reached its apogee during the reign of Sir Edmund Du Cane, chairman of the Prison Commission from 1877 to 1895? Secondly, to what extent and for what reasons were effective reforms set in motion by his successor Sir Evelyn Ruggles-Brise, who was in charge of the system until 1921? Since the publication of Foucault's *Discipline and punish* in 1977 and the critical application of his insights to the English context by Michael Ignatieff and David Garland, the narrative of continuous improvement driven by humanitarian sentiment has been untenable. It is evident that the combination of bureaucratic order, moral aggrandizement and rationalist ambition, later reinforced by the claims of the behavioural social sciences, generated unprecedented mechanisms for subjugating the personalities of the powerless. But equally there is no case for simply inverting the old Whiggish history and presenting change as the inexorable loss of liberty. Throughout the modern period, careful attention needs to be paid to the timing and substance of the principal turning-points, to the variable relation between theory and practice and above all to the complex and unresolved tension between reform and retribution in the penal system.

Penal servitude

The manner in which the regime of penal servitude was entrenched in the years following the final abandonment of transportation left as little room as possible for casual kindness. Unlike the expanding police service, rigorous organization pervaded every aspect of the prisons, from the management of the staff to the diet and disciplining of the convicts. With the possible exception of the workhouses and some of the more ambitious public schools, no other institutions in the country were so completely bound by regulation. Following several serious prison disturbances and a public panic about garrotting, which was partly blamed on prisoners released on licence – the "ticket-of-leave men" – a royal commission recommended in 1863 that the deterrent element of prisons should be further enhanced at the expense of rehabilitation. It endorsed hard fare, hard labour and a hard bed and argued that "the moral reformation of the offender" should not hold "primary place in the prison system". There were to be no more hammocks and only remedial education for those still unable to write their names. This approach was endorsed by a House of Lords select committee chaired by Lord Carnarvon, which demanded that the local prisons must conform to the practices of the convict establishments. The proposals were given force in the 1864 Penal Servitude Act and the 1865 Prisons Act, which also attempted to impose the use of separate cells on the local prisons. A further Prison Act in 1877 finally destroyed all pretence that the community controlled incarceration. In the interests of both uniformity and reducing the rates, the administration of the local institutions was passed to the central prison commissioners, JPs retaining only a vestigial role as members of visiting committees. The access that concerned citizens such as John Howard once had to the cells and their inhabitants was removed. The high walls kept the prisoners in and the neighbouring community out. What went on inside was determined by Du Cane and his staff of warders, most of whom were recruited from the armed services.

The essence of Du Cane's regime was the absolute predictability of punishment founded on the complete uniformity of procedure. As he explained in his *Punishment and prevention of crime* in 1885, "A sentence of penal servitude is, in its main features, and so far as concerns the punishment, applied on exactly the same system to every person subjected to it. The previous career and character of the prisoner makes no difference in the punishment to which he is subjected." The nine months' solitary confinement was imposed on all convicts to break them out of the way of life that had brought them before the courts. Thereafter, the only way in which the individual personality of a prisoner could affect his treatment was through the elaborate system of marks, by which minor privileges could be gained and lost according to how hard he laboured at the set tasks. The stated object was to draw the prisoner towards virtuous behaviour rather than compel him. The summit of achievement was rewarded by one half-hour visit and one letter sent and received every three months. Productive labour in workshops was largely replaced by laborious public works, such as excavating docks, or harsh, repetitive, mechanical tasks that approached the margins of deliberate torture. In Du Cane's eyes the virtue of winding the crank and walking on the treadmill was that they conformed to the principles of regularity and less eligibility. No labour in the outside world could be more monotonous or tiring than the routines that now faced convicts. Picking oakum became a favourite task because it could be undertaken in silence inside the cell.

The ambition of reforming the prisoner remained a real though subordinate element of the system. The principal objectives were punishment and deterrence, but it was anticipated that the passage through the stages of the sentence would encourage a convict to rebuild his moral self. Particular importance was attached to the initial period of solitary confinement. "During this time", explained Du Cane, "he becomes open to lessons of admonition and warning; religious influences have full opportunity of obtaining access to him; he is put in that condition when he is likely to feel sorrow for the past and to welcome the words of those who show him how to avoid evil for the future." Although the chaplains played a supporting part, the essence of the process was the long, lonely struggle between the soul and the Almighty. Men and sometimes women, drawn mostly from the least prosperous and least educated sections of society, found themselves

Figure 15.1 Prisoners on the treadwheel, Stafford Gaol, 1869–71 (copyright Staffordshire Museum Service).

exposed to the Protestant approach to salvation in its purest and bleakest form. The schoolmaster's role in this process was confined to ensuring that the prisoner was capable of reading the Bible. As with the workhouses, the only public buildings of comparable size in the period, the state provided the physical context for reconstructing the moral self, but the responsibility for making the journey to salvation was left to the sinners. They had chosen of their free will to break the law, and they must choose of their own volition the path back to righteousness. If the opportunity was not taken, and Du Cane often entertained doubts about whether the lowest of the convicts were capable of reflection and self-analysis, there was nothing else that could be done for them.

Variation in punishment

There is no disputing the relentless ordering of the penal system in the final quarter of the nineteenth century, but the impression given in the official reports, that the experience of those found guilty in the courts was as rigid as the stones out of which the prisons were built, was in several senses misleading. The deliberate stripping away of the dignity and individuality of the prisoners encouraged the warders to indulge their personal whims and feelings. The more total the process, the greater the licence to petty tyranny. The mark system and the structure of internal punishments, which included flogging, gave them enormous power over those in their charge. Every prisoner knew that there were rules within the rules, minor variations in conduct, speech or gesture that one warder would permit and another visit with curses, blows or more formal sanctions. Even the predilections of the governor's pets could become a factor in the prisoners' lives. Although there were fewer instances of outright neglect and persistent brutality than in the early-nineteenth-century system, and every prison now had its own doctor to provide some surveillance of physical suffering, the prisoners had no basis for external appeal against the conduct of their gaolers. Variation was also present in the reaction of the prisoners to their punishments. However determined Du Cane was to ignore background and personality, it remained the case that some prisoners were more capable of withstanding the solitary confinement and hard labour than others. Amid the general dulling of strength and spirits, there were frequent cases of mental and physical breakdown, at this stage largely hidden from public knowledge.

More generally, the judicial process itself was at variance with the principle of rational, repetitive order. Setting aside the powerful element of discrimination that influenced whether the police brought the defendant to court in the first place, those who determined the sentences enjoyed extensive latitude. In theory, the discretion of the courts was complementary to the rigidity of the prisons. Du Cane justified his disregard of the previous career and character of the prisoner on the grounds that, "it is for the Courts of Law, who have, or should have, a full knowledge on these points, to consider them in awarding the sentence". He saw it as his duty merely to ensure that the judge could be certain of the consequence of his decision. The emergence of the modern penal system was accompanied by a restatement of the independence of the judiciary. Parliament was free to specify the minutest details of the prison regime, but neither it nor the Home Office had the right to dictate to judges how they interpreted the law. The consequence was what Jabez Balfour described as a "flagrant inequality of judicial sentencing", a scandal greater in his view than any shortcoming of the prisons themselves. This was notably the case with white-collar criminals, who throughout the period were treated with a general leniency interspersed with an occasional exemplary sentence, and with persistent petty offenders, who could find themselves sent down for seven or more years' penal servitude for the third theft of a hen or an item of clothing.

In the closing years of the century examples were brought to public attention of personal idiosyncrasy in sentencing, not just by ignorant or prejudiced amateur magistrates, but by the most senior judges in the land. The element of chance and the gulf between practice and any discernible standard principles became too much even for Du Cane, who campaigned with increasing vigour for a more orderly treatment by the judges of prisoners' personal conditions. However, various attempts to codify practice on a European model came to nothing, as did more modest proposals to set an agreed tariff of sentences. It was left to the unfortunate but uncircumcised Adolf Beck, who probably had more influence on the reform of policing and punishment than any single individual other than Peel, to provoke a change. An inquiry into the judicial errors that had led to his conviction and reconviction highlighted the sheer contingency of the factors that had freed him and finally brought home the need for a formal system of review. In 1907 the Court of Criminal Appeal was set up, with the power to amend a sentence imposed on an erroneous interpretation of the law or of the facts in a case. Although the discretion of the judges was not directly circumscribed, the decisions of the Appeal Court did begin to establish working guidelines to sentencing practice.

In this period, confinement in a convict or local prison became the standard punishment attached to existing and newly legislated crimes. The last transport ship had set sail in 1867, and capital punishment was by the late 1890s imposed in only seven in ten thousand indictable convictions. At one level, this meant that incarceration became the experience of very large numbers of men, women and children. Around the turn of the century, nearly two hundred thousand a year heard the prison doors close behind them. Yet only a small and declining minority of these underwent the full horrors of the 14-year penal-servitude sentence described in such painful detail by Balfour. During Du Cane's reign, the average length of non-penal sentences fell from 48 to 36 days. Two-thirds of all those entering prison were out within a fortnight, and only one in a hundred served more than 12 months. Penal servitude, which was designed as the substitute for transportation, was visited on just 2 per cent of those convicted of indictable offences in 1896. In 1891, the minimum period for this form of punishment was reduced from five years to three, and this became the most common length of sentence. Balfour was among only one in ten convicts serving more than five years.

The preoccupation of the historiography of punishment with the totalitarian drama of long-term penal servitude is in some respects perfectly justified. Although the sentence was imposed on a small proportion of prisoners, in the early years of Du Cane's reign the convicts accounted for a third of the prison population on any one day. This form of punishment and the purpose-built institutions in which it was implemented were designed as the ultimate embodiment of contemporary penal policy. The centralization of prison administration, consolidated by the 1877 act, meant that all other forms of imprisonment were treated as modifications of the convict model. Here theory became reality, and was in turn examined and debated through proliferating forms of official and unofficial discourse. At Portland, Pentonville and Dartmoor, the distance that the system had travelled from the ramshackle structure of bodily punishments and town lock-ups was most clearly measurable. Yet it remained the case that for the majority of those sentenced to detention, prison was little more than a passing inconvenience, one more episode of misfortune in a life filled with uncertainty and hardship. There were no months in solitary confinement and long years accumulating and losing small privileges; rather the temporary exchange of an overcrowded and vermin-infested tenement for a more private and somewhat less insanitary cell. The diet might be the absolute minimum that contemporary nutritional science would permit, but it was at least regular. The doctors might not be too zealous but they were more accessible there than in a typical slum, and following the reforms the danger of succumbing to an infectious disease or epidemic was smaller inside the walls than outside. True, prison remained less desirable than the workhouse, which in general was less desirable than any free existence, including, at least for the young, petty crime and prostitution. But if the worst happened, it was for most of those sent down a transitory rather than a transforming event.

The female offender

This was especially the case for female offenders, who in the 1880s made up a fifth of the local prison population and a tenth of those in convict establishments. There was a steady growth in the number of women who underwent very short sentences of 14 days or less, mostly for drunkenness and related crimes. In these instances, the distance between the outside world and the prison cell was not large. The sojourn behind bars was too brief to permit much punishment or any reform. The prisoners came out as noisy, insubordinate and deprived as they went in. The most distinctive element of the experience was some much needed attention to what were frequently serious health problems. The rate of recidivism for this sector of the prison population was higher than for males and growing. In local prisons in 1880, five times as many women as men had more than ten previous convictions. This pointed partly to the irrelevance of prison as a response to alcoholism and partly to its temporary attractions. Women who had become detached from family or community support systems were even more likely than men to find themselves faced with a stark choice between freedom and food. An absolute lack of resources or an overwhelming need for medical

Figure 15.2 Morning prayers in the female's prison, Stafford Gaol, 1869–71 (copyright Staffordshire Museum Service).

assistance, particularly in respect of a childbirth, could dramatically reduce fear of the courts and their sanctions.

The small minority of those in local prisons who served more than three months and the female convicts, whose numbers fell from around a thousand sentences a year in the early 1860s to just 34 in 1900, underwent a harsher experience, but one that in comparison with the men was less rigorously preoccupied with punishment. The governing model of femininity laid especial emphasis on the susceptibility to moral influence and the potential for the moral direction. Female prisoners were held to be less hardened than male prisoners and more open to improving influence, and by the same measure women prison staff were seen to have a natural role in reforming the characters committed to their care. The prison system was a notable exception to the otherwise male preserve of law enforcement. The attack on the corrupt aspects of the old system required that male gaolers were kept as far away as possible from vulnerable female prisoners. As warders and eventually governors, women came to exercise more institutional power and responsibility than in almost any other contemporary walk of life. In their work, more attention was paid to individual personality than in Du Cane's standard model. The rules were interpreted with greater latitude, the internal punishments were less severe, and greater intimacy was encouraged with and between the inmates. This led to complex patterns of resistance, conflict and accommodation, especially when the relationships acquired a physical aspect. In prison, as in the world outside, female homosexuality was not regarded as a serious problem. There is little evidence that much reform occurred, the staff having no professional background and negligible training. Without the possibility of labouring on outside public works, the life of the female convict was more monotonous than the male, but less physically destructive.

The young offender

The direction of change in this phase of penal policy was thus more complex than at first appears. While Du Cane's regime was becoming ever more rigid, the number of offenders consigned to penal servitude halved, as did the number of local prisons. This reflected not only the general fall in the crime figures but also a double shift in sentencing policy, from longer to shorter periods and, as the century drew to a close, from prison to non-custodial forms of punishment. As with the New Poor Law, the other great manifestation of bureaucratic intervention of the period, reform began at the periphery and reached the centre by degrees. The first retreat from the dominant emphasis on non-individualized punishment was registered at the bottom of the system. The youthful nature of the offending population presented an immediate problem as incarceration became the standard penalty in the middle decades of the nineteenth century. In 1880 there were still six and a half thousand children of 16 and under in prison, and nine hundred below the age of 12. The great majority of these had been sentenced for minor thefts or behavioural misdemeanours. Growing concern was expressed at their removal from any kind of nurturing influence and at their exposure to the depraved habits of hardened adult criminals for no greater cause than breaking a window or making off with a mouthful of food. During the succeeding half century, attempts were made both conceptually and physically to separate this cohort of offenders from the remainder of those undergoing confinement. While adult penal policy was stressing the singularity of the process of punishment, the approach to convicted or potential young delinquents was increasingly merged with initiatives in schooling and child welfare.

The acceptance by the state of its responsibility for educating the children of the lower orders, most notably in the provision of a national system in 1870 and of compulsory attendance in 1880, was paralleled in the field of crime. The inspected schools were designed to take over from parents the task of instilling self-discipline and respect for the law: when they failed to do so, the solution was not to abandon teaching for punishment, but rather to establish a more disciplined environment in which the malleable personalities could be reshaped. The industrial schools gave moral, educational and work training to children under 14 who had come before the courts for particular offences or more generally for lack of effective parental supervision. A deliberate attempt was made to blur the distinction between actual lawbreaking and the perceived potential for doing so. The central purpose of the schools, which were privately run but officially subsidized and inspected, was reform, not retribution. By the end of the century, their role was complemented by truant and day industrial schools set up under the education acts. At the same time the reformatory schools, which at their inception in 1854 had been intended to provide a closer alternative to prison for children between 12 and 16, gradually lost their penal quality. When the requirement that the first fortnight of a sentence should be spent in prison was abandoned in 1899, they came to be seen as merely the more senior version of the industrial schools, and were formally merged with them in 1913.

By the beginning of the twentieth century, children under the age of 12 had almost disappeared from the prison system, and those under 16 had fallen to a thousand. Fearful as it was of the juvenile criminal, the state could not bring itself to abandon incarceration altogether, and even in the epochal Children Act of 1908, which abolished penal servitude for children and young offenders, prison was retained as an option for those between 14 and 16 whose character was held to be particularly depraved. Their cases, however, would now be heard by special juvenile courts, staffed by magistrates with particular knowledge of this age group and empowered to take welfare issues into account when determining the length and form of punishment. By this time, the concern to enhance the element of reform had spread to what in social theory was coming to be recognized as a distinct and important subgroup of the population, those navigating the choppy waters between childhood and adulthood. A flurry of reports in the Edwardian period raised concerns about the transition from school to permanent employment, and within the penal system experiments were launched at Bedford, Borstal and Dartmoor prisons to develop a form of imprisonment appropriate to the particular character of the adolescent offenders, "the young hooligans", as Ruggles-Brise described them, "well-advanced in crime". Their apparent success led to the establishment under the Prevention of Crime Act 1908 of a new category of punishment. Offenders aged 16 to 20 were to be sentenced to a term of one to three years, which could be shortened by good conduct or lengthened if the conditions of the licence were transgressed. They were to be housed in a separate building and exposed to a routine of physical exertion, formal education and work training. Inmates were selected on the basis of their exposure to criminal habits and their capacity for reform.

From the outset the Borstal system implied that much greater attention was to be paid to the personalities of the offenders than in the conventional system. In theory, the regime represented the traditional model of punishment infused with the public-school ethos. Subordination and self-reliance was to be instilled through energetic team activity interspersed with moral and intellectual instruction. After a while, the Borstal inmates were grouped into houses with their own housemasters, who were to generate corporate pride and conformity to the new traditions. If the factory provided an inspiration for early-nineteenth-century reformers, the public school constituted a model for those of the early twentieth century. In practice, the first institutions were staffed not by classically educated teachers but by hardened prison warders, who tended to fall back on the routines of strict discipline and endless mechanical labour. Nevertheless, the first studies of recidivism among "Borstal boys" appeared to show an encouraging improvement over the conventional prison, which still dealt with the less tractable cases.

The emergence of the twentieth-century system

The increasing efforts to distinguish delinquent children from criminal adults was part of a broader process of change in the two decades before the outbreak of the First World War. The turning-point was the critical report of the Gladstone Committee in 1895 and the consequent retirement of Du Cane. The new era was signified by the appointment of a more liberal chairman of the Prison Commission, Evelyn Ruggles-Brise, and the passage of a new Prison Act in 1898, which led to an amelioration of the harsher aspects of penal servitude, including the abolition of the treadmill and the crank and the reduction of physical punishment for transgressions of prison rules. Local boards of visitors replaced the ineffectual visiting committees, giving outsiders greater powers of inspection and inmates better opportunities to appeal against their treatment. Greater association was permitted among prisoners, and the system of earned remission was extended from the convict establishments to the populous local prisons. The most immediate cause of reform was a revival of the humanitarian concern for the welfare of prisoners, now informed by more scientific measurements of physical and psychological suffering. It became easier to calculate the damage done by incarceration to long-term prisoners and more difficult to detect its benefits. Whilst Du Cane might point to the fall in the official crime rate as evidence of the effect of deterrence, his critics emphasized the apparent rise in recidivism as proof of the failure of moral reformation. The Gladstone Committee's report coincided with the downfall of Oscar Wilde; his impassioned protests at his own prison experience and the suffering he witnessed amongst fellow inmates, including children, did much to confirm the feeling that a more constructive approach to punishment was required. "Something was dead in each of us", he wrote in *The ballad of Reading Gaol* in 1898, "and what was dead was Hope."

The direction of change was shaped by two emerging approaches to deviant behaviour that had quite different sources but overlapping conclusions. The first was the scientific study of the criminal personality, which replaced the discourse of choice and sin with one of biology and inheritance. Forms of neo-Darwinism developed into the eugenics movement, which explained antisocial conduct in terms of the transmission of personality types between generations. In its most extreme manifestation it implied that punishment was irrelevant and reform hopeless. Instead, steps should be taken to prevent the inadequate from reproducing and to subject to more specialized medical treatment those constitutionally incapable of observing the law. The second approach stressed the possibility of a broad, integrated attitude to achieving a more humane and responsible community. The emphasis moved from the civil war of individual conscience to the collective struggle to improve the ethical behaviour of society and the physical conditions that underpinned it. Where the eugenics movement was driven by the fear of racial decline, the liberal welfarism was drawn on by a new confidence about the possibility of social progress and a new faith in the constructive role of the state. Liberal critics of the former foresaw the total destruction of basic human rights; conservative opponents of the latter envisaged a slide towards full-blown socialism. Both approaches, however, stressed the authority and relevance of professional experts in a range of disciplines outside the narrow and secretive world of prison administration. And both argued that closer attention should be paid to the different backgrounds and requirements of individual offenders.

In the event, the change of direction at the beginning of the twentieth century was more confused and less complete than either of the theories demanded. This was partly because of the sheer physical inertia of the system. Even more than in the schools, the impact of practical reforms and theoretical revolutions was always conditioned by structures that contained the prisoners and the staff which ran them. The immense nineteenth-century prison-building programme endowed the service with a network of solidly constructed institutions based on increasingly obsolescent penal practices. During the first half of the twentieth century, the only significant alteration to the environment of punishment was the continuation of the programme of closing the older, smaller buildings, which left the Victorian monoliths yet more dominant in the prison landscape. Although the 1898 act provided better training for staff, the resilient traditions of military organization operated as a kind of disciplinary flywheel, qualifying the impact of the more innovative reforms, especially in respect of young offenders. Whatever its application to the prisoners, the theory of inherited characteristics was ever more relevant to their warders.

Alternatives to prison

For the most part, the more radical changes were confined to the perimeters of the system. Of greatest long-term importance were the attempts to curtail the role of imprisonment for those who had committed less serious offences. In the early years of the twentieth century, half of those committed to local prisons lost their freedom as a consequence of their failure to pay often quite small fines imposed for equally trivial misdemeanours. Most drunks, for instance, received institutional punishment only at the second remove as they expiated their original financial penalty. This procedure cost the state twice over and rendered largely inoperative a device that was designed to restrict the prison population. After several failed attempts at reform, the Criminal Justice Administration Act of 1914 tackled the problem by requiring magistrates to give time to pay a fine, providing the defendant had a fixed abode. By 1921, the number committed for non-payment had fallen from 85,000 to 15,000. During the succeeding decades, fines increasingly became an alternative to, rather than a cause of, imprisonment. A wider range of offences were punished by financial sanctions, and the Money Payments Act of 1935 further deterred magistrates from using prison sentences by requiring them to inquire into the indigence of defaulters. By 1947, almost four-fifths of those convicted in the criminal courts suffered financial penalties, and of the half-million fines imposed, less than three thousand eventually led to prison.

For those whose offences were neither repetitive nor committed in the heat of the moment, a second alternative to prison was consolidated and extended in this period. The long-standing practice of releasing an offender on recognizances had been given a statutory existence in the Criminal Jurisdiction Act of 1879, and in 1887 Du Cane had introduced probation for first offenders. But neither device was widely used, and the task of turning the footsteps of young criminals back to the paths of righteousness was left in the hands of voluntary societies, whose funds and expertise were neither adequate nor reliable. Eventually, the continuing growth of recidivism and the widening gap between the potential and the practice of the device forced a more systematic reform. In 1907, the Liberal Government passed the Probation of Offenders Act, which provided for a period of between one and three years' supervision by trained probation officers for transgressors thought capable of benefiting from it. As with so many welfare reforms of the period, its significance lay more in the principles it embodied than in its immediate impact on the problem. The act formally recognized the existence of a common field of operation between the legal system, which determined the destinations of convicted defendants, the nascent social-work profession, which supplied the personnel and the methodology of the probation service, and the schools, whose headmasters were integrated in the process of reforming the younger offenders. From magistrates to High Court judges, those passing sentence were now engaged with sources of expertise and practice outside the police officers and prison governors who in the latter part of the nineteenth century had dominated penal activity.

Less successful were the attempts to develop alternative forms of confinement for those who did not seem capable of responding to conventional punishment. As the concept of addiction took form towards the end of the nineteenth century, the treatment by the courts of persistent drunks attracted increasing attention. These reappeared before the magistrates so frequently as to suggest that prison was operating as neither a penalty nor a deterrence. The emerging theory of inebriation argued that the cause of the problem was the overwhelming of the moral sense by some combination of environment and alcohol. Rather than retribution, this category of offenders required a regime of reform too specialized and intensive to be undertaken in the surroundings of a prison. Attempts in 1879 and 1888 to establish a system of licensed private retreats failed to address the problem, and in 1898 the Inebriates Act specified the creation of separate institutions to which habitual drunkards or those committing crimes under the influence of alcohol could be sent for a course of rehabilitation lasting up to three years.

In the first decade of the act's operation, only two in a thousand of those convicted for drunken behaviour were committed to reformatories, and a decade later the scheme was effectively abandoned. The problem was partly that most of the new centres were to be provided by local authorities, who were reluctant to accept the responsibility, and partly that the method of treatment was ineffective and uncertain. When the inmates, who were mostly women, showed little signs of benefiting from traditional forms of moral exhortation, the emphasis began to shift towards newer devices of therapeutic intervention. But if they were designated as mentally ill, then there was little case for confining them in what remained an extension of the penal system. At the same time, their offences were too trivial and their intellectual infirmity too variable to fall within the scope of the "McNaghten Rules", which since 1843 had separated a small number of defendants deemed incapable of understanding their acts or distinguishing right and wrong from the overwhelming majority of offenders held to be in possession of their free will. The criminally insane were housed in Broadmoor from 1863, supplemented by Rampton from 1910, where their treatment gradually evolved from an exclusive reliance on occupational therapy and rhubarb to the application of the techniques of a secure mental hospital. For sick alcoholics and other mentally inadequate offenders, an intermediate solution was devised in the Mental Deficiency Act of 1913, which enabled the courts to divert to medically run institutions those deemed in some way mentally ill.

Change and continuity

The structure of punishment bequeathed to the interwar period was much more complex than that of the heyday of Du Cane's regime, and rather less consistent. The series of reforms from the late 1890s onwards had softened the stark outline of punishment and deterrence and allowed into the field an increasing range of professional experts. Enquiries into the background and individual characteristics of offenders had become widespread, and prison was no longer the common destination of those convicted in the courts. The ambition of rebuilding the personalities of especially malleable offenders was now entrenched within the system. Constructive attempts had been made to connect penal policy with the broader enterprise of reforming the economic and social conditions of the section of the population from which most prisoners came. At the same time, the more draconian prescriptions of the eugenicists had been firmly resisted. Although many influential penologists took an interest in the pioneering studies of hereditary criminality, they remained sceptical about the conclusions. It was evident that more account needed to be taken of types of mental infirmity when determining the treatment of prisoners, but such medical intervention was still confined to the periphery of the system. The dominant assumption remained that, unless proved otherwise, criminals were personally responsible for their actions and fully capable of estimating the consequences. Their failure was a matter of morality rather than psychology. They possessed reason and judgement, and the primary function of penal policy was, as it had been during the last quarter of the nineteenth century, to exact punishment on those who had transgressed the law and to deter those who were contemplating doing so.

An underlying factor in the pre-1914 reforms was the perception that the war against crime was going well. Victory was far from complete, but the containment of the rise in offences eased the burden on the prison system and suggested that it was performing a positive function for society as a whole, if not for all those who passed through it. This general sense of optimism lasted well into the interwar period and permitted further relaxation of the old regime. Ruggles-Brise departed in 1921, and for the rest of the period the dominating influence was Alexander Paterson, who believed that offenders should be sent to prison "as a punishment, not for a punishment". The Borstal regime, now staffed by more appropriately trained officers, became increasingly energetic and ambitious in the claims made for its reforming capacity, and the adult prison system began to take on some of its characteristics. Physical education was much more widely available in the form of individual exercises and team games. A growing number of teachers, a race regarded with enormous mistrust in Du Cane's time, worked inside prison walls. A wider range of recreational facilities was provided, including in some cases the new technology of the wireless. The broad arrows on the prison uniform disappeared in 1921, as did the convict crop, and regular shaving was introduced.

Increasingly the distinction between penal servitude and ordinary imprisonment was blurred. The enforced separation of convicts was suspended in 1923 and abolished in 1930. The following year it was abandoned in local prisons, and thereafter convicts and short-term prisoners were increasingly treated alike and allowed to mix within the same institutions. In the mid-1920s the prison commissioners set themselves the task of "protecting society by training offenders, as far as possible, for citizenship". The period of solitary confinement at the beginning of penal servitude was abolished on the grounds that rather than engaging in moral reconstruction, "a man brooding alone in his cell became morose and vindictive". More work training was provided, and an earning scheme was introduced that allowed prisoners to labour for small sums of real money rather than marks or privileges. The probation service, whose role was extended by the Criminal Justice Act of 1925, was by the end of the 1930s dealing with more than half of those convicted for indictable offences. A further fifth were fined, leaving just under a quarter who were punished by imprisonment. Corporal punishment, whose role had been declining before the war, virtually disappeared as a sentence and as a disciplinary device within the prisons.

In one sense there was a linear progression from the changes in the Ruggles-Brise era to the Criminal Justice Act of 1948, which consolidated the interwar reforms. The two most feared elements of the late-Victorian system, penal servitude and flogging, now formally ceased to exist, and further attempts were made to reduce the use of prisons by the introduction for petty offenders of attendance centres where they could perform useful labour in their free time, and detention centres for young offenders whose character was not in need of the rigours of Borstal. However, the scale of change was neither as great nor as uncontested as might appear. The fall in the official crime figures had bottomed out and was now beginning to rise with accelerating speed. Uncertainty about progressive policies surfaced in 1932 when the governor of Dartmoor attempted to revert to earlier forms of discipline and provoked the most serious riot for more than half a century, which caused the destruction of the entire central block. The growing number of outsiders at work in the prisons, whether as teachers, instructors, chaplains, doctors or welfare workers, provoked intermittent misgivings within the system, the more so when the visitors used their access to generate a series of hostile commentaries.

The official reports constructed a narrative of progressive treatment, but the critics and the intermittent prison autobiographies described a system in which the innovations merely made more palatable what remained a harsh, punitive experience lived out in precisely the same cells that had housed Du Cane's convict population. If there were more social workers in the prisons, there were just as few lavatories. In the 1950s, slopping out was still the standard practice, and as the chairman of the Prison Commission delicately put it, "the normal habits of large numbers of the prison population still fall short of refinement". Prisoners still spent the night on the hard plank beds prescribed in 1863. Until the new building programme signalled by the 1959 white paper "Penal practice in a changing society", only two new prisons had been constructed since 1900, Camp Hill on the Isle of Wight in 1912 and Eversthorpe in 1957, which like all its predecessors was based on the Pentonville model of 1842. Forty new institutions covering the whole range of penal treatment were planned, partly in an effort to adapt the physical structures to the changed penal practices, and partly to cope with the rising prison population, which was already causing significant overcrowding. By now, there were 22,000 prisoners, twice as many as before the war, and despite the increasing use of non-custodial sentences the figure was set to double again by the 1980s. The most consistent feature of the period covered by this chapter is that each succeeding regime of prison commissioners closed more prisons than it opened. In this sense, the late 1950s marked the end of an era, but it was far from clear that the building programme would outpace the growth in demand and make possible the eradication of the Victorian legacy.

After the controversies and upheavals of the Edwardian period and the succession of innovations in the following decades, two fundamental truths remained. In the first place, most of those who entered prison left too rapidly for the process to have any measurable impact on their moral or physical wellbeing. Despite the continuing efforts to find non-custodial alternatives for young and petty offenders, three-quarters of sentences were for three months or less. In more stable economic and social structures, the impact of such temporary interruptions to a free life may have been greater, but for most of this transient population, the gravity of the experience bore little relation to the weight of theory and debate that had now built up around the penal system. Secondly and conversely, for the minority of those serving substantial sentences, it was no easier than ever it was to demonstrate that they came out better or fitter citizens than they entered. The depths of suffering had been reduced, but it was, in spite of the games and the classes and the radios, still a process destructive of body and soul alike. "In reality", wrote an ex-prisoner in 1956, "it is a place of punishment wherein a few reformative elements have been incongruously and unprofitably planted."

Chapter 16
Epilogue

A 1996 televised video-recording showed two crooks poking a pole with a hook on the end of it through the letter-box of a clothing store and pulling out garments from a display unit. Little did they realize that they were replicating a method first described by Thomas Harman in 1566 in his *Caveat for common cursitors*. Dickens's Fagin (*Oliver Twist,* 1837–8) had his real-life precursor in the London alehouse keeper and fence of 1585 described above in Chapter 2. The method of house-breaking recorded in Charles Reade's novel *"It is never too late to mend"* (1856) could act as a useful manual for the modern burglar. There are many continuities in criminal method although, as we have shown, criminals have always adapted their methods to take advantage of new opportunities and employed the latest technologies. There are also continuities in types of crime. The following abbreviated court account of urban violence leading to a homicide could have come from any age. Was it 1306, 1506, 1706, or 1906?

> Robert Clark and William Walker, Liverpudlians travelling from Chester to Liverpool, started to quarrel. They came across Walker's cousin, William Brown. The two cousins sided against Clark. The quarrel led to violence. Brown pulled a knife and threatened Clark, who fled in terror down an alley-way. Brown and Walker followed him, Walker brandishing his knife. In self-defence Clark also produced a weapon, and in the ensuing fray Walker was killed.

This case, as it happens, comes from 1306. There are, it would seem, certain constants in the history of crime and, to a lesser extent, in the history of punishment.

The two most obvious continuities concern the nature of crime and the identity of the criminal. Throughout our history, most crimes have been against property rather than against the person. Crime was and is a way of making a living or supplementing the resources of those denied access to an adequate lifestyle. Despite the increasing concern about violence in the last decade, 93 per cent of all recorded crime between July 1994 and July 1995 comprised burglary, theft, fraud, forgery, criminal damage and arson. The stealing of other people's possessions dominates the category of property offences, as it always has done. All that has changed over the decades is what is stolen. The most recent figures confirm the impact of the motor car on criminal behaviour in this century; more than a half of theft offences and a quarter of all recorded crime comprising theft of or from vehicles. Some of these cars are of great value and are stolen by professional thieves. But now, as throughout the past, most unlawful redistribution of goods is casually undertaken and yields only casual sums of money. Despite the enormous growth in consumer goods and the accompanying ravages of inflation, a quarter of burglaries in the early 1990s resulted in no quantifiable loss of property, and a further 45 per cent involved goods worth less than £100.

Violence, as has long been the case, has an influence on popular perceptions of crime that is quite disproportionate to its actual incidence. In recent decades this tendency has been entrenched as the growth in violent crimes has outstripped that of property crimes; and within the category, the more serious offences against the person have increased more rapidly than the less serious. The one exception to this pattern is the most serious of all acts of violence. In the early 1950s the homicide rate peaked at just over 400 a year. In 1994, a quarter of a century after the abolition of the death penalty, it had risen to 729, which, however, still represents one of the slowest levels of increase for any kind of offence. Despite the increasing availability of firearms, almost 90 per cent of murders are committed by the time-honoured means of sharp or blunt instruments, hitting, kicking or strangling, burning, drowning or poisoning. The only truly modern method of causing death recorded in the current returns is using a motor vehicle deliberately to kill – a dozen or so cases each year.

The chapters in this book constitute an uncompleted history of the transition from an informal to a formal means of defining and dealing with transgressive behaviour. As the centuries passed, the agencies of law and order increased their dominion over individual and communal conduct, and in turn were appealed to by a growing range of people in a widening range of circumstances. Ever since serious attempts were made to express crime in quantifiable terms, questions have been raised about the gulf between those criminal acts known to the police and those, in terms of the prevailing definitions, that were either endured or dealt with by other means. In recent years, unrecorded crime has become known as the "dark figure", a concept that elides the problems of professional statisticians and the difficulties of everyday victims. Attempts are now made to count the previously uncounted by various devices, of which the most systematic is the British Crime Survey. This indicates that still, after all the "advances" that have been recorded in this book, more offences are concealed from the police than are reported to them. Among the motives cited are those that would be familiar to past generations – distrust of the competence or neutrality of the police and courts, disinclination to accept official definitions of criminal behaviour, dislike of the trouble, expense and sometimes physical danger of using the law, and desire to deal with problems within the family and neighbourhood. The survey also finds, however, that the gap is continuing to close, with a marked rise in reporting from 31 to 43 per cent in the decade from 1981, which suggests that the real rise in lawbreaking over this period may have been less steep than the recorded figures implied. Such complexities confirm that movements in criminal statistics should not be taken now or at any time in the past as an accurate reflection of actual changes in behaviour and experience.

Whether they were fighting in alley-ways or picking pockets, most of those who caused trouble to the judicial system were young and male; they still are. Outside of prostitution, which remains a constant theme throughout a thousand years, women appear less frequently in criminal statistics and normally for petty offences, except in cases of family violence. For some sectors of the population, challenging the prevailing forces of law has constituted a male rite of passage. More generally the time of life when men were most detached from social, educational and economic structures represented the peak period of temptation. As history has merged with the present, the average age of male offenders has kept pace with the extension of educational provision, advancing from 14 to 18. However, there are now fears that rather than retreat to the paths of legality as they progress into their twenties, as once happened, these men remain on the wrong side of the law on a scale that has rarely been found in the past. For the smaller cohort of female offenders, on the other hand, the peak age of criminality has stayed at 14.

The average male criminal is now the same age as the average first-year undergraduate, and indeed at the university from which this book comes, the police have recently complained of the difficulty of visually distinguishing between the students and the outsiders seeking to deprive them of their cars and stereo systems. However, most of the prison population continues to be drawn from the sector of society that has the poorest access to education and the levels of occupational security and mobility that it brings. The recent dramatic increase in opportunities for international fraud and embezzlement by means of the sophisticated manipulation of information technology has merely widened still further the long-standing gulf between the minority of highly skilled professional criminals and the large majority of casual thieves whose activities are a measure not of extensive planning and calculation but rather of their complete absence.

In crime, as in other forms of welfare provision, much of the redistribution that takes place is from the poor to the poor. It remains the case that the most vociferous advocates for more extensive policing and more repressive punishment are those who statistically are least vulnerable to assaults on their person or property. The young men who commit most violence are also the greatest victims of it. They tend to steal from inner-city tenants who surround them, not from distant rural home-owners. Insecurity of income begets loss of possession, while security of income begets fear of the dispossessed. The perception and reality of danger still have an inconsistent relation. It can be shown, for instance, that the elderly, whose apprehensions have multiplied in recent years, face the lowest risk of assault of any age-group. The proximity of offender to victim, most dramatically displayed in the tendency of the murdered to be known or related to their killers, is one of the great constants in this history. If the breakup of families and communities is causing a growth in criminal behaviour, the substance of crime reveals just how complex and real such social groups remain.

Criminality can itself become a tradition for an area, a group, or even a family. Members of a distinctively named Cannock Chase family appear as minor lawbreakers in both sixteenth-century and late-twentieth-century court records. How far these traditions are constructed by outside labelling, by continuities of material surroundings or by cultural or even biological inheritance has long been a matter of debate. We find the Elizabethan observer Thomas Harman noting how criminals brought up their children to be criminals, and Victorian commentators placing poor parenting at the centre of their explanations of criminal behaviour. At the beginning of the twentieth century, eugenicists sought to reinterpret tradition as science, an exercise that is taking on a new form in the modern era with attempts to isolate the so-called "criminal gene". The greatest and most persistent projection of the deviant tradition, however, has been in the shape of outsider national or racial minorities, whether the Welsh, Scots and Irish in medieval and early modern England, the Jews, Chinese and again the Irish in Victorian and Edwardian England or, more recently, Black immigrants. In the present day, 12 per cent of the male prison population in England and Wales are from minority ethnic groups, yet such minorities comprise just 5 per cent of the total population.

Explanations of crime that lay sensational emphasis on manufactured facts and that in turn have a disproportionate influence on policing and punishment constitute their own intermittent tradition in this history. From the temporary imposition of harsh penalties in the mid-sixteenth century in response to widespread rioting and disorder, to the deeply influential but largely unfounded garrotting panic of the 1860s, to the storms that have swept across penal policy in the immediate past, rational discourse has frequently been pushed to the margins of official practice. There is little historical evidence that being "tough on crime" has ever worked. Just as increases in criminal behaviour have often been an index of a sense of exclusion from the mores and lifestyles of the elite, so intensifications of punishment regimes have resulted from a loss of confidence in the values and behaviour of the lower orders. A fall in the crime rate has generally been a cause not a consequence of a change in penal policy. In the broader historical context, the current shift to longer sentences and harsher prison regimes seems no more than a colonic spasm in a permanently stressed condition.

The famous dictum of the interwar prison commissioner Alexander Paterson, that criminals were sent to prison as, and not for, a punishment, echoed the prescription of the great Roman jurist Ulpian, that "Prisons indeed ought to be employed for confining men, not for punishing them." Equally the desire to use incarceration for retribution can be traced back to the emergence of canon law in the early Middle Ages. Neither reform nor punishment can be expelled from the modern penal system; we are imprisoned in an endless struggle between them.

The line between fact and fantasy in the public discourse about crime has never been easy to draw. Since the Middle Ages at least, lawbreaking and lawbreakers have been prime sources of popular entertainment. From the medieval Robin Hood ballads, to early modern chap-books on cony catching, to nineteenth-century true-life trial publications, to modern film and television, more money may have been made out of criminals than by criminals. The bottomless public fascination with crime has consistently propelled depiction towards dramatization, and condemnation towards romanticization. In his 1867 preface to *Oliver Twist* Dickens complained that he had "read of thieves by scores; seductive fellows (amiable for the most part), faultless in dress, plump in pocket, choice in horse-flesh, bold in bearing, fortunate in gallantry, great at a song, a bottle, pack of cards or dice-box, and fit companions for the bravest". He had, by contrast, set out "to paint them in all their deformity, all their wretchedness, in all the squalid misery of their lives". None the less, he was forced to defend himself from the charge that he had sentimentalized the character of Nancy, whose love for Sikes offended conventional assumptions about the barrier between virtue and vice. The contribution of the Victorians to the discourse about crime was to invent powerful new forms of amusement while at the same time establishing new standards of professional objectivity in the recording and analysis of criminal behaviour. If modern criminology has taught us to be wary of the claims of the latter, the contemporary entertainment industry has made little advance on the former. *Oliver Twist* is now encountered most frequently in the form of a musical that empties the original of any resemblance to the culture it sought to portray.

Many of the changes that have taken place during the final third of the twentieth century may be seen as variations on themes and conflicts that can be located at many junctures in earlier periods. However, there are perhaps three areas where the extension of established patterns has been so great as to separate the recent past from the present on a scale that is rarely to be found in parallel forms of social and institutional history. The most obvious is the sheer volume of recorded crime, which has risen from about one per hundred population in the 1950s to five in the 1970s and to ten in 1994. The only comforts that the present government may take are that the figure has grown at a fairly consistent rate, with occasional small annual falls, whichever party has controlled the Home Office (although on average the rate of growth has been slightly higher under Conservative administration than under Labour), and that in the industrialized economies, with the exception of Japan, crime rates have increased generally with affluence and urbanization (although between 1987 and 1994 the increase in England and Wales was the second highest of 19 comparable countries). While the prison population has been prevented from rising in proportion by a continuing extension of non-custodial sentences, it is now fluctuating at around the fifty-thousand level, double the figure in the 1950s. The prison-building programme, which was beginning to gain momentum as this history finished, has still left the service less able to cope with the demand on its capacity than when it started.

In an attempt to exploit the modernizing forces that seemed to be promoting criminal behaviour, the state and its agencies have succeeded only in compounding the crisis in public confidence. There has for many centuries been a slow erosion of lay participation in the criminal justice system. In medieval and early modern England all men were required to participate in the hue and cry; peace-keeping was a universal obligation. Many ordinary men were required to serve a term as a peace-keeping officer such as a constable or tithing man. Local laymen initiated and carried out prosecutions. A much higher proportion of the male population were required to participate in court proceedings as suitors, witnesses, jurymen and court officers than is the case today. In recent decades, the criminal justice system has slipped further out of community control into the hands of the professionals. In the early 1990s, the move to statutory sentencing, most notably in the Criminal Justice Act of 1991, has restricted the capacity of the judiciary to perform its time-honoured if often only symbolic role of modifying the rigours of the law and its consistent bias towards protecting the person and property of the better off. At the same time the enthusiastic exploitation by the police of technologies of communication and surveillance have further distanced them from the communities they are employed to serve. Performance indicators may rise, but public estimation of the competence and integrity of the forces shows little sign of regaining the lost levels of the post-war decades.

Perhaps the most striking epilogue is that of the boys born in the coronation year of 1953, the beginning of the new Elizabethan age after the rigours of depression, war and austerity. One-third of this cohort now have a conviction for an offence on the "standard list", which includes all the indictable and some of the more serious summary offences. By the time those growing up in our present society have reached their forties, the figure will be still higher. What has gone, perhaps for ever, is the optimism that characterized the Victorians who founded the modern systems of policing and punishment. It is no longer believed that progress requires only rational reform and committed public service. As the state turns towards the market to run its prisons, so the electorate turns away from the public sphere for a solace to its fears. And as the century draws to an end, the proportion of the population that can be listed as neither victims nor perpetrators of crime is dwindling into insignificance. In the most direct sense possible, this history ends with us all.

Glossary

affeerers elected manorial officials who set the level of individual amercements at manor courts

ale-tasters elected manorial officials who regulated the food and drink trade in a village or town

amercement financial punishment set by custom or by-law in manor courts

Archdeacon's court lowest level of church court

arson wilful setting on fire of another's or one's own property

assault violent attack upon another person

assizes twice-yearly royal court held in each county normally at the county town. Presided over by visiting Westminster judges, it dealt *inter alia* with the more serious criminal cases

benefit of clergy the right of a cleric to be tried in a church court; this right became extended to criminals who could read. Felons successfully claiming benefit of clergy were branded on the brawn of the left thumb, not executed. A reading test was imposed to establish clerical status. Branding acted as a proof of first conviction. On the second the offender was hanged

benefit of the belly women convicted of a felony who successfully claimed to be pregnant had the death sentence respited until after the birth of the innocent child. Often this reprieve was turned into a full pardon

borough courts very like manor courts in their procedures but located in towns

Borstal special system for the separate imprisonment and hopefully the rehabilitation of young offenders

burglary house-breaking with intent to thieve, originally at night

canting criminal argot of the sixteenth and seventeenth centuries

capital punishment punishment which imposed the death penalty

chap-books cheap popular literature of the early modern period

coining the illicit casting of metal to make fraudulent coinage

coin-clipping paring coin to collect the silver or gold clippings

common scolds a person (usually a woman) accused of being quarrelsome

common serjeant medieval equivalent of a QC

corporal punishment punishment which inflicted pain on the body, most commonly whipping

consistory court the bishop's court

constable elected or appointed peace-keeping officer

cony-catcher Sixteenth-century criminal; the cony was the victim

copyholder peasant farmer who held his land by copy of a manor court roll

court leet a manorial court with criminal jurisdiction

crank mechanism by which criminals were required to lift heavy weights as part of hard labour. Into a small box (which looked like a large coffee mill) fixed to the cell wall went a handle, the resistance of which was regulated by weights and a screw. If the screw was tightened, the handle was harder to turn. An automatic counter recorded the number of times the handle was turned. Prisoners could be required to turn the crank up to 1,800 revolutions in an hour and for two or more hours at a time

embezzlement the fraudulent diversion of money and so on to one's own account or benefit

enclosures the assignment of formerly common land to private ownership, often involving hedging it around

felony a serious crime subject to the death penalty

Fenians members of a group of Irish nationalists committed to the overthrow of English rule by physical force

forgery counterfeiting, falsifying elements of documentation, especially the authenticating signature

fraud criminal deception with intent to benefit the deceiver

game laws ancient laws protecting the rights of the propertied classes to hunt specified species of animal and birds for sport

garrotting highway robbery by throttling the victim

grand jury the county jury which decided whether or not there was a case to answer

grand larceny stealing goods to the value of one shilling or above

Habeas Corpus Act Under this legislation a writ could be issued requiring that a person accused of a crime be present in court at the time of his trial and that they be not be convicted in absentia

hard labour imprisonment with heavy bodily toil imposed upon convicts

High Commission ecclesiastical court

hundred sub-division of a county, sometimes called a wapentake

hulks the hulls of superannuated ships moored in river estuaries as temporary prisons but in fact in use for many years

Inns of Court The organisations of London lawyers (now just barristers)

justice of the peace magistrate

King's Bench Westminster court with criminal jurisdiction

laissez-faire the political philosophy which places the emphasis on the maximum individual effort and the minimum of state intervention

magistrate later term for a justice of the peace

manor court local customary court

manorial steward the presiding judge at a manor court

misdemeanour minor criminal offence

overseers of the poor locally elected or appointed officials charged with looking after the poor on behalf of a parish

peculiar a parish (or other benefice) outside of the bishop's jurisdiction

peine forte et dure punishment designed to make a defendant enter a plea

penal servitude imprisonment with hard labour

penance shaming punishment imposed by church courts

penitentiaries the new prisons of the nineteenth century which sought not simply to offer retribution and to deter but to reform

petty larceny stealing goods valued at less than a shilling

petty sessions court presided over by JPs meeting more frequently than quarter sessions – usually monthly -normally on a hundred basis

pillory wooden framework into which an individual was locked upright for public ridicule for a set period of time

press-gang body of men charged with securing by force individuals to serve in the navy or the army

probation the release of criminals especially first offenders on license and under supervision to complete their sentence in the community as long as they exhibit good behaviour

procuring to secure the services of another person especially a woman for purposes of sexual gratification

quarter sessions court which met four times a year in each county. Presided over by JPs. Dealt with cases that were more serious than those handled by petty sessions but less serious than those which came before the assizes

receiving the acceptance of stolen goods with a view to selling them to others

recidivism re-offending after a period of imprisonment; relapsing into criminal behaviour

recognizances legal instrument binding an individual to obey the order of a court.

recusant Catholics who refused to go to the Anglican church

reeve manorial official

remand prisoners prisoners in custody awaiting trial and therefore not yet found guilty

sidesmen or questmen assistants to the churchwardens

stews brothels

statutory crime offences created by the passing of more and more legislation, especially from the early nineteenth century onwards

Star Chamber equity court dealing mainly with riots

stocks a device which clamped the legs of a person between two planks. Used as a punishment for minor offences and sometimes, in remote villages, as a holding device before an accused person was brought to court.

Ten Commandments God's law given to Moses on Mount Sinai (Exodus ch. 20)

tithes ecclesiastical tax of one-tenth of the produce and harvest of the land paid for the support of the clergy and parts of the Church

tithings groups of neighbours in a village having mutual responsibility to report on each other's misdemeanours

tourn a minor court held twice a year and presided over by the sheriff

treadmill appliance for producing motion by stepping on and off steps attached to a revolving cylinder; used in prisons as a form of hard labour

treason criminal act against the sovereign and the sovereignty of the state

trial juries juries sworn to try a case

Tyburn public place of execution in London

uprightman gang-leader of early modern criminals

vestry the laymen charged *inter alia* with upholding church law in a parish. Later it became the group of people taking political decisions within a parish. A "closed" vestry consisted of a narrow oligarchy. An "open" vestry was more democratic in its make-up

wapentake a hundred

watch the group of people patrolling the streets of a community at night time looking for wrongdoers

Bibliography

Medieval

Bellamy, J. *Crime and public order in the later Middle Ages* (London and Toronto, 1973).

Hanawalt, B. *Crime and conflict in English communities* (Cambridge, MA, 1979).

Harding, A. *The law courts of medieval England* (London and New York, 1973).

Keen, M. *The outlaws of medieval England* (London and Toronto, 1961, rev. 1977).

Early modern

Addy, J. *Sin and society in the seventeenth century* (London, 1989).

Beattie, J. M. *Crime and the courts in England, 1660–1800* (Oxford, 1986).

Brewer, J. & J. Styles (eds). *An ungovernable people: the English and their law in the seventeenth and eighteenth centuries* (London, 1980).

Brinkworth, E. R. C. *Shakespeare and the bawdy court of Stratford* (London, 1972).

Bushaway, R. W. "Grovely, grovely and all grovely": crime and conflict in the English woodland. *History Today* **31**, May 1981, pp. 37–43.

Cockburn, J. S. *A history of English assizes 1558–1714* (Cambridge, 1972).

Cockburn, J. S. (ed.), *Crime in England, 1550–1800* (London, 1977).

Emmison, F. G. (ed.). *Elizabeth life: home, work and land* (Chelmsford, 1976) [part 3 (pp. 197–333) is an extended essay with numerous examples of various aspects of the Elizabethan manor courts of Essex].

Gatrell, V. A. C. et al. (eds). *Crime and the law: the social history of crime in western Europe since 1500* (London, 1980).

Harvey, P. D. A. *Manorial records*, British Records Association, "Archives and the user", no. 5 (1984).

Hay, D. War, dearth and theft in the eighteenth century. *Past & Present* **95**, 1982, pp. 117–60.

Hay, D. et al. (eds). *Albion's Fatal Tree: crime and society in eighteenth-century England* (London, 1975).

Herrup, C. B. *The common peace: participation and the criminal law in seventeenth-century England* (Cambridge, 1987).

Ingram, M. *Church courts, sex and marriage in England, 1570–1640* (Cambridge, 1987).

Judges, A. V. (ed.). *The Elizabethan underworld* (1930) [collection of documents].

Kent, J. *The English village constable, 1588–1642: a social and administrative study* (Oxford, 1986).

McLynn, F. *Crime and punishment in eighteenth-century England* (Oxford, 1989, 1991).

Marchant, R. A. *The church under the law* (Cambridge, 1969).

Moir, E. *The justice of the peace* (Harmondsworth, 1969).

Munsche, P. B. *Gentleman and poachers: the English game laws 1671–1831* (Cambridge, 1981).

Salgado, G. *The Elizabethan underworld* (London, 1977).

Sharpe, J. A. *Crime in early modern England, 1550–1700* (London, 1984) [the best introductory text].

Sharpe, J. A. *Judicial punishment in England* (1990).

Stevenson, J. *Popular disturbances in England, 1700–1832*, 2nd edn (London, 1992).

Styles, J. & J. Brewer (eds). *An ungovernable people: the English and their law in the seventeenth and eighteenth centuries* (London, 1980).

1800–1960

Bailey, V. (ed.). *Policing and punishment in nineteenth-century Britain* (London, 1981).

Carson, W. G. White-collar crime and the institutionalisation of ambiguity: the case of the early factory acts. In *Crime and society, reading in history and theory*, M. Fitzgerald et al. (eds)(London, 1981) pp. 134–47.

Conley, C. *The unwritten law* (Oxford, 1990).

Davis, J. A poor man's system of justice: the London police courts in the second half of the nineteenth century. *Historical Journal* 27, 1984, pp. 309–35.

Donajgrodzki, A. P. *Social control in nineteenth-century Britain* (London, 1977).

Emsley, C. *Crime and society in England 1750–1900* (London, 1987).

Emsley, C. *The English police* (Hemel Hempstead, 1991).

Forsythe, W. J. *The reform of prisoners 1830–1900* (London, 1987).

Forsythe, W. J. *Penal discipline, reformatory projects and the English Prison Commission 1895–1939* (Exeter, 1990).

Garland, D. *Punishment and welfare: a history of penal strategies* (Aldershot, 1985).

Gatrell, V. The decline of theft and violence in Victorian and Edwardian England. In *Crime and the law. The social history of crime in western Europe since 1500*, V. A. C. Gatrell, B. Lenman, G. Parker (eds) (London, 1980), pp. 238–337.

Gatrell, V. Crime, authority and the policeman state. In *The Cambridge social history*, vol. 3, F. M. L. Thompson (ed.) (Cambridge, 1990), pp. 243–310.

Gatrell, V. *The hanging tree* (Oxford, 1994).

Hay, D. & F. Snyder (eds). *Policing and prosecution in Britain, 1750–1850* (Oxford, 1989).

Home Office. *Criminal statistics: England and Wales 1994* (London, 1995).

Ignatieff, M. *A just measure of pain: the penitentiary in the Industrial Revolution* (London, 1978).

Jones, D. J. V. *Crime, protest, community and police in nineteenth-century Britain* (London, 1982).

Jones D. J. V. The new police, crime and people in England and Wales, 1829–1888. *Transactions of the Royal Historical Society*, 1983, pp. 151–68.

McLintock, F. H. & N. H. Avison. *Crime in England and Wales* (London, 1968).

Mannheim, H. *Social aspects of crime in England between the wars* (London, 1940).

Miller, W. *Cops and bobbies – police authority in New York and London, 1830–70* (Chicago, 1977).

Morris, T. *Crime and criminal justice since 1945* (Oxford, 1989).

Palmer, S. *Police and protest in England and Ireland, 1780–1850* (Cambridge, 1988).

Petrow, S. *Policing morals – the Metropolitan Police and the Home Office* (Oxford, 1994).

Radzinowicz, L. & R. Hood. *A history of English criminal law and its administration from 1750,* vol. 5 of *The emergence of penal policy in Victorian and Edwardian England* (Oxford, 1990).

Reiner, R. *The politics of the police* (London, 1992).

Robb, G. *White-collar crime in modern England* (Cambridge, 1992).

Samuel, R. *East End underworld* (London, 1981).

Steedman, C. *Policing the Victorian community* (London, 1984).

Stevenson, J. & R. Quinault *Popular protest and public order* (London, 1974).

Storch, R. The plague of the Blue Locusts: police reform and popular resistance in northern England, 1840–57. *International Review of Social History* **20**, 1975, pp. 61–90.

Thompson, F. M. L. Social control in Victorian Britain. *Economic History Review*, 1981, pp.189–208.

Weinberger, B. The police and the public in mid nineteenth-century Warwickshire. In *Policing and punishment in nineteenth-century Britain*, V. Bailey (ed.) (London, 1981), pp. 65–93.

Wiener, M. J. *Reconstructing the criminal: culture, law, and policy in England 1830–1914* (Oxford, 1990).

Zedner, L. *Women, crime and custody in Victorian England* (Oxford, 1991).

Index

abortion 44
abram-man 20
Ackton Hall Colliery 223
Act of Union, 1800 113
Act of Settlement, 1701 70
addiction 205–6, 240
Adulteration of Food Acts, 1860, 1872
  and 1875 130, 155
adultery 12, 43
Aethelbert 5
Aethelstan 2
affeerers 40
affrays 26, 41
age of consent 200
Alcatraz 227
ale-tasters 40
alehouses 27, 41, 48, 52–3, 58, 65,
  104, 245
alibis 26
Aliens Act, 1905 224
Alstonfield (Staffs.) 39
alternatives to prison 239
amercements 39
amputations 24
anarchists 224
Anarchy (the) 8
Anatomy Act, 1832 130
Angler 20
Anglicanism see Church of England
Anglo-Saxon justice 3–6
animal-maiming 114
anti-Catholicism 119, 120
anti-police riots 151
anti-ritualist 119
anti-Truck 115
apprenticeships 21, 104
approvers 10–11
Archdeacon's Court 33
Argentina 227
armed forces 203, 213
army 109, 112, 117, 145–6, 148–50,
  151, 156, 199, 223

arson 114, 121, 245
Artisans and Labourers Dwelling Act,
  1868 137
Ascoli, David 216
Ascot 201
assault 121, 134, 164, 178, 184, 188,
  203, 205
Assize of Clarendon 8
Assize of Northampton 9
assizes 28–30, 48–9, 50, 56, 62, 64–5,
  67, 74–6, 80, 82, 87, 133
attendance centres 242
Australia 162–3, 167, 171, 173
Automobile Association 207–8

Bailey, James and Thomas 164
Balfour, Jabez 227, 232
Bamford, Samuel 110
banishment 10
bank fraud 187
bank robbers 191
bankruptcies 132, 187–8
banks 132–3, 190
Barings 132
Barnardo's 182
Barons of the Exchequer 7
Bartholomew's Fair (London) 23
bastardy 12, 37, 44
Beattie, J. M. 61, 67, 75–6, 80, 83
Beck, Adolf 215, 232
Bedford and Bedfordshire 152, 160,
  236
Beech, John 133
beggars 20, 128, 152, 196–7
beheading 24
Belgravia 118
benefit of clergy 74–6, 81–2, 85,
benefit of the belly 75–6
Bengal 215
Bentham, Jeremy 115, 158, 168
Benton, Nathan 164
Berkshire 122

bestiality 184
betting 200–202
Betting and Gaming Act, 1960 202
Betting Houses Act, 1853 200
Bible 230
bicycle 215
bigamy 43
Billings, Samuel 164
biological inheritance 248
Birkenhead 224
Birmingham 107, 148
Birmingham Prison 169
black immigrants 248
black propaganda 224
Black Country 115
blackmail 45
Blackstone, Sir William 75, 167
Blake, Lord 118
blanketeers 110
blockage riots 95
blood sports 122
Blood, J. T. 154
Bloody Code 157
Board of Trade 138
boards of visitors 237
body-snatching 130
Boer War 181
bogus shares 187
Bonaparte *see* Napoleon
Bonner's Fields 117
book-keeping 132
bookmakers 200–202, 219
books of orders 55–6, 58
Booth, William 120
borough courts 4, 38, 45
borough forces 211
borough lock-ups 169
boroughs 144–5, 148–9, 154, 156
Borstal 182–3, 236–7, 242
Boss of Britain's underworld 183
Bottomley, Horatio 187
Boulton, George 166
Bow Street Day Patrol 144
Bowmer, Margaret (Lady) 45
boys *see* pretty and rent
brandings 23
Brandreth, Jeremiah 110
Brassington, William 166
bread 124, 130
bread and water diet 170
breaking and entering 165–6
brewing 120, 194

bribery 202, 208
Bridewell (London) 23, 44
Bright, John 118
Bristol 21, 114
British and Foreign Schools Society 106
British Crime Survey 246
Broadmoor 241
brothels 128, 198–200 *see also* stews
Brotherton, General 147
Brown, Thomas 166
Brown, William 245
Bryan, Joseph 164
buggery 29, 203
building societies 134
Burdett, Sir Francis 110
bureaucratic 193
Burgess, Guy 204
burglars and burglaries 29, 121, 128, 134, 143, 150, 177, 188–9, 215, 245
Burke, Edmund 107
Burn, Richard 57
Burn, W. L. 103, 104
Burslem (Staffs.) 164, 166
Bushaway, R. W. 91
Butler, Josephine 150, 199
Buxton, Thomas Fowell 159, 161
by-laws 40

Camp Hill 243
cannabis 206
Cannock (Staffs.) 33, 39, 45
Cannock Chase (Staffs.) 30, 248
canon law 249
Canterbury (Kent) 12, 33
Canterbury Savings Bank 186
canting language 20
capital and capitalism 124, 137, 139, 150–51, 186, 188, 198
capital offences and punishment 23–4, 73–7, 82–3, 85, 125, 142, 157–9, 165–6, 171, 173, 179, 232
Capper, Joseph 167
Captain Swing 113,
card-sharps 20
Cardiff 206
Cardington (Beds.) 160
Carlisle 113
Carnarvon, Lord 228
Carpenter, Mary 172, 180
carters 22
Carthusian monks 24

carting 79
Cartwright, Sir William 155
cash-orientated society 129, 139
casual thieves 247
casual wards 197
Catholic Association 113
Catholic Emancipation 113
Catholics 18, 26
Cato Street Conspiracy 111
Caveat for common cursitors 20, 245
cells 149, 233
centralization and central government
146–8, 150, 155–6, 168
Ceylon 216
Chadwick, Edwin 147, 162
chap-books 20, 249
chaplains 229, 243
charge rooms 149
charities 197
Chartists and Chartism 111, 114,
115–17, 151, 166, 223
Chater, Daniel 88
chemists 216
Cheshire 27
Chester 27, 29, 39, 148, 245
chief constables 153, 155, 209, 213,
217–18
child abuse 26
children 129, 135, 161, 179, 182–3,
195, 204, 235–6
Children Act, 1908 180, 236
Chinese 248
Chipping Ongar (Essex), 36
cholera 137
Christian, Edward 122
Christian mission and conscience
127, 131, 162
church courts 6, 12, 33–8, 79
Church and King mobs 107
Church of England 104, 106
Church of England Temperance
Society 172
churchwardens 34, 51–6
Cinque Ports 30
City of London 187
Clare family 165–6
Clare, May 166
Clark, Robert 245
class 141, 150, 183, 200, 208, 222–3
clerical justices 57
clothing 181, 189–90, 199, 232
cocaine 195, 206

cock fight 143
Cockburn, J. S. 75
coin-clipping 24
coining 90, 131, 165, 186, 214
Cold War 204
colliers *see* miners
Colquhoun, Patrick 63
Combination Acts, 1799 109, 113
commerce 139, 186–8, 205
committee of magistrates 211
common scolds 40
common serjeant 28
Common Pleas 9
communal hostility 212
Communist Party 224
companies 190
company directors 187
company law 186–7
compulsory attendance in 1880 236
compurgation 5
Congregationalists 160, 172
Conservative Party 250
consistory court 33
constable *see* parish constables
consumer society 150, 190
Contagious Diseases Acts, 1864, 1866
and 1869 199
convicts 163, 167, 171–2, 227, 242
cony-catchers 23
Cook, Thomas 195
copyholders 20, 40
Corn Laws, 1815 108
Cornwall (Duchy of) 30
coroners 9–10, 26–8, 50
corporal punishment 6, 28, 79–80,
159, 163, 170
corrupt practice 133
Corrupt Practices Act, 1883 119
corruption 216, 225
Cottrill, Isaac 153–4
Council in the Marches of Wales 30,
47
Council of the North 30, 47
Counter the (prison) 25
county asylums 171
county constabularies 149
county court 49
county forces 211
county gaol 50, 169
county interest 169
County and Borough Police Act,
1856 147, 154, 177, 209

County Clare, Ireland 113
Coupland, Hannah 166
court and criminal statistics 121, 124,
  151–3, 178–9, 181–2, 185, 193–4,
  198–90, 203, 205, 207, 220, 247
courts leet 38, 55
court officers 250
Court of Criminal Appeal 232
Coventry 107
Coventry and Lichfield (diocese) 33
Cox, Edward 136
cranks 170, 229, 237
Crawford, William 169
crime and criminal behaviour
  120–21, 124, 126, 135, 141, 145, 148,
  149, 150, 152, 177–9, 180–82, 184,
  187–8, 190–91, 202–3, 207
crime rates 225, 245, 248
crime-prone generation 125, 139, 166
Crimean War 148, 199
crimes against the person 132, 139
crimes of violence 121, 135–6
criminal class 125–7, 139, 187,
  190–91, 222
criminal conspiracies 215
criminal damage 245
criminal gene 248
criminal justice system 250
criminal personality 238
Criminal Investigation Department
  216
Criminal Jurisdiction Act, 1879 239
Criminal Justice Act, 1991 250
Criminal Justice Administration Act,
  1914 239
Criminal Justice Act, 1855 221
Criminal Justice Act, 1948 242
Criminal Law Amendment Act, 1885
  203
Criminal Law Amendment Act, 1912
  203
Criminal Record Office 216
criminally insane 241
criminology 185, 249
Cromwell, Oliver 7
Cromwell, Thomas 45
Cruikshank, George 131
cuckoldry 43
curia regis 6
currency 121
custodial sentences 157, 159, 167,
  172, 208

cut-pursing 20, 24
cutlery trade 119

dairy owners 129
Danelaw 3
Dangerous Drugs Acts, 1920 and 1923
  206
Dartmoor 170, 233, 236
Davies, Joseph 166
Dawes, Dr 128
de Veil, Thomas 58
dearth 188
death penalty see capital punishment
debt 131, 153, 161, 220
Defence of the Realm Act 224
deformed children 136
defrauding see fraud
Dekker, Thomas 20, 43
delinquent children 237
demanding money 197
demonstrations 224
deodand 9–10
depressions (economic) 111, 125,
  127, 170, 189–90, 196–7, 199
detectives 152, 216
deterrence 83–5, 163, 228–9
Devon Quarter Sessions 27
Dialogus de Scaccario 11
Dickens, Charles 20, 105, 245
diet 162, 170, 228, 233
discipline 171, 212, 228
diseases 21
disorderly behaviour 122, 248
dissenters 107
distilling 122
disturbances 107–14, 116–7, 119–20
disturbing the peace 182
Dixon of Dock Green 209
doctors 213, 231, 233, 243
dog-racing 202
Dogberry 209
Donajgrodzki, A. P. 104
Doncaster (Yorks.) 45
double standards 199
Dowd, Michael 166
Doyle, Conan 216
drink and drunkenness 38, 105, 120,
  122, 125–6, 134–7, 152–3, 166, 181,
  183–5, 189, 191, 193–5, 197–9,
  201–7, 212, 218–9, 220, 233, 240
driving 193
drovers 22

drownings 24, 246
drugs 20, 177, 193, 204, 206–8
Du Cane, Edmund 228
ducking stool 78
Dudley, Catherine 165
Dumont, Etienne 158
Durham 30

Eardley, John 164
East End 182–3
East Midlands 115
Eden, Sir Frederick 167
Edinburgh Review 149
education 103, 105–6, 127, 161, 170,
 181–3, 201, 204, 228, 236–7
Edward the Confessor 7
Edward VI (1547–53) 24
Eirenarcha 57
elderly 248
elections 114
electric telegraph 201
electroplating 214
elementary schools 214
Eliot, F. P. 109
élites 150
Ellis, Havelock 203
embezzlement 49, 133, 153, 186–8,
 190, 247
Emergency Powers Act, 1920 224
Emma Silver Mining Company of Utah
 186
employers and employment 105, 114,
 180–84
Emsley, Clive 126, 130, 142, 149,
 157, 169
enclosures 93–6, 98, 106, 114, 123,
 126
Engels, Frederick 127
English Civil War 18
entertainment 135
epidemic 233
Essex 29, 34
Etruria (Staffs.) 143
eugenicists 238, 248
evangelicals 160–62
Eversthorpe 243
Exchequer 7
excise duty 194
excommunication 34
Exeter (Devon) 21, 107
Explosives Act, 1875 155
extradition 227
eyre system 7, 28

factories 103, 147
factory acts 133, 138
factory inspectors 108
Fagin 20, 245
false prospectus 187
family and family life 103, 104, 135–7,
 178, 180, 182–3, 189, 197–8, 202, 247
fantasy 249
Farrington, William 36
felons and prosecution societies 26,
 28, 124, 142–3, 159, 207
female delinquency 183, 233
Fenians 145, 171, 223, 227
fictitious mortgages 133
Fielding, Henry 49, 65, 67
Fielding, Sir John 59, 141
film 249
financial services 186–7
fines and fining 82–3, 130, 160,
 172–3, 202, 208, 239
fingerprinting 215, 218
Finsbury Court 44
fire-service 154
firearms 246
fires 143
First World War 103, 120, 154, 195,
 197, 206, 220, 224, 237
fixed-point system 217
flogging 136, 159, 163, 173, 231, 242
food 106, 181, 189–90, 195
food riots 55
football 106, 182
football pools 202
foreign spies 224
foreigners 21, 24
forest law 6
forgers 131, 159, 183, 187, 215, 245
fornication 12, 43, 104
fortune tellers 196
Foucault's *Discipline and punish* 228
Founsing Besse 44
Fox, John 165
framework knitters 115
fraud 128, 131, 132, 134, 185–6,
 188, 227, 245
Fraud Squad 187
French 111, 112
French Revolution 107
French system of anthropometry 215
French Wars 108
friendly societies 132–3
Fry, Elizabeth 160, 161–2, 173

fuel 189
full employment 212

gagging acts, 1817 108
Galley, William 88
Galley-Chater 89
Galton, Francis 215
gambling 41, 134–5, 181, 193, 200–201, 204
game laws 49, 122
Gaol Fees Abolition Act, 1815 160
gaols see prisons
Gaols Act, 1823 168
Garland, David 228
garrotting 137, 159, 170, 177, 228, 248
Gatrell, V. C. H. 150, 154
gender 183
general elections 223
Germany 203
girls 200
Gladstone Committee in 1895 237
Gladstone, W. E. 118, 205
Glanvil 11
gleaning 129
Gloucestershire 42
Godfrey's Cordial 204
goods in transit 129
Gough, Richard 68–9
government 142, 146, 150, 155
governors 235, 242
Gower, Lord 109
Grafton, Duke of 147
grand jury 27–8
grand larceny 74–5, 80–81
Grant, Albert 186
grants see subsidies
Great Depression 178, 189
Great Revolt (1381) 17, 39
Greatbach, George 166
greed 181, 188
Greene, Robert 20
Greenwood, James 130
Greenwood, Walter 191
Greg, R. H. 138
Grey, Lord 114
Grey, Sir George 147–8, 154
Griffiths, A. 126
gross indecency 203
Grosvenor, Lord 118
Grundy, Sam 201
guns 209

Habeas Corpus Act, suspension of, 1817 108
Habitual Criminals Act, 1869 121
Hambleton Hannah 164
Hammond, J. L. and Barbara 107
Hampstead 118
hand-loom weavers 115
Hanley (Staffs.) 142–3, 164
harbours 147
hard labour 159, 162, 170, 173, 228, 203
Harding, Arthur 182, 191
Harding, Broadhurst 165
Harman, Thomas 20, 23, 245, 248
Harris, Thomas 36
Harrison, Christopher 75
Harrison, Royden 118
Harrowby, Lord 111
Hartshorne, John 164
Harvey, J. C. and W. K. 132
Harvey's Bank 132
Haughton, John 157
Hay, Douglas 61, 89, 125
Heath, Priscilla 166
Hendon 216
Henry I (1100–35) 7
Henry II (1154–89) 8
Henry VII (1485–1509) 17
Henry, Sir Edward 215
hereditary criminality 241
Hereford 113
heresy 24
Herschel, William 215
Hertfordshire Assizes 29
Hext, Edward 63
high constable 53–4, 66
high court judges 240
High Commission (court of) 18
High Holborn 152
highway robbery 128, 137, 166
Hill, Billy 183, 191
Hill, Matthew Davenport 172
Holmes, Sherlock 216
Home Office 146, 148, 154–5, 211, 215, 218, 223, 231, 249
Home Office Committee on Detectives 217
Home Secretary 168, 225, 211
homeless poor 3
homicide 121, 136, 178, 180
homicide rate 246
homosexuality 193, 203–4, 208

Hood, Robin 18, 123, 249
hooligans 177, 180–81
horse races 201
horse thieves 20, 24
Horsley, Canon 188
hospitals 103, 131
Houghton, W. E. 104, 105
householders 143
housemasters 237
houses of correction 49, 58, 82
How criminals are made and prevented
(1913) 188
Howard, John 50, 86, 160, 162–3,
167, 173, 228
Howard League 159
Howarth, George 134
Hudson, George 186
hue and cry 250
hulk fever 163
hulks, 160, 162–3, 166–7
humanitarianism 104, 181
Hume, Joseph 113
hundredal juries 51–2
hundreds 4, 25, 54, 56–8
Hue and Cry and Police Gazette 59
Hue and Cry 142
hunger 198
hunger marches 224
Hungerford (Lord) 45
husbands 134, 135–7, 139, 178, 220
Hyde Park riots 118, 223
Hylls, William 37
hypodermic needle 206

identity parades 215
Ignatieff, Michael 169, 228
illegal street trading and soliciting 152
illegitimate and deformed children
136, 139
illicit still 143
importuning 203
imprisonment 50, 80–82, 85, 111,
114, 117, 131, 135–6, 159, 164, 166,
199, 202 *see also* prisons
improvement commissioners 143
incest 43
indecency 44, 203
India 215
industrial revolution 178, 186
industrial schools 172, 180, 236
Industrial Schools Act 1857, 172
industrializing 189

industry and industrial society 103,
105–9, 113–15, 117–20, 127, 152
Ine, King 6
Inebriates Act 240
infanticide 22, 35, 136–7, 178, 180
infectious disease 233
inflation 106
information technology 247
informers 216
Innes, Joanna 82
Inns of Court 21
insane *see* lunatics
insider knowledge 132
Inskip, John 164
inspector of prisons 160
inspectorate of constabulary 148, 155
inspectors and inspectorate 131, 138,
145–6, 149, 156, 169, 172
instructors 243
insurance companies 132
international crime 215, 247
Intoxicating Liquors Act, 1872 194
Ireland and the Irish 20, 113, 119,
222–3, 248

Jack the Ripper 137
Jennings, Nicholas 23
Jews 2, 21, 215, 248
jobs 115, 189
Jones, David 150–51
Jones, Sir Thomas 64
journalists 191
journals 142
judges 221, 231
juries 27, 75–7, 158, 173, 221, 250
juries of presentment 8
justices of the peace 11, 26, 47,
48–50, 53–9, 63–6, 68, 82
see also magistrates
justices in eyre 7, 9
justices's clerk 27
justiciar 7, 8
juvenile convicts 163
juvenile courts 179, 236
juvenile delinquency 172, 180, 182
juvenile establishment 163
juveniles 21, 106, 172, 173, 179, 191,
206, 235

Keele (Staffs.) 45
Kensit, John 120

Kent 27, 42, 142, 180, 184
Kent, Joan 53, 66
Kerr, Dr Norman 205
Kettle, Richard 164
King's Bench 9, 30

labelling deviancy 219
Labouchere, Henry 203
labour 125, 159
labour exchange 224
Labour Party 224, 250
labouring poor 193
laissez-faire 120, 123, 137, 187
Lambarde, William 27, 57
Lambeth (Surrey), 25
Lanarkshire 117
Lancashire 42, 117, 151, 153, 168, 171
Lancaster (Duchy of) 30, 42
Lancaster 170
Landau, Norma 65
Lane End (Staffs.) 165
larcenies 121, 165, 177–8, 184, 188, 190
Lateran Council (1215) 10
Latin 6, 39
laudanum 204
lavatories 243
law 177, 180, 182, 185, 187–8, 190, 193–4, 200, 220
law and order 210
law officer 131
laws of contract 129
lawyers 209, 213
lay participation 250
Leedham, David 164
leet jury 53
legislators 201
lesbiansim 203
libel 203
liberal state 216
liberal welfarism 238
Liberal government 223, 240
Liberator Building Society 227
liberties 3
Lichfield (Staffs.) 28
Lichfield Cathedral (Dean and Chapter of) 33
Lighting and Watching Act, 1833 145
limited liability 186
Lindop, James 166
Lisbon Tramways Company 186

Lister, Samuel 64
literacy test 214
Liverpool 206, 245
Liverpool Street station 182
Lockett, Thomas 26
loitering 181, 196
London 20–25, 30, 110, 123, 128, 132–3, 137, 141–2, 144, 146, 149, 151, 154, 196, 206, 223, 245
London General Omnibus Company 129
London Working Men's Association 115
Longton (Staffs.) 119, 128, 132–3
Longton and Fenton Building Society 133
lords lieutenant 49
Love on the dole 191, 201
Lowe, Alexander 164
Luddism 109, 121
Lunacy Act, 1890 206
Lunar Society 107
lunatics 134, 171, 173

Maberley, Colonel 116
machine-breaking 108–9, 114, 121
Mackintosh, Sir James 157
Magdalen College, Oxford 45
magistrates and magistracy 108, 111–12, 119, 129, 133, 136, 139, 141–2, 144, 146, 149, 152, 155–8, 163, 166, 168, 184, 195–6, 199, 201–2, 207, 219–21, 240
magistrates' court 196
Maintenance of Wives Act, 1886 220
male rite of passage 247
malicious woundings 207
Manchester 107, 111–12, 119, 148, 172, 184, 222
Manchester court leet 39
Mannheim, Hermann 182
manors 51, 146
manor courts 12, 38–42, 82
manorial steward 39
manufacturers 138–9, 143
market-watching 143, 155
martial law 23
Marxist 150
Mary (1553–8) 18
mass entertainment 195
Master and Servant Act, 1867 223
Matheson and Jardine 132

Matrimonial Causes Act, 1878   220
matrimony   104
Mayhew, Henry   20, 127–8, 131–2, 190
Mayne, Sir Richard   118
McNaghten Rules   240
Mental Deficiency Act, 1913   241
mentally ill   240, 241
Messina   191
Methodists   123
metropolis *see* London
Metropolitan Police Act, 1829   142, 144–5
Metropolitan Police Force   118, 146–7, 152, 155, 211, 215–16, 218
MI5   224
middle classes   127, 132, 136, 150, 152, 154, 157, 167, 171, 183–4, 188, 199, 207–8, 220
middle-class crimes and offenders   124, 137, 139, 150
Middlesex Justice Act, 1792   58, 142
Middlesex Quarter Sessions   22
Middlewich (Ches.)   27
Midland Revolt (1607)   18
military drill   214
military *see* army
militia   64
Mill, John Stuart   105
Millbank   168
millocrats   157
miners   116, 129
ministrales   9
minority ethnic groups   248
Moir, Esther   56
Molesworth Commission   167
money   135, 160, 186–8
Money Payments Act, 1935   239
moral investigators   198
morality   241
morphine   206
morse code   215
mothers   21, 181
motor cars   185, 193, 196, 207, 215, 219, 222, 246
motorized patrols   215
mugging   191
Muir, Charles   200
Municipal Corporations Act, 1835   144–5, 147
murder   8, 24, 29, 137, 143, 158–9, 178, 183, 207, 246

Murphy, William   119
mutilation   159
mutual improvement societies   127
My prison life   227
Mysteries of police and crime (1902)   126, 131
myths about crime   18–21

nail makers   115
Nantwich (Ches.)   27
Napoleon   105, 108–9
Napoleonic Wars   139, 189
narcotics   206
national criminal record   215
national force   211
national penitentiaries   169, 173
National Council for Civil Liberties   224
National Insurance Acts, 1911   212
National Police College   214
National Society   106
National Society for the Prevention of Cruelty to Children   180
National Unemployed Workers' Movement   224
neo-Darwinism   238
nepotism   153
new model unions   119
new regulatory state   139
New Poor Law *see* Poor Law
New South Wales   163, 167
Newcastle under Lyme   119, 143, 153, 165
Newgate   158, 160–61
Newington   23
Newmarket   201
newspapers   115, 125, 135, 137, 139, 165, 177, 182
night patrols   143
night-walkers   143
Nightingale, Florence   205
non-custodial sentencing   159, 160, 171, 173, 250
non-penal sentences   232
nonconformity   202
Norden, John   40
Norman Conquest   6–7
Norman French   6
Northamptonshire   147
Northern Ireland   120
Northwich (Ches.)   27
Norwich (Norf.)   21

Notting Hill and Nottingham race riots 225
Nottingham 107, 114

O'Connell, Daniel 113
oakum 170, 229
Oath of Supremacy 24
off-course gambling 219
offences against the person 134, 136
Official Secrets Act 224
Old Bayley (London court) 24
Oliver Twist 245, 249
opium 204–6
order 177, 180, 188, 190, 193
organized sport 195
orphans 21
Orwell, George 197
outlaws 18
overseers of the poor 47–8, 51, 53–4, 56
Owen, George of Henllys 63–4
Oxford 45

Paget, Lord 90
Palmer, Enoch 133
Palmerston, Lord 148
Panopticon 168
parents and parenting 126, 128, 139, 180–82
Paris Sûréte 216
parishes 51–4, 146, 149
parish constables 30, 51–9, 66–7, 212, 221
parish priest 45
Parker, Alice 45
Parkhurst 227
Parliament 133, 143, 158, 160, 187, 196, 231
Paterson, Alexander 242, 249
pathologists 216
Patriche, Mary 45
pawn shop 135
pawnbroking 191, 199, 220
peculiars 33
pederasts 22
pedlars 196
Peel, Sir Robert 59, 144, 168, 209, 212, 232
peine forte et dure 28
penal servitude 228, 232, 242
penal theory 190
"Penal practice in a changing society" 243

Penal Servitude Act, 1853 171
Penal Servitude Act, 1864 228
penance 34, 43–4
Pendleton (Lancashire) 153
Penitentiary Act, 1779 85, 167
penny capitalism 198, 201
penny post 214
pensions (police) 153–6, 212–13, 211
Pentonville 169, 233
Pentrich Revolution, 1817 110
performance indicators 250
perjury 159
person 245
personal observation 218
Peryn, Thomas 41
Peterloo, 1819 111, 112
Petrow, Stefan 220
petty constable *see* parish constables
petty crime 142, 233
petty juries 52
petty larceny 75, 79, 80–81, 215
petty offenders 231
petty sessions 47, 53, 57–8, 65, 82, 221
petty theft 122, 126, 128, 133, 139
philanthropy 103, 172, 220
phone-tapping 108, 224
photography 215, 218
physical assault 182
physical education 242
pickpockets 20, 124, 128, 247
pillory 24, 77–8, 136, 159, 173
pimps 200
pipe-rolls 7, 8
piracy 24
Pitt, William the Younger 108
Place, Francis 113
plain-clothes policemen 152, 199
plaintiffs 219
Plug Plot Riots, 1842 116, 144, 153, 166
poachers and poaching 41, 89–90, 97, 114, 122, 130
poisoning 24, 246
Poisons and Pharmacy Act, 1868 205–6
police and policing 108, 114–24, 129, 133, 135, 137, 141–9, 150–56, 164, 168, 171, 177–9, 181–2, 184–5, 190–98, 200–208, 213, 220, 250
police boxes 217
police court missionaries 172

police riot 224
police stations 149, 151, 154, 202
police strikes of 1918 and 1919 213
police training school in London 214
Police Act, 1840 147
Police Act, 1890 211
Police Act, 1964 209
Police Federation 213
Police Service Advertiser 154
political reform 112
political refugees 224
politicians 223
Pollock, Lord 133
poor 184, 188, 194, 198, 208, 220, 222
poor laws 27, 47, 51, 56, 58, 69, 107, 113, 115–16, 144, 146–7, 151, 155, 168, 196–7, 235
poor parenting 248
poor rates and poor relief 27, 136, 143
Poor Law Act, 1601 51, 69
Poor Man's Guardian 150
popular amusements 120
popular opinion 111
popular perceptions of crime 246
population changes 17, 124
pornography 44, 196
Portland 227, 233
post office and postmasters 104, 108, 116, 212, 214
Postal espionage 223
Potteries 147, 153, 164
Pottersbury (Salop) 147
poverty 127, 129, 160, 181–2, 188–9, 190–91, 198, 200
Prescott (Lancs.) 42
press-gang 106
Preston, William 187
pretty boys 22
Prevention of Crime Act, 1908 237
Price, Richard 64, 107
price-setting 95
Priestley, Joseph 107
Prigger of prancers 20
Prince Regent 110
Principles of punishment 136
printers 129
prison administration 233
prison building 238
prison discipline 170
prison disturbances 228

prison inspectorate 169
prison library 227
prison officers 171, 209
prison uniform 242
prison visiting 172
prison workshops 227
Prisons Act, 1865 228
Prison Act, 1877 228
Prison Act, 1898 237
Prison Commissioners 228
prisons and prisoners 50, 131, 137, 143, 157–8, 160–63, 168, 171–3, 177, 179, 183, 187, 189, 197, 228, 239
privileges 229
Privy Council 30, 56
probation 163, 171–3, 240
Probation of First Offenders Act, 1887 172
Probation of Offenders Act, 1907 240
procuring 128, 200
professions and professionalism 104, 144, 149, 152, 154–6, 185, 205
profits 186
prohibition 194, 201–2
promotion (police) 153, 155–6
propertied 142–3, 189, 193, 207
propertied classes 188
property 132, 134, 137, 139, 142, 144–6, 152, 156, 166, 177, 182, 184–5, 187–8, 190, 208
property qualification 221
prosecution societies 142
prosecutions 124, 158, 219
prostitution 20, 25, 41, 43–5, 128, 134, 166, 184, 185, 191, 193, 197–9, 198–9, 201, 204, 218, 233, 247
Protestant Truth Society 120
public analysts 130
public disorder 189
public health 137
public houses 135, 201, 208
public order 120, 145, 150, 197, 204, 200, 205
public panic 228
public prosecutor 124
public schools 228, 237
public works 229
Public Order Act, 1936 224
punishment 50, 73–86, 179, 191, 196, 207, 229, 238
puritanism 25
Purleigh (Essex) 37

Quakers   134, 160–61
qualifying examinations (police)   214
quarter sessions   26–8, 47–9, 50–5, 57–8, 63, 65, 67, 82–3, 87, 97, 146
Queensberry, Lord   203

radicals   110–13
radio-controlled police car   215, 217
Radzinowicz, Sir Leon   148–9
ragged schools   127
railways and railway companies   104, 132, 138, 186
Rampton   241
rape   8, 24, 29, 41, 183–4, 203
Ratcliffe Highway murders   137
ratepayers   152, 218
Ratsey's ghost   19
Rayleigh (Essex), 38
Reade, Charles   158, 162, 245
rebellion   23
receiving   128, 165, 178
recidivism   191, 233, 237, 239
recognizances   26
recorded crime   247, 249
recording and analysis of criminal behaviour   249
recreations   151
recruits   212
recusants   26
Redding, Cyrus   123
reeve   40
reform and reformers   34, 108, 111, 158, 160, 163, 220, 236, 238
Reform Bill, 1832   124
Reform League   118
Reformation   18, 33, 43
reformatories   179–80, 236
Reformatory Schools Act, 1854   172
refugees   21
Register of Habitual Criminals   215
registers of local inhabitants   218
regulatory offences   172–3
regulatory state   130, 138
regulatory system   187
rehabilitation   85, 228
religion   103, 105
Religious Census of 1851   105
remand prisoners   161, 173
remission   237
rent boys   203
Report on Rural Constabularies   147
Requests (court of)   30

respectability   103, 105, 111, 153, 155, 185–9, 191, 193, 195, 201, 205, 208
Restoration   17
resurrection men   130
retribution   84–5, 236, 249
Richards, W. J.   108
Richter, D.   151
rick-burning   114
Riot Act   114
riots and rioters   95, 107–9, 114, 116–18, 122–3, 146, 151, 242, 248
see also disturbances
Ritschel, George   67
ritual cleansing   84–5
river crime   128
robberies   121, 142–3, 185, 198
Rochdale Savings Bank   134
Rochester (Bishop of), 24
Rolleston Report   206
Romilly, Sir Samuel   157
rough music   68
Rowan, Charles, Metropolitan Police Commissioner   146
rowdy activity   219, 222
Rowntree, Seebohm   190
royal commission   202
Royal Commission on the Rural Constabulary   126, 145
Royal Irish Constabulary   144
Royal Mint   214
Royle   Edward   124
Rudé, George   121, 166
Rugeley (Staffs.)   33, 39, 41, 45
Ruggles-Brise, Evelyn   228, 237, 242
Rule, John   92
Rural Constabulary Act, 1839   145, 147
Russell, Lord John   114

sackings   213
Sadleir, Michael   186
safe-breakers   214
safe-manufacturers   214
sailors   21
Salford   112
Salisbury (bishop of)   33–4
Salisbury (Wilts.)   21
Salvation Army Riots   120
sanctuary   10
Sandon (Essex)   37
Sandys, Edward (Archbishop)   45

savings 188
school attendance officer 181
school for pickpockets 20
schools *see* education
Scotland Yard 126, 187, 214
Scots 248
Second Reform Bill, 1867 118
Second World War 178, 196, 202, 207–8, 225
secondary punishment 159
secret ballot 119
secret policemen 216
Secret Service Bureau 224
sedition 122
Select Committee on the Police 147–8
Select Committee on Criminal and Destitute Juveniles 141
self-help 107, 187
sentences 111, 231–2, 243
separate systems 169, 242
sergeant (police) 155, 213
sex 135, 183–5, 191, 197–8
sexual offences 8, 24, 29, 34, 41, 43–6, 158, 178, 180
sexual taboos 42
Shakespeare, William 43, 45, 141
shaming punishments 77–9
share-rigging 187
Sharpe, J. A. 82, 84
Shaw, Charles 167
Sheffield "outrages" 119
sheriffs 3, 8, 27, 49–50, 5–6
shire courts 4
shoplifting 185
Shufflebotham, Hugh 165
sidesmen or questmen 34
Sidmouth, Lord 108
Sikes, Bill 249
silence 229
silent system 169, 171, 173
sin 181
Sindall, Richard 188
Six Acts, 1819 112
Skeleton Armies 120
slavery 3, 6
sleeping out 197
slopping out 243
slums 187, 190
Smiles, Samuel 107, 127
Smith, John 215
Smith, Sidney 167

smuggling and smugglers 88–90, 97, 123, 128
Social aspects of crime between the wars 182
social control and discipline 104, 105, 120, 169
social purity 193
socialism 202
Society for the Improvement of Prison Discipline 168
Society for the Study of Inebriety 205
socio-political crime 87–99
sodomy 45, 184
soldiers 21, 23
soliciting 128, 200
solicitors 219
solitary system and solitary confinement 159, 162, 169–70, 170, 173, 227, 242
sorcery 35
South Sea Bubble 186
Southwark (Surrey), 20, 22
Southwark stews 44
Sowthbemflete (Essex), 36
special constables 148, 153–4
Special Irish Branch of the Metropolitan Police 223
Spence, Thomas 111
spies 108, 150–52, 204, 216
Stafford 26, 28, 33
Stafford coroner 26
Stafford gaol 165, 230, 234
Staffordshire 26–8, 30, 39, 41, 45, 109, 115–17, 133, 147, 153, 158, 166
Staffs Advertiser 165
Stamford Rivers (Essex), 37
standard list 250
Star Chamber 30
Starr-Bowkett 134
state 177–8, 180, 193, 194, 201
state control and intervention 107, 138
State of Prisons in England and Wales 160
statistics 177, 180, 188–90, 202, 218
see also court and criminal statistics
statutory crime 137
statutory penalties 173
statutory sentencing 250
Steedman, Carolyn 144, 146–7, 149, 152–4
Stennett, Samuel 160

Stephen (1135–54)   8
Stephen, Sir James   157
Stephens, Revd J. Rayner   116
stereo systems   247
stereotypes   218
Stevenson, John   114–55
stipendiary magistrates   221
Stock Exchange   186
Stockport   119
stocks   79, 159, 173
Stoke-on-Trent   119, 157
Stone (Staffs.)   164
Storch, Robert   150–51
strangling   246
street betting   200
street offences   200
street trading   152, 182
Street Offences Act, 1959   200, 202
streetwalkers   198–9
streets   181, 183, 191, 196
strikes   151, 223
strip searches   227
Styles, John   90, 92
subcontracting   138
subsidies   148–9, 154, 156, 211
suffragettes   224
suicide   162, 169
suitors   250
Summary Jurisdiction (Married
  Women) Act, 1895   220
Summary Jurisdiction Act, 1879   221
Sunday observance   122
Sunday schools   106, 127
Sunday trading   118
Superintendents   153–4
Surrey   142
surveillance   150, 220
surveyors of the highway   51, 53–4
Sussex Assizes   29
swindlers   128, 187
Symons   C. T.   216
syndicalists   118
system of marks   228

Tasmania   167
Taylor, A. J. P.   103
Taylor, W. C.   145
teachers   243
team policing   217
technology   214, 250
teenagers *see* juveniles
telegraph   215

telephone   217
television   249
temptation   212
Ten Commandments   36
Test and Corportion Acts, Repeal of,
  1828   113
Thames (River)   25
Thames Police Office   142
The ballard of Reading Gaol   238
*The justice of the peace and the parish
  officer*   57
The road to Wigan Pier   197
The Times   152, 163
theft   29, 40, 139, 150, 166, 183–5,
  191, 209, 220, 222, 245
theology   127
thief-takers   142
thieves   128, 178, 190, 191, 220
Thistlewood, Arthur   111
Thompson, E. P.   109, 112,123
Thompson, F. M. L.   105
Thompson, Flora   151
Thomson, Basil   224
ticket-of-leave system   163, 171, 228
tithes   114, 123
tithing man   250
tithings   40
tolls   123
Tomes, Nancy   136
Torrens' Act, 1868   137
torture   229
Tottenham Court Road   118
tough on crime   248
tourn   49
town lock-ups   233
Town Police Clauses Act, 1847   145
towns   123, 141, 143, 146, 193, 196,
  198
toys   181
trade offences   24
trade recession *see* depression
trade unions   113, 119, 223
Trade Union Act, 1871   119
tradition   248
Trafalgar Square   118
traffic offences   181
trafficking   170
training (police)   152, 154, 214, 221
tramps   196–7
transportation   80–81, 85–6, 111,
  117, 148, 157–8, 162–7, 169, 171,
  173, 227, 232

Transportation Act, 1718   81–2
treadmill   170, 229, 237
treason   24, 122
Treason Trials Bill, 1696   70
trial by ordeal   5, 8
trial by battle   7
trial juries   27–8
Trotter, Eleanor   54
truck *see also* anti-truck   129
true-life trial publications   249
Tunstall (Staffs.)   166
turf frauds   216
turnpike riots   95
turnpikes   123
Turpin, Dick   128
Twemlow, Mr   166

Ulpian   249
underemployment   190
undergraduate   247
unemployed workers' riot of 1886   223
unemployment   153, 180, 189, 196–7
unemployment insurance   189
unfair trading   128
uniforms   141, 151–2, 154, 213
unionize   213
Unitarians   107
universities   103
unsecured overdrafts   132
upper class   152
uprightman   20
urbanization and urban world   106, 109, 120, 122, 127, 145, 151, 156, 187, 200, 201
USA   169
Uttoxeter (Staffs.)   154
Uxbridge (Earl of)   94, 96–7

vagabonds   19, 26
Vagrancy Act, 1824   196
Vagrancy Act, 1898   203
Vagrancy Act, 1935   197
vagrants and vagrancy   23, 49, 143, 152, 162, 193, 196–8, 201, 203, 218
vandalism   24, 181
venereal disease   199
vestry   34, 53, 145
vice   43, 191, 206
victims   124–5, 135, 158, 183–6, 188–9, 193, 195, 198–9, 207, 218, 248
Victoria   223

Victorian boom   188
Victorian commentators   248
village   146
Vincent, Howard   216, 223
violence and violent crime   125, 135, 136, 139, 148, 151, 178, 180, 182–5, 188–9, 195, 246
visit   229
visitations (ecclesiastical)   34
voluntary resignations   212

wagering   201
wages   114
Wakefield (Yorks.)   42
Walker, William   245
Wall Street crash   189
Wallis, William   37
Walpole, Spencer   118
Wapping   142
war   109, 125, 182, 213
war against crime   241
war-time slump   197
Ward, Thomas   37
warders   227, 231, 235
watch   65
watch boxes   143
watch committees   210–11
watchmen   141, 143, 145
water   122
weather   189
Webb, Beatrice and Sidney   162
Wedgwood, Colonel "Jos"   119
Wedgwood, Josiah II   143
Wedgwood, Josiah   104
weights and measures   114, 128–9, 145–6, 155
Weinberger, Barbara   209
welfare state   212
welfare workers   23
Wellington, Duke of   114
Welsh   20, 248
Wesleyan   116
West Riding of Yorkshire   147, 151
Western Australia   167
Westminster   21–2, 110, 144
Whig historians   150
Whigs   114, 149
whipping   23, 159–60, 173
white slaves   200
White, R. J.   106, 112
white-collar class   202
white-collar crime and offenders

171–2, 185–6, 188
white-collar criminals   231
Whitehaven (Cumberland), 119
Wife Beaters Act, 1882   136
wife-beating   37, 135–6, 159, 220
Wilde, Oscar   203, 238
William the Conqueror (1066–87)   7
Wiltshire   34
Wimbledon (Surrey)   110
wireless   242
Witan   2
witchcraft   29, 37
witnesses   218–19, 250
wives   105, 135–7, 178, 200, 205, 220
Wolfenden, Lord   204
Wolverhampton (Staffs.)   28, 119
women   134–8, 159, 183–5, 196,
   198–9, 206, 221, 240
women's rights   199
wood theft   49, 91–2
Wood, Isaac   165
Wood, Thomas   26
Woodford, Elizabeth   165
Worcester   114
work   103, 122, 127–9, 161, 170,
   181, 185, 189

work training   237
workplace   181
workplace crimes   128
workhouses   79, 103, 107, 115, 131,
   143, 151, 189, 199, 228, 230, 233,
working classes   103, 105–6, 115, 118,
   120, 125, 127, 131–2, 135–7, 150–51,
   153–4, 156–7, 170, 181, 187–8,
   190–91, 194–5, 199, 201–2, 208,
   219–220, 222, 248
working-class families   190, 199, 201,
   205,
working-class victims   219
workshops   229
Wormwood Scrubs   227
wrecking   91, 123
Wright, Thomas   172
Wrightson, Keith   66
writ: *mort d'ancestor*   10
writ: *novel disseisin*   10
Wyatt's Revolt (1554)   23

year-books   11
yeomanry   112
York   12, 21, 33–4, 114, 185
Yorkshire   7, 22, 42, 45

LaVergne, TN USA
20 April 2010
179873LV00001B/28/A